The Spirit of Hope

Jürgen Moltmann

The Spirit of Hope

Theology for a World in Peril

WESTMINSTER
JOHN KNOX PRESS
LOUISVILLE • KENTUCKY

Published in the United States of America by
Westminster John Knox Press
Louisville, Kentucky

Copyright © 2019 WCC Publications

First published in Switzerland in 2019 as
Hope in These Troubled Times by WCC Publications

19 20 21 22 23 24 25 26 27 28—10 9 8 7 6 5 4 3 2 1

Translated by Margaret Kohl and Brian McNeil

Cover design by Allison Taylor
Cover image: Hope *by Sharon Cummings*
Book design and typesetting: Michelle Cook / 4 Seasons Book Design

Library of Congress Cataloging-in-Publication Data is on file at the Library of Congress, Washington, D.C.

ISBN-13: 9780664266639

Most Westminster John Knox Press books are available at special quantity discounts when purchased in bulk by corporations, organizations, and special-interest groups. For more information, please email SpecialSales@wjkbooks.com.

Contents

Preface

WE LIVE IN TROUBLED TIMES, ONE CAN AFFIRM WITHOUT exaggeration. Yet what are the roots of our troubles, and what might be the realistic basis for hoping that we can surmount them? How can we, as Christians, frame an honest and theologically tenable worldview to guide our lives and work in this perilous context?

In this volume, I attempt to answer these questions by offering a set of recent reflections on such topics as the ecological challenge, interfaith relations, solidarity and compassion, and terrorism in the name of religion. I focus on the upcoming ecological reformation of Christian theology and spirituality. The path goes from the earth into the city, from the soul into the senses, in order to encourage new experiences of God and new human self-experiences in earth's community.

I also explore, in a second part, some of the underlying theological issues raised by these concerns and the roots of our difficulties and dilemmas in modernity itself. "Thinking hope" requires but also enables a reassessment and reappropriation of these legacies, in both their promising and problematic elements.

So Part One focuses on renewing theology and reasserting hope today, while Part Two explores the historical and theological sources of our situation and our future. Though drawing on my recent volume *Hoffen und Denken* for this volume, I have also added essays and selected chapters that most directly address our contemporary situation and its roots in the Christian tradition and, most particularly, in the ambiguities of modernity. Sources are listed following the notes in this volume. I am grateful to the late Mrs. Margaret Kohl, with whom I worked for many years, for many of the English-language drafts of these chapters, as well as to the Rev. Dr Brian McNeil, for revisions of some translations and new translations of others.

Christian hope draws the promised future of God into the present day, and prepares the present day for this future. As Immanuel Kant rightly said, thinking in the power of hope is not the train-bearer of reality: instead, it goes ahead of reality and lights its way with a torch. The historical-eschatological category is the category of the *novum*, that which is new: the new spirit, the new heart, the new human being, the new covenant, the new song, and ultimately, the promise: "Behold, I make all things new" (Rev. 21:5).

I hope that readers will agree: in light of our faith, as Christians we can honestly assess and face the full force of humanity's contemporary challenges yet also experience and instil a realistic hope of transcending them.

PART ONE

Facing the Future

Chapter 1

A Culture of Life in the Dangers of This Time

IN THIS CHAPTER I GRAPPLE WITH WHAT HAVE BEEN MY MOST URGENT concerns for some time: a culture of life that is stronger than the terror of death, a love for life that overcomes the destructive forces in our world today, and a confidence in the future that overcomes doubt and fatalism.[1] These issues are for me most urgent because with the poet Friedrich Hölderlin I believe strongly:

> *Wo aber Gefahr ist, wächst*
> *Das Rettende auch.*
> [But where there is danger
> Salvation also grows.][2]

We should inquire whether and to what extent this hope bears weight as we explore the possibilities of a culture of life in the face of the real annihilations with which our world is threatened. I will begin by addressing some of the dangers of our time in the first section, and in the second section offer some answers by considering dimensions of a world capable of supporting life and in a quite literal sense a world that is worthy of love. At the end I return to the first verse of the poem by Hölderlin: "Near is God, but difficult to grasp."[3]

The Terror of Universal Death

The unloved life

Human life today is in danger. It is not in danger because it is mortal. Our life has always been mortal. It is in danger because it is no longer loved, affirmed, and accepted. The French author Albert Camus wrote after the Second World War, "This is the mystery of Europe: life is no longer loved."

I can attest to this. I remember the experiences of the war with continuing horror. My generation was destined for a murderous war in which it was no longer a matter of victory or peace, but only of death. Those who suffered in that monstrous war knew what Camus meant: a life no longer loved is ready to kill and is liable to be killed. The survivors experienced the end of terror in 1945, but we had become so used to death that life took on a "take it or leave it" atmosphere because it had become meaningless.

The 20th century was a century of mass exterminations and mass executions. The beginning of the 21st century saw the private terrors of senseless killings by suicidal assassins. In the terrorists of the 21st century, a new religion of death is confronting us. I do not mean the religion of Islam, but rather the ideology of terror. "Your young people love life," said the Mullah Omar of the Taliban in Afghanistan, "our young people love death." After the mass murder in Madrid on 11 March 2004, there were acknowledgments by the terrorists with the same message: "You love life, we love death." A German who joined the Taliban in Afghanistan declared, "We don't want to win; we want to kill and be killed." Why? I think because they view killing as power and they experience themselves as God over life and death. This seems to be the modern terrorist ideology of the suicidal assassins. It is also the mystery of crazed students who in the United States and Germany suddenly shoot their fellow students and teachers and end up taking their own lives.

I remember that we had this love of death in Europe some 60 years ago. "Viva la muerte," cried an old fascist general in the Spanish Civil War. Long live death! The German SS troops in the Second World War had the saying "Death gives, and death takes away" and wore the symbol of the skull and bones. It is not possible to deter suicidal assassins, for they have broken the fear of death. They do not love life anymore, and they want to die with their victims.

Behind this terrorist ideological surface a greater danger is hidden: Peace, disarmament, and nonproliferation treaties between nations share an obvious assumption, namely, that on both sides there is the will to survive and the will to live. Yet what happens if one partner does not want to survive but is willing to die, if through death that partner can destroy this whole "wicked" or "godless" world? Until now we have had to deal only with an international network of suicidal assassins and individual students overcome by a death wish. What happens when a nation possessing nuclear weapons becomes obsessed with this "religion of death" and turns into a collective suicidal assassin against the rest of the human world because it is driven into a corner and gives up all hope? Deterrence works only so long as all partners have the will to live and want to survive. When it is of no matter whether one lives or dies, one has lost the fear that is necessary for deterrence. Those who are convinced for religious reasons that they must become a sacrifice in order to save the world can no longer be threatened with death. Those who clamor for the "great war" even if it means their own destruction are beyond deterrence.

The attraction of destroying a world that is considered "rotten," disordered, or godless can obviously grow into a universal death wish to which one sacrifices one's own life. "Death" then, becomes a fascinating divinity inflaming a desire for destruction. This apocalyptic "religion of death" is the real enemy of the will to live, the love of life, and the affirmation of being.

The nuclear suicide programme

Behind this present political danger endangering the common life of the nations there also lurks an older threat: the nuclear threat. The first atomic bomb dropped on Hiroshima in August 1945 brought the Second World War to an end. At the same time, it marked the beginning of the end time for the whole of humankind. The end time is the age in which the end of humankind is possible at any moment.

No human being could survive the "nuclear winter" that would follow a great atomic war. Remember that humankind was on the cusp of such a great atomic war for more than 40 years during the Cold War. It is true that since the end of the Cold War in 1990 a great atomic war is not as likely. We live in relative peace. Yet there are still so many atomic and hydrogen bombs stored up in the arsenals of the great nations (and some smaller ones as well) that the self-annihilation of humankind remains a distinct possibility. Sakharov called it "collective suicide": "Whoever fires first, dies second." For those 40 years we depended for our security on "mutually assured destruction."

Most people had forgotten this atomic threat until President Barack Obama, in a speech delivered in Prague in 2009, revived the old dream of a world free of atomic bombs and started new disarmament negotiations with Russia.[4] Then, many of us became aware again of this destiny hanging like a dark cloud over the nations. Strangely enough, we feel the presence of the nuclear threat publicly in what American psychologists call "nuclear numbing." We repress our anxiety, try to forget this threat, and live as if this danger were not there. Yet it is gnawing at our subconscious and impairing our love of life.

The social conditions of misery

A general impairment of life also exists in miserable social conditions. For more than 40 years, we have heard repeatedly and everywhere the charge that, despite all political efforts, the social gap between rich and poor is widening. It is not just in the poorer countries of the two-thirds world that a small, rich sector of the population rules over the masses of the poor. In the democracies of the developed world, the financial asset gap between financiers, on the one hand, and low-income workers, welfare recipients, the unemployed, and those not able to work, on the other hand, takes on obscene proportions. Yet democracy is grounded not only in the freedom of citizens but also in their equality. Without social justice in life opportunities and the comparability of life circumstances, the commonweal dies and with it what holds society together falls apart. Trust is lost.

Since the democratic revolutions in England, the United States, and France, the political task in the European states has been the balancing of individual freedom and social equity. The deregulation of the economy and fiscal institutions wrought by American politics, with all its destructive consequences, has led to an imbalance between freedom and equality that has become life-threatening for many people. It has led to their disempowerment and poverty. A capitalism that is no longer politically controllable through the commonwealth becomes an enemy of democracy because it destroys the common meaning of the society. We find ourselves on a social slippery slope. Climbing on the social ladder brings anxiety. In the modern competitive society, the losers fall off, the winners ascend, and "the winner takes all." The anxiety of life creates nothing but the anxiety of existence for modern human beings. Yet is anxiety a good incentive for life, for work, and for happiness?

The ecological conditions of world destruction

Unlike the nuclear threat, climate change is not only a threat but already an emerging reality everywhere. It is not only a latent problem but also very much a matter of public consciousness. People know it because they can see it, feel it, and sometimes smell it. The biosphere of the planet earth is the only space we have for life. The globalization of human civilization has reached its limits and is beginning to alter the conditions of life on Earth.

The destruction of the environment that we are causing through our present global economic system will undoubtedly seriously jeopardize the survival of humanity in the 21st century. Modern industrial society has thrown out of balance the equilibrium of the earth's organism and is on the way to universal ecological death, unless we can change the way things are developing. Year after year, vulnerable species of animals and plants die out. Scientists have shown that certain chemical emissions are destroying the ozone layer, while the use of chemical fertilizers and a multitude of pesticides is polluting our drinking water and making the soil infertile. They have shown that the global climate is already changing, so that we now are experiencing an increasing number of "natural" catastrophes, such as droughts and floods, expanding deserts, and intense storms – catastrophes that are not simply natural but are also caused by human activity. The ice in the Arctic and the Antarctic is melting. In the coming century, scientists predict that coastal cities such as my hometown, Hamburg, and coastal regions such as Bangladesh and many South Sea islands will be flooded. All in all, life on this earth is under threat. Why is this so? With some irony one may say: Some do not know what they are doing, while others do not act on what they know.

This ecological crisis is fundamentally a crisis wrought by Western scientific and technological civilization. Yet it is a mistake to think that environmental problems are problems for the industrialized countries of the West alone. On the contrary, ecological catastrophes are intensifying even more in the midst of already existing economic and social problems of countries in the developing world. Indira Gandhi was right when she said, "Poverty is the worst pollution." Despite the well-documented "limits to growth," the ideology of permanent "growth" continues unabated with its specious promise of solving social problems. We know all this, but we are paralyzed and do not change our economy or our lifestyle: We do not do what we know is necessary to prevent the worst consequences. This paralysis may be called "ecological numbing." Nothing accelerates an imminent catastrophe so much as the paralysis of doing nothing.

We do not know whether humanity will survive this self-made destiny. This is actually a good thing. If we knew with certainty that we would not survive, we would do nothing; if we knew with certainty that we would survive, we would also do nothing. Only if the future is open for both possibilities are we forced to do today what is necessary to survive tomorrow. We cannot know whether humankind will survive, so we must act today as if the future of life depends on us and trust at the same time that our children and we will survive and thrive.

Must a human race exist or survive, or are we just an accident of nature? We can ask cynically: Didn't the dinosaurs come and go?

The question of existence:
Whether humanity should be or not be

More than seven billion human beings already live on earth today. This number likely will grow rapidly. An alternative future is that the earth could be uninhabited. The earth existed without human beings for millions of years and may survive perhaps for millions of years after the human race disappears. This raises an even deeper question: Are we human beings on earth only by chance, or are we human beings a "necessary" result of evolution? If nature showed a "strong anthropic principle," we could feel "at home in the universe" (Stuart Kauffman). But if a strong anthropic principle of this kind cannot be demonstrated, the universe gives no answer to this existential question of humankind. Looking to the universe for an answer to the question of our reason for being, we encounter the sad conjecture of Nobel–Prize winning physicist Steven Weinberg: "The more the Universe seems comprehensible, the more it also seems pointless."[5] The silence of the world's expanses and the coldness of the universe can lead to despondence. In any case, neither the stars nor our genes say whether human beings should be or not be.

How can we love life and affirm our being as humans if humanity is only an accident of nature, superfluous and without relevance for the universe, perhaps only a mistake of nature? Is there a "duty to be," as Hans Jonas claimed? Is there any reason to love life and affirm the human being? If we find no answer, every culture of life is uncertain in its fundamentals and built on shaky ground.

A Culture of Life Must Be a Culture of Common Life in the Human and the Natural World

Can we live with the bomb?

Are the dangers growing faster than what can save us? I think we can grow in wisdom, but how? President Obama's dream of a "world without atomic weapons" is an honourable one, but only a dream. Human beings will never again become incapable of what they can do now.

Whoever has learned the formula of atomic fission will never forget it. Since Hiroshima in 1945, humankind has lost its "atomic innocence."

Yet the atomic end time is also the first common age of the nations. All the nations are sitting in the same boat. We all share the same threat. Everyone can become the victim. In this new situation, humankind must organize itself as the subject of common survival. The foundation of the United Nations in 1945 was a first step. International security partnerships can serve peace and give us time to live, and someday perhaps a transnational unification of humankind will keep the means of nuclear destruction under control. Through science we learn to gain power over nature. Through wisdom we learn to gain control of our power. The development of public and political wisdom is as important as scientific progress.

The first lesson we learn is this: Deterrence does not secure peace any more. Only justice serves peace between the nations. There is no way to peace in the world except through just actions and the harmonious balance of interests. Peace is not the absence of violence, but the presence of justice. Peace is a process, not a property. Peace is a common way of reducing violence and constructing justice in the social and global relationships of humankind.

Social justice creates social peace

The gap between the poor and the rich widens, but the alternative to poverty is not property. The alternative to poverty and property is community. One can live in poverty when it is borne in common with others, as was the case in Europe in the years of hunger after the Second World War. It is injustice that makes poverty insufferable. The spirit of communal solidarity and mutual help was demolished by the flight from taxes, which in turn aroused the anger of the people. If everyone is in the same situation, then all give mutual help. If we remove equality, because one wins and the other loses, then mutual help also vanishes. By "community" here I mean the visible community of solidarity as well as the inner togetherness of society in social balance and social freedom. It is not football games that unite a society; it is social justice that creates lasting social peace.

The individualism that says "Everyone is his or her own neighbour, looking out for himself or herself" makes human beings powerless. The fragmenting of work by making it temporary, insecure, and without benefits harms the life planning of those at the mercy of the system and destroys their future. In communities of solidarity, human beings are strong and wealthy, that is, wealthy in relationships with neighbours and friends, companions and colleagues on which they can depend. They are thus made strong by being recognized and by being esteemed as worthy. Many helpful actions emerge in such communities, such as child care, the care of the sick and aged, associations of the disabled, and the hospice movement.

"Market position" and "competition" are certainly strong incentives for work, but they remain humane only in the framework of a common life, and that means only within the bounds of social and ecological justice. There are dimensions of life that may not be determined by the market logic because they follow other laws. Patients are not "customers" of doctors and nurses, and students are not "consumers" of the science and research of the university.

Reverence for life

Because human society and the natural environment compose the total life-system, when there is a crisis of dying in nature, there emerges a crisis of the whole life-system as well. What we call today the "ecological crisis" is not only a crisis in our environment but also a total crisis of our life-system, and it cannot be solved by technological means only. It also demands a change in our lifestyle and a change in the basic values and convictions of our society. Modern industrial societies are no longer in harmony with the cycles and rhythms of the earth, as was the case in pre-modern agrarian societies. Modern societies are predicated on progress and expansion of the projects of humanity. We reduce the nature of the earth to "our environment" and destroy the life-space of other forms of life. Nothing works so much destruction as reducing nature to no more than an environment for humans.

We need a change from the modern domination of nature to a "reverence for life," as Albert Schweitzer teaches us. "Reverence for life" is respect for every single form of life and for our common life in the human and the natural world and for the great community of all the living. A postmodern biocentrism will have to replace the Western and modern anthropocentrism. Of course, we cannot return to the cosmos-orientation of the ancient and pre-modern agrarian world, but we can begin the necessary ecological transformation of the industrial society. To achieve this, we must change our concept of time. The linear concept of progress in production, consumption, and waste must give way to the concept of the cyclical time of "renewable energy" and a "recycling economy." Only the cycles of life can give stability to our world of progress. Yet as long as the children of Ghana bear the burden of recycling our electronic scrap, we must say the recycling economy is still the economy of poor people. The Earth Charter of the United Nations from 2000 points in the right direction: "Humanity is part of nature. All other life forms of nature have their worth independent of their worth for human beings." We are "part of nature," and can therefore survive only by preserving nature's integrity.

The love of life in times of danger

Human life is not only a gift of life but also a task of being human. To accept this task of humanity in times of terror requires the strength and courage to live. Life must be affirmed against terror and threat. To put this in simple terms: Life must be lived, and then the beloved life, which is the common life in the human and the natural world, will be stronger than the threat of universal annihilation. I see three major factors for this courage to be and the courage to live.

First, human life must be affirmed, because it can also be denied. As we know, a child can grow and live only in an atmosphere of affirmation. In an atmosphere of rejection, the child will fade away in soul and body. Experiencing affirmation allows children to affirm themselves. What is true for the child is true for human beings throughout their lives. Where we are accepted, appreciated, and affirmed, we are motivated to live; where we feel a hostile world of contempt and rejection, we retire into ourselves and become defensive. We need a strong affirmation of life that can deal with such negations of life. Each yes to life is stronger than every negation of life, because it can create something new against the negations.

Second, human life is participation. We become alive where we feel the sympathy of others, and we stay alive where we share our life with others. As long as we are interested, we are alive. The counterproof is obvious: indifference leads to apathy, and apathy is a sickness unto death. Complete lack of participation is a completely unlived life; it is the dying of the soul before physical death.

Third, human life is alive in the pursuit of fulfilment. Human life gains its dynamic from this inborn striving. "The pursuit of happiness" is, since the writing of the Declaration of Independence, one essential human right. To pursue one's happiness is not only a private human right but also a public human right. We speak of the "good life" or the "meaningful life," meaning a life that lives out its best potential in the public life of a good and harmonious society. When we take this "pursuit of happiness" seriously, we encounter the misfortune of the masses of poor people and begin to suffer with the unfortunate. The compassion by which we are drawn into their passion for life is the reverse side of the pursuit of happiness. The more we become capable of the happiness of life, the more we become also capable of sorrow and compassion. This is the great dialectic of human life. "But where there is danger, salvation also grows." How is salvation growing? I have tried to show how being can take in nonbeing, how life can overcome death through love, and how deadly contradictions can be changed into productive differences and higher forms of living and community. I am reminded of a famous affirmation by the German philosopher Friedrich Hegel, a friend of Hölderlin since their student days at Tübingen University. Hegel wrote in his *Phenomenology of Mind* (1807), "Not a life that shrinks away from death or remains untouched by devastations, but a life that endures death and bears death in itself is the life of the Spirit." Consciously lived life is a beloved life that endures the contradictions of death and finds the courage to live through its dangers.

"Near Is God, and Difficult to Grasp"

I conclude by allowing the theologian in me to speak and declare the Christian faith:

- Should humanity be superfluous? Or are we superfluous?

- Is there a duty to survive, or are life and death simply a "take it or leave it" matter?

- In the evolution of life, are we an accident of life?

The existential questions of humankind are answered not only by rational arguments, but first of all by a prerational assurance or lack of assurance that guides the interests of our reason.

"Difficult to grasp is God," wrote Hölderlin, not because God is so distant from us human beings, but rather because God is "near." What is "near," indeed nearer to us than we are to ourselves, is "not to be grasped" by us, for we would need distance for that. If, however, we were "grasped" by the nearness of God, we would know the answers to our existential questions:

- In the eternal yes of the living God, we affirm our fragile and vulnerable humanity in spite of death.

- In the eternal love of God, we love life and resist its devastations.

- In the ungraspable nearness of God, we trust in what is saving, even if the dangers are growing.

Chapter 2

The Hope of the Earth:
The Ecological Future
of Modern Theology

TODAY WE STAND AT THE END OF THE MODERN AGE AND AT WHAT has to be the beginning of the ecological future of our world, if our world is to survive. A new paradigm is in the process of developing, a paradigm which links human culture and nature differently from the way they were linked in the paradigm of modern times. The modern age was determined by the human seizure of power over nature and its forces. These conquests and usurpations of nature have now come up against their limits. All the signs suggest that the climate of the earth is changing drastically as a result of human influence. The icecaps of the poles are melting, the water level is rising, islands are disappearing, droughts are on the increase, the deserts are spreading, and so forth. We know all that, but we are not acting according to what we know. Most people are closing their eyes or are as if paralyzed. And yet nothing hastens on the catastrophes as much as a paralyzed inactivity.

In our culture, we need a new understanding of nature and a new picture of the human being – and that means a new experience of God. Here, a new ecological theology can help us. Why theology, of all things? Because it was modern theology which determined the relationship to nature and the concept of the human being in the modern age. The determining concept was the lordship over the world which was to be exercised by the godlike human being. It was the interpretation of God without the world and of the world without God. It was the mechanistic concept of the earth, and of all non-human dwellers on the earth, which had to be "subdued" or "subjected."

There is an old joke: Two planets meet in space. The one asks: "How are you?" The other one replies, "Oh, I'm not at all well. I'm ill. I have *homo sapiens*." The other answers, "I'm sorry to hear that. That's really bad. I have had it too. But never mind – it will pass." That is the new planetary perspective on humanity. Will this human planetary sickness pass because the human race does away with itself, or will it pass because the human race becomes wise and heals the wounds which it still continues to inflict on the planet earth down to the present day?

The New Picture of the Human Being: From the Centre of the World to Cosmic Integration, Or: From the Arrogance of World Domination to Cosmic Humility

Before we human beings "till and keep" the earth and assume any rule over the world or any responsibility for creation, the earth cares for us. It creates the conditions that are favourable for the human race and has preserved it down to the present day. It is not that the earth is entrusted to us: we are entrusted to the earth. The earth can live without us human beings, but we cannot live without the earth.

We can demonstrate this from the modern way of reading the biblical accounts of creation, for the biblical creation stories are deeply rooted in the consciousness and the subconscious of modern Western men and women.

According to the modern reading, the human being is "the crown of creation." Only the human being has been created to be the image of God, and to rule over the earth and all earthly beings: "Subdue the earth . . . and have dominion over the birds of the air and over every living thing that moves upon the earth" (Gen. 1:28). According to Psalm 8:6, God has "given man dominion over the works of his hands; has put all things under his feet." Consequently, the human being is supposed to "subdue" the earth and all the human's fellow creatures like a pharaoh. According to the second creation account, humans are rather supposed to "till and keep" creation like a gardener. That sounds milder and more respectful, but even so, in both creation stories the human being is the determining subject, and the earth with all its inhabitants is the human's object. This is what Max Scheler described as the human being's special place in the cosmos.[1] These biblical texts are more than 2,500 years old, but it was only 400 years ago, during the Renaissance, that they became "modern."

In the Renaissance era, this biblical picture of human beings was accentuated: they were now at the centre of the world. Pico della Mirandola provided the classic text in 1486, in his discourse *De hominis dignitate, On the Dignity of the Human Being.* He begins with a quotation from the Islamic scholar Abdallah: "There is nothing in the world more deserving of admiration than the human being," and he sees the human as "coming forward from the ordered sequence of the universe, an object of envy not only for the animals but also for the stars, indeed even for the other-worldly intelligences," the angels.[2]

> The nature of other beings is according to their nature determined by Us (i.e., God) through predetermined laws and is thereby kept in confines. But you are not restricted by any confines that cannot be overcome, but according to your own free will (in the hand of which I have laid your destiny) shall even predetermine that very nature. I have set you in the center of the world . . . so that as your own, completely free and honorably acting sculptor and poet, you yourself may determine the form in which you wish to live.

This "center of the world" is not merely the centre of the earth; it constitutes the centre between heaven and earth as well. As the image of the Creator, the Renaissance man is "his own creator" and – as is often said today – his own invention. The world is subject to the rule of law in the form of necessity, but the human being is its free master. Humans makes themselves "the measure of all things," the inventor of their own selves, and the lords of their own world.

The Englishman Francis Bacon proclaimed that "knowledge is power"; this was a proclamation that moulded the German educational system right down to my own youth. He linked the scientific and technological acquisition of power over nature with a dream of redemption: as God's image, the human being was created for rule over nature. Through the Fall, humans lost this divinely determined rule. Through science and technology the human acquires "a restitution and reinvesting (in great part) of the sovereignty and power which he had in his first state of creation."[3] But whereas, according to the Bible, human rule over nature was justified by the fact that the human being was created to be God's image, Bacon argued in the reverse direction: human beings' rule over nature proves that they are the image of God. What picture of God does this imply? In the same way that God is the Lord of the universe, so the human being as God's image is destined to be lord of the earth. In this analogy, the only one of all God's attributes that remains is God's almighty power.

In his *Discourse on the Method of Rightly Conducting Reason* (*Discours de la méthode*, 1692), the French philosopher René Descartes went a step further.[4] Through science and technology, the human being becomes "the lord and possessor of nature." Descartes split the world up into the *res cogitans* of the human mind and the *res extensa* of nature. In nature, the thinking mind sees only objects of measurable extension. The reduction of the knowledge of nature to calculations became the foundation of modern science. This is the *reductio scientiae ad mathematicam* – the reduction of science to mathematics.[5] In this way, Descartes reduced the human body to being the measurable locality of the human soul. And from this his pupil, the physician LaMettrie, drew the conclusion: *L'Homme machine* (Man the Machine, 1748).

According to the new ecological way of reading the same creation narratives in the Bible, the human being is the last being God creates and therefore the most dependent of all God's creations. For their life on earth, human beings are dependent on the existence of animals and plants, air and water, light, daytime and night-time, sun, moon, and stars, and without these things they cannot live. Human beings exist only because all these other creatures exist. The other creatures can all exist without the human being, but human beings cannot exist without them. So it is impossible to conceive of the human being as a divine potentate, or as a solitary gardener, over against nature. Whatever their "special position" and their special tasks may be, human beings are one created being in the great "community of life," and part of nature.[6] Before the divine "breath" is breathed into the human being, as the second creation account tells, the human is "dust from the ground" (Gen. 2:7), and before human beings "till and keep" the earth, they know: "You are dust, and to dust you shall return."

According to the modern view of the human being, the human being as God's image is God's deputy and representative on earth. The human is an earthly person or hypostasis of the eternal God. In the pre-modern view of the human being held by the church fathers, the human being as person was at the same time a "hypostasis of the whole cosmic nature." Before human beings are an *imago Dei*, they are an *imago mundi*, a microcosm in which all previous life forms are integrated. The ecological picture of the human being says that "if we are to understand what it means to be human in the widest sense, we must start with the interactions and milieus in which human beings occur and from which they live; and that means beginning with the genesis of the cosmos, the evolution of life, and the history of the consciousness."[7]

According to the biblical traditions, God did not breathe the divine Spirit into the human being alone, but into all God's creatures.

> *When thou hidest thy face, they are dismayed;*
> *When thou takest away their breath, they die and return to*
> *their dust.*
> *When thou sendest forth thy Spirit, they are created;*
> *and thou renewest the face of the ground. (Ps. 104:29-30)*

We can deduce from this that if the character of human beings as image of God is due to the Holy Spirit which dwells in them, then all created beings in which God's Spirit dwells are God's image and must be respected accordingly. At all events, human beings are so closely connected with nature that they share in the same distress and in their common hope for redemption. Men and women will not be redeemed from transience and death *from* this earth, but *together with* the earth.

Paul heard the "groaning" of those who are moved by the Spirit of God as they wait for the redemption of their bodies. He therefore also heard the "groaning" of the non-human creation by which he was surrounded (Rom. 8:22-23). He was convinced that it is God's Spirit itself which lets us and the whole creation sigh for redemption from the fate of death. The Spirit who is now present is the beginning of the new creation, in which death will be no more, for it is the Spirit of Jesus' resurrection and the comprehensive presence of the risen one. Orthodox theology has expressed this in its hope not only for the deification of humanity but for the deification of the cosmos too. "The whole of nature is destined for the glory which humanity will partake of in the kingdom of the completion."[8]

Human beings are part of nature, in their own character, in their destiny, and in their hope for life. So they do not stand at the centre of the world. If they are to survive, they must integrate themselves into nature and into the community of their fellow beings. They are not entitled to the arrogance of power over nature and the liberty to do with it what they like. Their attitude should rather be characterized by a "cosmic humility"[9] and by an attentive respect in all their interventions in nature. It is only when we become aware of our dependence on the life of the earth and on the existence of other living things that we shall turn from being what Luther called "proud and unhappy gods" into truly human human beings. True knowledge is not power; true knowledge is wisdom.

God and the World: From the Distinction between God and the World to the Trinitarian Doctrine of Creation: From a Godless World to the World in God, and God in the World

Modern theology has ascribed the fundamental distinction between God and world to the biblical belief in creation. The world proceeds, not from God's eternal nature, but from God's free resolve. If it had proceeded from God's eternal nature, it would be divine itself. It would then be self-sufficient, like God, grounded in itself and perfect. But as

God's creation, heaven and earth are worldly, heavenly and earthly, but not divine. Modern interpretation stresses that the Israelite belief in creation has de-divinized, de-demonized and, in the modern sense of the word, "secularized" it. *"Profana illis omnia quae apud nos sacra,"* said Cicero, in his worldly Roman piety, talking about the godless Jews: "for them, everything which for us is sacred is profane." With their belief in creation, Israel abolished the fertility cults in Canaan, as the story of Elijah relates. That is why modern scientists like Sir Isaac Newton appealed to the Bible when they expelled the Aristotelian "soul of the world" from their worldview and interpreted the world as a soulless mechanism. In Israel the taboos of the ancient oriental religions of nature already found an end. Nature became the world of human beings.

"Subdue the earth." Modern theologians took this up and delivered nature over to scientific research and the technological utilization by human beings. Scientific methods themselves became value-free, agnostic, or atheistic in tendency. The strict theism of modern times banished God into the mystery of transcendence, in order to have the world for human beings in a transcendence-free immanence. Ultimately speaking, in the theology of modern times God was thought of as world-less, so that the world, being God-less, could be dominated, and so that men and women could live in it without God. If God is only in the world beyond, this world can be subjugated, free of God, and moulded according to one's own ideas.

Arnold Gehlen aptly sums up the result:

> At the end of a long spiritual and cultural history, this view of the world as an *"entente secrète"* – the metaphysics of harmonizing and conflicting life forces – has been destroyed. It has been destroyed by monotheism on the one hand and, on the other, by the scientific and technological mechanism for which monotheism itself first cleared the path when it de-demonized and de-divinized nature, God and the machine have survived the archaic world, and now confront one another quite alone.[10]

The most frightening thing about this vision is that between the transcendent God and the world as machine, human beings as we know them no longer exist. They have become not God but a machine.

But there is a more profound ecological understanding of creation. The Creator is linked with creation not only outwardly, but inwardly too. Creation is in God, and God is in creation. According to the original Christian doctrine, the act of creation is a trinitarian proceeding: God the Father creates the world through his eternal Word in the power of the divine Spirit. The world is a non-divine reality, but it is interpenetrated by God. If all things are created by God the Father, through God the Son, and in God the Holy Spirit, then they are also from God, through God, and in God.

Thus, for us there is only one God, the Father, from whom are all things and for whom we exist, and one Lord, Jesus Christ, through whom are all things and through whom we exist (1 Cor. 8:6).[11]

In his treatise on the Holy Spirit, Basil says: "Behold in the creation of these beings the Father as the preceding cause, the Son as the creating (cause), and the Spirit as the perfecting (cause), so that the ministering spirits have their beginning in the will of the Father, are brought into being through the efficacy of the Son, and are perfected though the aid of the Spirit."[12] If we see the act of creation as a trinitarian proceeding of this kind, then it cannot be ascribed merely to "God the Father, the Almighty"; it has to be ascribed with equal weight to the Son and the Spirit too. Nor is it an act "outwards" (*ad extra*); it is an act in the life of the whole Trinity. Inasmuch as through his energies the Spirit acts, invigorates, and lives in all created beings, God is present in creation, and creation has its continued existence in God. If, as Basil says, the Spirit is "the perfecter," then all created beings are directed through the energies of the Spirit toward their future perfecting and are driven toward that. According to biblical traditions, the "perfecting" of creation means that the triune God "indwells" his consummated creation, and that all created beings then participate in God's eternal aliveness (Rev. 21:1-3).

What follows from this trinitarian view of creation is the concept of a world shot through by the Spirit. In the power of his Spirit, God is in all things and all things are in God. We can also conceive of the divine Spirit in the world as a force field though which all things are energized.

In the mediaeval world, Hildegard of Bingen experienced the world in this way: "The Holy Spirit is life-giving life, Mover of the universe and the root of all creation, refiner of all things from their dross, brings forgiveness of guilt and oil for our wounds, is radiance of life, most worthy of worship, wakening and reawakening the universe."[13] In the Reformation era, we find a similar pronouncement in John Calvin's *Institutio*: "For the Spirit is everywhere present and sustains, nourishes and enlivens all things in heaven and on earth. That he pours out his power into everything, and thus promises all things existence, life and movement, is evidently divine" (I, 13, 14).

In the trinitarian doctrine of creation, the work of the transcendent Father is linked with the immanent outpouring divinity of the Holy Spirit. As a result, the created world must be viewed as divine, inasmuch as it is sustained and moved by divine forces. This is not "pantheism," for God and the world are differentiated. Nor is it "panentheism," which says that all things are "in God." The fact that God through God's Spirit is present in all things is best expressed in the Old Testament and Jewish Shekinah doctrine: God desires to "dwell" in the midst of his people Israel. God will "dwell" in the new creation forever, when all things are full of God's glory (Is. 6:3). We find this idea in its New Testament form in Paul and John. Patristic theology calls it "perichoresis," mutual indwelling: God in the world – the world in God. "He who abides in love abides in God and God abides in him" (1 John 4:16).

"Subdue the Earth – Which Is the Mother of Us All"?

Modern theology has always seen the earth only as something which human beings are supposed to "subdue," according to the first creation account. But in the book of Sirach 40:1, the earth is called "the mother of us all." Can one subdue one's own mother? Can one exploit her, destroy her, and sell her?

Modern ecological theology starts from the assumption that the earth is our "home": "Humanity is part of a continually developing universe. Our home earth offers living space for a unique and diverse community of living things . . . To protect the earth's ability to live, its diversity and its beauty is a sacred duty."[14]

In order to "subdue" the earth, human beings have to degrade it into an object which can be scientifically investigated and ruled by technology. It must be robbed of its subjectivity. The "soul of the world," which was revered from time immemorial, is necessarily lost. This was the outcome of the mechanistic worldview which the sciences have disseminated for the last four hundred years.[15] Modern chemistry goes back to Robert Boyle, who wanted to speak only of "mechanism" instead of nature. Isaac Newton outlined a world picture of the cosmic machine, which functions like the mechanism of a clock. It is so perfect that its time can run backwards and forwards. The metaphysical premise for the mechanistic worldview is that the world has been created in finished and complete form, once and for all. Its idea of God is deism, according to which God, as the architect of the world, has created it in such perfection that it needs no further divine interventions. God would contradict his own perfection if he subsequently had to correct his work by way of miracles. It is no wonder that the French physicist Laplace answered Napoleon's question about God by saying: "Sire, I had no need of this hypothesis." The world mechanism can be explained by itself, if it is perfect.

But if the world is imperfect and not yet finished, the mechanistic worldview fails to function, because it only describes the world's reality but does not take into account its potentiality. According to what evolutionary biology tells us, it may be said that only a small part of the potential diversity of life forms has as yet been realized. The forms of life which are possible cannot be envisaged. In a nature open to the future, even natural laws are not timeless; they are changeable "habits of nature."[16]

The new astro-sciences have shown the interactions between the non-living and the living spheres of our planet earth. The result is the idea that the earth's biosphere, together with the atmosphere, the oceans and land masses, forms a unique complex system which has the capacity to bring forth life and to create habitats. That is James Lovelock's much-discussed Gaia theory.[17] In spite of the poetical name of the Greek goddess given to it, this theory does not mean a deification of the earth. But the earth is viewed as a living organism which brings forth life and creates habitats.

If we understand life in the narrow biological sense, then the earth is not "living," because it does not reproduce itself. But it must be called more than living, because it brings forth life. Nor it is an "organism," like the biological organisms we know. It is more than an organism, because it brings forth organisms. The earth is a determining subject of its own particular kind, incomparable and unique. The earth is not a fortuitous accumulation of matter and energy; it is neither blind nor dumb. It is intelligent, because it brings forth intelligences. At a particular point in its evolution, the earth began to feel, to think, to be conscious of itself, and to feel reverence.[18] We human beings are earthly beings. So we do not confront the earth as its determining subject; instead, in our human dignity we are part of the earth and members of the earthly community of creation. We ourselves are "fellow creatures" with other living things. This cosmic feeling of community is more comprehensive than all the sectors of nature which we can know and dominate. So today it is time to move the sacredness of the earth into the centre and for us to integrate ourselves consciously into the earthly community.

The Gaia theory corresponds entirely to the wealth of biblical traditions about the earth.

According to the first creation narrative, the earth is not subservient to human beings; it is a great creative creation and in this respect unique. It brings forth life, it "brings forth living creatures according to their kinds: cattle and creeping things and beasts of the earth according to their kinds" (Gen. 1:24). The evolution of life and the history of the earth are closely interlocked. The earth not only offers the living space for a diversity of living things. It is also the womb which brings life forth.

The earth belongs to the covenant with God. Behind the covenant with Noah – "with you and your descendants after you, and with every living creature that is with you" (Gen. 9:9-11) – lies God's covenant with the earth: "I set my bow in the cloud, and it shall be a sign of the covenant between me and the earth" (Gen. 9:13). This covenant puts the earth into a direct connection with God. It is the earth's divine secret.

The rights of the earth in its covenant with God are brought to bear in the laws about the Sabbath: "In the seventh year there shall be a Sabbath of solemn rest for the land (earth)" (Lev. 25:4). The earth has a right to its Sabbath rest, so that it can regenerate its fertility. Anyone who disregards the earth's Sabbath turns the land into a desert and will be forced to leave it (Lev. 26:33).

The divine Spirit is the creative power of life, *Spiritus vivificans*. It is "poured out on all flesh" (Joel 2:28), that is to say on all living beings. If "the Spirit from on high" is poured out on us, as we read in Isaiah 32:14, 16, then "the wilderness will become a fruitful field and justice will dwell in the wilderness . . . and the effect of righteousness will be peace."

One very important point is that the earth hides within itself the secret of salvation: "Let the earth open, that salvation may sprout forth, let it cause righteousness to spring up also" (Is. 45:8). The prophet Isaiah even calls Israel's Messiah "a fruit of the earth" (Is. 4:2).

According to the Christian doctrine of reconciliation, God through Christ has "reconciled the cosmos" (2 Cor. 5:19). God has "reconciled" the cosmos so that "all things will be united in Christ, things in heaven and things on earth" (Eph. 1:10; Col. 1:20). The risen Christ is the cosmic Christ, and the cosmic Christ is "the secret of the world"; he is present in all things. The cosmic Christ is ultimately the coming Christ, who will redeem the world and fill heaven and earth with his justice and righteousness. According to the apocryphal gospel of Thomas, "I am the light that is over all, I am the All, the All has come forth from me, and the All returns to me again. Cleave a piece of wood, I am there. Lift up a stone and you will find me" (v.77).

Natural Theology: The Presupposition for Revealed Theology or Its Future?

We now come to a particular theme of Christian theology which is becoming especially topical in the ecological turn to the earth and everything connected with that. This theme is natural theology. But whereas traditionally, natural theology meant an indirect knowledge of God through nature, what we need today is an indirect knowledge of nature by way of God. The ecological crises are destroying the contexts and cohesions of life on earth. In order to preserve them in the face of destructive forces, we need an affirmation of the earth which is stronger than these forces, and an unconquerable love for life. Is there any greater affirmation and any stronger love than belief in the presence of God in the earth and in all the contexts of its life? We need a theology of the earth, and a new spirituality of creation.

Christian traditions interpreted "natural theology" as a knowledge of the existence of God and his nature that was gained from "the book of nature," with the aid of the innate reason of human beings. This natural, reasonable knowledge of God is not as yet a Christian knowledge of God, but it serves as its universal premise:

"God, the beginning and end of all things, can be perceived with certainty from created things through the light of human reason." So declared the First Vatican Council.[19] This definition goes back to Thomas Aquinas, according to whom Christian theology is the theology of supernatural revelation. It presupposes natural theology in the same way that grace presupposes nature. The natural knowledge of God belongs in the forecourt of supernatural knowledge of God; it is not an object of faith, but it is a reasonable preparation for faith. With the help of the cosmological proofs of God, every reasonable person can know that there is a God, and that God is one.

This is the way pre-modern Protestant theology also understood natural theology: there is a knowledge of God derived from "the book of nature" and a supernatural knowledge of God derived from "the Book of Books." A natural knowledge of God is inborn in the human being in the conscience and is acquired through the perception of God's activity in nature. Natural theology is based on "natural religion." Through this knowledge, however, one will only become wise; one will not be saved. Salvation is conferred only through God's communication of himself in his revelation through Jesus Christ. The phenomenon of "natural religion" goes back to creation. It is left over from the paradisiacal knowledge of God that was enjoyed by the first human beings. It was obscured through the Fall, but it served to preserve human beings and is the foundation of their yearning for God. The supernatural revelation of God brings knowledge of God's grace, and with that, a restoration of the paradisiacal knowledge of God. Revealed knowledge does not do away with natural theology or replace it, but rectifies it and completes it.

Natural theology is not revealed theology, nor is it in competition with revealed theology. When Karl Barth wrote his *No!* to natural theology in 1934, he overlooked this difference.[20] The real issue at that time was the political theology of the so-called German Christians and the Nazis, the "Blood and Soil" ideology. Through the knowledge of God's self-revelation, a person will be saved but not wise; through the knowledge of God in nature, the person will become wise in dealings with the earth, but not saved. Human beings will be happy only when they are both saved and wise. Karl Barth later took up this point again in his doctrine of lights.[21]

In 1946, my teacher Hans-Joachim Iwand had already postulated a thesis:

> Natural theology is not that from which we set out but the light towards which we draw. The *lumen naturae* is the radiance of the *lumen gloriae* . . . The reversal required by theology today is to assign revelation to our own aeon, while assigning natural theology to the aeon to come. The theme of true religion is the eschatological goal of theology.[22]

He is supported by the prophetic traditions of the Old Testament: "I will put my law within them and will write it upon their hearts . . . And no longer shall each man teach his neighbor and say: 'Know the Lord', for they shall all know me, from the least of them to the greatest, says the Lord" (Jer. 31:33-34). That is the promised "new covenant." Then the knowledge of God will dwell in the land; then all minds will be full of God's glory; then God's particularist promise to Israel will be universally fulfilled. When God appears in a new Real Presence and in a new Real Presence appears to this God-alienated world, the knowledge of God will be so "natural" and so self-evident that no one will have to "teach" anyone else: they will all know him and will all do the good because God's law is written in their hearts, so that there is no need for anyone to admonish others. When this new day of God begins, Christian theology will dissolve itself, because it has been fulfilled.

If this theology in the kingdom of God's glory is the true "natural theology," then "natural religion" here, and the natural theology which is now possible for human beings, is no more than an advance radiance and a promise of their future.[23] But that means that a realistic theology of nature in its present condition sees all things as being true promises of their own future in the kingdom of glory. All things are transparent to their future.

A realistic theology of nature gives expression to the "sighs and groans of creation" and its longing to be liberated from transience. This earth is not a paradise, but is caught up in a history of order and chaos. Natural theology is a vision of its good future in the coming of God. So in the present condition of the earth, true natural theology is not a final condition; it is a *theologia viatorum*, a theology of those who are on the way. All created beings are with us on this way, in suffering and hope. The harmony of human culture and nature is a companionship on that way. The "restless human heart" corresponds to a restless world.

The natural theology thus described is a theology of the Holy Spirit and of the wisdom of God. The divine Spirit who indwells all things is the present bridge between creation in the beginning and the kingdom of glory. For that reason, the essential thing at present is to perceive in all things, and in all the complexes and interactions of life, the driving forces of God's Spirit, and to sense in our own hearts the yearning of the Spirit for the eternal life of the future world.

The Spirituality of the Senses:
The Mysticism of the Lived Life

There is a reason of ideas and a reason of feeling, there is the *esprit de géometrie*, said Pascal, and the *esprit du coeur*. Spirituality is a direction given to the heart. In spirituality, we turn to the place where we experience God's Spirit. For a long time this was a spirituality of the soul and of inwardness. In one of his poems, the Protestant mystic Gerhard Tersteegen advised the reader: Close the gateway of thy senses and seek God deep within.

But this can also be a spirituality of the senses, if the Holy Spirit is experienced in nature, as in the cosmic mysticism of Hildegard of Bingen and in Francis of Assisi's *Canticle of the Sun*. Then we do not have to "withdraw" into an innermost space; on the contrary, we must go out of ourselves and experience the outer world with all our senses. We must throw ourselves into the arms of life. This cosmic mysticism certainly runs counter to the trend of Western spirituality ever since Augustine, but it is what is needed today, for an ecological future of human beings and the earth.[24]

Our bodily senses link us with the world. We do not have to use them only in order to live and work. One must cultivate them as well, develop them and enhance them with reverence for life and for the presence of the living God.

It is true that with our eyes we see things in the world, but we have not learnt to contemplate them. It is only when we are still and contemplate that we perceive the beauty of a tree or the character of a flower. It is only when we look and open ourselves to the impression of what we see in front of us that we love things and other people for their own sake.

With our ears we hear the sounds of the outer world, we hear noise, voices, music. But have we learnt to listen, the self-forgetting listening to the other person, to what is new? Judaism and Christianity are religions for listeners: "Hear, O Israel . . ." begins the Sh'ma Israel, and Mary "heard" the angel's voice and took its words to heart. There is not only a hearing with the ears; there is a hearing with the heart as well. This is a profound hearing with the whole of the body. It "goes through and through us," as we say.

God breathes through the whole creation. If we are seized by his Spirit of life, then an undreamt of love for life awakens in us and our senses are aroused: "Our senses and our hearts enflame, our hearts with heavenly love inspire." So runs Rabanus Maurus's hymn for Pentecost.

In order to resist cynicism about the annihilation of life in our world today, we must overcome the increasing indifference and coldness of heart. The new mysticism of life breaks through this inner paralysis, this coldness toward the suffering of other people, and the failure to see the sufferings of nature. Those who begin to love life – the life we share – will resist the killing of human beings and the exploitation of the earth and will fight for a shared future.

They will fight with an open heart for a common future. They will pray with open eyes, and will listen to the sighs of oppressed creation.

When we love God
we embrace the whole world.
We love God with all our senses in the creations of God's love.
God waits for us in all that we encounter.

Chapter 3

A Common Earth Religion: World Religions from an Ecological Perspective

Is GLOBALIZATION MAKING MODERN WORLD RELIGIONS OUT OF LOCAL beliefs? What changes are required of the world religions in the light of the new ecological perspective on the earth?

In this chapter, I begin by critically taking stock of a globalization that takes no care of the globe, and modern world religions that have no thought for "the world." I will then explain how the earth sustains the life of every religion on it. My question is this: Do we need an "earth religion" as the overarching framework in which world religions can encounter one another and live side by side in harmony?

World Religions in the Age of Globalization

The global village

Globalization makes itself felt in every area of life. Since much has already been written about this topic, I will limit myself to a brief description of current trends.

Through the image of the global village, we can see that because of modern means of communication and transport, we are all neighbours, as in a traditional village. Communication creates communion, with no regard for traditional boundaries and distances. Telephones, fax machines, the Internet, e-mail, and so on enable us to communicate with each other with almost no delay at all. Individuals in different nations can be close as never before. Air travel bridges vast distances.

We are beginning to share one space; time delays are vanishing; physical distance is shrinking; interdependencies are growing. Our lives are more and more tightly intertwined. Events in Europe have consequences in Africa; changes in China affect us all; the collapse of the US real estate market brought the finances of many nations to their knees. The different peoples of the world are merging into one humanity. Different cultural traditions are melding together. The economy is globalizing markets and production systems. Wealth and poverty are being globalized by the banks. Just as in a traditional village, we are all related and we all share in the sorrows and joys of our common life.

There is one partner in this process that has not yet had its say, for almost nobody listens to its voice: that is the earth, our common home and the source of all life. We globalize our civilization with no concern for the strengths and weaknesses of the globe itself. We globalize our human economy at the expense of the earth's resources. We call this "progress," but our climb up the ladder of progress pushes down other life forms on this earth and threatens the fragile conditions for life itself. Every year, thousands of species become extinct; the climate deteriorates; the deserts expand; the sea level rises. We all know *The Limits to Growth* – the 1972 study by the Club of Rome – but we pay those limits barely any attention.[1]

In what follows, I offer an outline of other political and economic developments, after which I will draw out what this all means for the world religions.

From world politics to earth politics

I see this approach developing in three stages:

(1) Until the Second World War, the peoples of the world were politically organized in *nation states*. When faced with global challenges, such as the nuclear threat, those nations responded with international treaties. They founded the United Nations, yet no nation would relinquish any of its sovereignty to the Security Council. No transnational institutions were created. Responsibility for finding political solutions to mutual threats lay – and still lies – in the realms of national foreign policy.

(2) However, the greater the universal dangers become, the less chance any individual nation has of ensuring peace and protecting life. This is why some 30 years ago, at the height of the Cold War, German physicist and philosopher Carl Friedrich von Weizsäcker demanded a paradigm shift from national foreign policy to world domestic policy,[2] repositioning the focus of political thought away from the vital interests of the individual nation toward the survival interest of humanity as a whole in this, the only world we have. Every nation must subordinate its own interests to those of humanity. Conflicts between nations must never be allowed to menace the continued existence of the human race. Ideological and religious claims to absolute truth must be relativized for the sake of the future of humankind.

(3) The next step that must be taken is the transition from such a world domestic policy to a common earth policy.[3] Ecological disasters do not stop at national borders; they threaten every nation. The death toll of tsunamis and earthquakes, famines and floods has evoked admirable human solidarity. However, at an international level, a large-scale strategy to face the ecological disasters of the future remains virtually impossible, because there are still so many conflicting national interests: a common earth policy needs transnational institutions. For a transnational peace policy, a firm foundation can be found in human rights. For the earth policy that is needed, we must codify and enforce the rights of the earth itself, "regardless of its worth to human beings," as is written in the UN Earth Charter. This view must also apply to other forms of life in nature. They must be protected for their own sake.

From a world economy to an earth economy

The 19th century saw the development, along with the nation state, of the national economy, or macroeconomics. The most important thing for a national economy is the regulated domestic market. External trade was termed the import-export business. It was promoted and regulated at first by international trade agreements. In many parts of the world, this remains the case. But the globalization of markets and production systems has given rise to transnational companies.

Since they were deregulated about 30 years ago (by Ronald Reagan and Margaret Thatcher), we have seen the emergence of transnational markets and transnational economic organizations. These global players in the world economy seem to have shaken off all political regulation; indeed, they seem to be beginning to regulate national policy themselves.

While national economies merge into one world economy, political institutions have not kept pace. This imbalance can be seen with painful clarity when populations must pay the price for damage done by transnational companies – from the oil industry to nuclear power. Through governments and non-governmental organizations, we must put pressure on the world economy to become an earth economy – one that pays for the harm it does and learns to take care of the natural world.

To destroy one's own livelihood or that of another people for short-term gain is stupid. The earth's resources, too, are limited and will one day be exhausted. There is no need to go into details here; we all know this. However, my point is different: obviously, the measure of progress and globalization is economic growth – quantitative growth on a linear time axis. Produce more; consume more. On this time axis, we move toward the future and leave the past behind. In economic terms, this means that consumption increases; we use more and more resources and leave more and more refuse behind us. Yet to transition toward an earth economy means to learn the earth's cyclical time, where strength can be reborn. To convert this earth wisdom into an earth economy will entail developing renewable energies and expanding the recycling industry, making new from old.[4] This approach will bring us into a qualitative kind of growth and stabilize our relationship with the natural world through balanced systems, giving rise to a bio-economy, which will respect and promote the regenerative powers of life.

World religions before globalization

World religions have existed since long before contemporary globalization. World religions are commonly understood to be those that claim universal validity, take their mission over many parts of the world, or cover large proportions of humanity. Moments in life – birth, coming of age, marriage and death[5] – are universally marked by celebration and religious observance: these are family religions, and they are found everywhere. The cycles of nature – the solstices, the phases of the moon, spring and autumn, seed-time and harvest – are also marked by celebration: these are nature religions, and they exist everywhere. World religions, however, are something more than this religious celebration of life's events, for they offer something universal. Just what do they offer?

Political religions emerged with the founding of states. These religions are invariably monotheistic: one god, one ruler, one empire, with the ruler also acting as high priest of heaven.[6] This is how the ancient emperor cults of Rome, Persia, China and Japan, Genghis Khan and the Indian Moguls were formed. In China, the "Son of Heaven" faced the children of earth as their lord and priest. His empire was as universal as the heavens that arch over the earth. The domain of his rule was concomitant with the heavenly domain of salvation.[7] Such political world religions have been an essential element of world empires right up into the modern era. Far from suppressing family and nature religions, political religions protect them and, within their territory, are thoroughly tolerant.

Buddhism is probably the oldest non-state world religion. It is a monastic religion of meditation and inner balance. Thus it fits comfortably with common family and nature religions and poses no conflict for the political religions of rulers. In Japan, it exists in harmony with both state and folk Shinto. Buddhism was popularized in China through scriptures brought from India and then translated. Even today, Buddhism works not through aggression but through appeal. Its universality lies not in its charisma but in its attractiveness. Buddhism is rarely exclusive. Buddhist practices can well be combined with other religious forms, as in the Three Religions Movement in Japan or the Five Religions Movement in Taiwan. Buddhism does not demand a monogamous relationship: you definitely can have other gods besides it.

The Abrahamic world religions are different. They are rooted in the exclusivity of the God of Israel. Christianity and Islam are referred to as religions of prophecy or religions of history because they are rooted in historic salvation events and spread the news of the universal significance of these events through active mission. They transform the particular exclusivity of the God of Israel into the exclusive universality of the One God, who has revealed himself in Christ or in the Koran. This is why their missions are aggressive and their faith exclusive. One must make a decision and submit to their faith. Not least, they have a tendency to take on the form of imperial political religions and set up Christian or Islamic empires. The Christianization of the Roman Empire gave rise to the empires of Europe, which ended in mutual destruction and collapse in the First World War. Even the USA is no longer "the empire."[8]

World religions since globalization

The pre-modern world was primarily an agrarian culture and was centred on the rhythms and cycles of the earth. We therefore talk of pre-modern cosmic religions. The industrial revolution signalled the dawn of the anthropocentric age. Humans no longer oriented their cultures by nature on earth or the stars in the sky; instead, they created their cultures according to their own ideas. The human being became the centre of the world, between heaven and earth, and the centre of its own self-created world.[9] The world was made into the world of the human being, and nature on earth was demoted to being merely the environment for human civilization.

At the hub of the pre-modern world lies the village, and the village lies in its own landscape. At the hub of the modern world lies the city, which often has no interaction with the landscape on which it stands, or even with the sun in the blue sky. Over 50 percent of all people today live in mega-cities, cities of 10 million to 35 million inhabitants, such as Mexico City, Lagos, and Chongqing. In these distended urban monsters, nature religion has died and the old family religions are losing their families. Religion is forced to focus on individualized human beings and on their needs. Today's urbanized, globalized world makes all religions world religions, if a number of conditions are fulfilled:

The first is the separation of religion and politics. Modern states are secular states and do not need a state religion. State religion does still exist in some parts of the Islamic world, and Myanmar has even made an official religion of Buddhism, but elsewhere, the wisdom of Jesus' words to "give to the emperor the things that are the emperor's, and give to God the things that are God's" (Mark 12:17) applies. This draws a clear dividing line between the worship of God and national interests.

Once religion is no longer a matter for the political common-wealth, it becomes a private matter. The modern world practises reli-gious tolerance by guaranteeing individual religious freedom: no one may be discriminated against because of his or her religion. All indi-viduals are free to choose their own religion, to change their religion or to belong to no religion.

The modern, globalized, urbanized world is therefore becoming a multi-religious society. Through missionaries, radio, television and the Internet, any religion can go global and gain adherents all over the world. So we have latter-day shamans in California and Tibetan Buddhists in Germany. The conditions outlined above and the media of the modern world have enabled every religion to have a presence in every part of the world. But in what form?

The world religions are freely accessible in a spiritual and reli-gious marketplace. As religious "products" they are subordinated to the desire of the religious "customer" – and that alters religions fundamentally. They are turning into opportunities for individual religiosity and, thus, into options that are universally open to every individual. However, taken to its extreme, this means a Judaism with no Torah, a Christianity with no Sermon on the Mount, an Islam with no Sharia, and Buddhist meditation with no asceticism: religion lite, patchwork religion. But a religion that makes no demands can offer no comfort.

Many Religions – One Earth

Gaia theory

"Earth" has many meanings, depending on context. When we talk in terms of air – water – earth, we mean the solid ground on which we stand. In religion, "earth" can stand for the duality of the world – heaven and earth, or the visible and invisible world.[10] In astronomical terms, we mean "the blue planet," whose beautiful image we have been enabled to see thanks to space flight. So, in the first sense, "earth" is the land, where we grow our crops and raise our livestock; in the second, it is the habitat of earthly life, in contrast to the heavens of the gods; in the third, it is our life source and our home.

Modern astronomical science has demonstrated the interdependency between the populated and unpopulated parts of our planet. This view has given rise to the idea that the biosphere of this earth, together with its atmosphere, oceans, and landmasses, forms one unique, complex system, and that this system can be understood, for the sake of comparison, in terms of an "earth organism," as it has the capacity to bring forth life forms and create habitats for them. This is James Lovelock's much-discussed Gaia hypothesis. Lovelock wanted to call the earth system he had described a "universal biocybernetic system with a tendency to homeostasis," but his neighbour, the poet William Golding, offered the Greek name "Gaia," after the goddess of the earth. And thus the theory became known as Gaia theory.

The Gaia theory is not an attempt to deify the earth, but an understanding of this planet earth as an organism that creates life and creates the habitats for life to exist in many forms.[11] The earth is not an agglomeration of materials and forces; it is not blind or deaf; nor is it simply the environment for human cultures. Rather, it is to be viewed as one great subject, bringing forth life, upholding life, creating the conditions necessary for life, neutralizing chemical compounds that are hostile to life and, not least, developing ever more complex forms of life. We humans are ourselves creatures of the earth. At a certain point in its development, the earth began to feel, to think, to become self-aware and to experience awe.[12] To truly understand our humanity, we must begin not with ourselves, but with the earth, the "nature subject." Gaia theory puts an end to the anthropocentrism of the modern world and clears the way for a democratic integration of the human race into the life of the earth system as a whole. This theory provides the bridge for the ecological reconstruction of our globalized world and our modern worldviews.

God – earth – humanity

The Abrahamic world religions, in contrast to nature religions, are known as "religions of history," since their God reveals himself in the world of humanity and is only secondarily recognized in the world of nature. This view sets up an anthropocentrism whereby humanity stands between the divine and the earthly: as the image of God, humanity is appointed ruler of the earth:

- the Divine;

- humanity;

- earth.

In the *Tao Te Ching*, we find a different order:
Man follows earth.
Earth follows heaven.
Heaven follows Tao.
Tao follows what is natural.[13]

I do not propose to go into a discussion here on Taoism's teachings on nature,[14] but merely to draw attention to this alternative order:

- Tao;

- heaven;

- earth;

- the human being.

The symbol in Taoism for the emergence of earth's myriad creatures is not the masculine image of creation, but the feminine picture of birth:

The beginning of the universe
is the mother of all things.
Knowing the mother, one also knows the sons.[15]

We must understand the earth to understand humanity. The ancient wisdom of the Hebrew Bible hints at this point, which forms the foundation for the Abrahamic religions. According to the creation story, the earth is commanded to "bring forth living creatures of every kind" (Gen. 1:24), and human beings themselves are "formed . . . from the dust of the ground" (Gen. 2:7). The Noahic covenant, which holds meaning for Jews, Christians and Muslims alike, is a twofold covenant. It is at once God's covenant with "[Noah] and [his] descendants after [him], and with every living creature" (Gen. 9:9-10), and God's covenant with the earth (Gen. 9:13) and every living creature. Thus the Noahic covenant is both, on the one hand, *God – human being – life – earth*, and, on the other, *God – earth – life – human being.*[16]

To me, this means that we must now forge dialectically a connection between these two modes of understanding: we must understand life and the earth from a human point of view and at the same time comprehend humanity and life from the perspective of the earth. It is earth that enables humanity to understand the heavens and the Tao, and it is through humanity that life on earth attains self-awareness.

The earth as the space for encounter and cooperation between world religions

In the past, the world religions have considered that their universal relevance and scope extended only as far as the human world. But if that human world is embedded in the nature of the earth and cannot survive without it, then the universal scope of the world religions in fact extends to Gaia itself.[17] They can be truly world religions only if they become earth religions, and view humanity as an integrated element in planet earth as a whole. If the missionary religions of history are to reach the ends of the earth, they must transform themselves into universal religions of the earth. To do this, they must rediscover the forgotten ecological wisdom and natural reverence of local nature religions. True, those mountain gods and river goddesses were worshipped only within their own lands, but the transformation of the world religions into earth religions will take place only when they globalize that local ecological wisdom and reverence for nature and enable the rights of the earth to be honoured. In the past, many adherents of the world religions have looked down on nature religions, thinking them primitive. As those religions metamorphose into earth religions, their members will acknowledge their error and seek to reinterpret that pre-industrial wisdom for our post-industrial age. For if the world religions cannot achieve this result, who can?

A South African friend told me the following story. Whenever his father wanted to make a canoe, my friend would have to chop down a tree. But in order to fell the tree, he would first have to ask the tree spirit for forgiveness. Then a Christian missionary came and said, "This is idolatry. Subdue the earth and chop down the tree." Yet now, environmentalists come and say, "No, no, your father was right. Trees and forests are a vital part of the earth's organism. If you have to fell a tree, ask the earth for forgiveness and plant a new tree in its place."

World religions are invariably focused on the world beyond; this is why they concentrate on immanent universality. The Nirvana of Buddhist religions and the God of the monotheistic religions both have their being beyond this world. Imperial political religions, too, raise the emperor up to the position of a son of heaven to contrast him against the children of earth. For these world religions, the "world" is not all there is; the world is mundane, painful, mortal, futile, and temporary. It cannot be a fitting home for an immortal human soul. Only the unseen world of heaven, the gods, or Nirvana can offer a soul salvation, peace, or a paradise of wishes that are unfulfilled on earth. With their focus on the world beyond, the world religions have offered comfort in the strangeness of this world, but have also made this world into a stranger. They have paid for their solace in the world beyond with a negation of this-worldly life. In so doing, they have themselves become contributing factors in today's ecological crisis. They have often spent more time preaching denial of earthly life than affirmation of it; they have often promoted respect for life more than love for it.

If the world religions are to reach "the ends of the earth," they must turn back to the earth and give it back the beauties and virtues that they have projected onto the world beyond.[18] They must abandon their denial of life, their capacity for violence and their promises of redemption in the world beyond.[19] To put it in secular terms, world religions must seriously engage with the ecological perspective and start by applying it to themselves. For if the earth can no longer support life, that means the end of the human world and the end of world religions.

The Hebrew Bible offers us an "earth religion" in the form of the Sabbath year. Every seventh year, the people are to leave the land fallow.[20] Two reasons are given: "so that the poor of your people may eat" and so that there may be "a Sabbath of complete rest for the land." Sabbath rest for the earth is blessed by God, for this year allows the land to become fruitful again. If the people observe the Sabbath for the earth, they will live secure in the land. If they disobey this command, they will be cast out of the land and scattered among the nations for 70 years, until God's land has recovered. This old story gives us a grave warning: if we fail to observe the earth religion and force the earth to bear fruit constantly, using artificial fertilizers, we will exhaust the ground and make it infertile. The deserts will spread, droughts will become more frequent, and eventually the human race will disappear from the earth that it has wrecked and abused.

My vision for the future of the world religions is well expressed in an image taken from China. Whenever I'm in China or Taiwan, I have always loved to buy the beautiful wall paintings found in those countries. Whatever else they depict, they always include a waterfall, bringing living water from heaven to earth. That's a powerful symbol. My dream is that one day, the religions of the world will flow like fresh water, from beyond into our world, making the joy of heaven the delight of earth and bringing the water of life from eternity into time. For all the world's religions, I long for the kingdom of God to come "on earth as it is in heaven."

Chapter 4

Mercy and Solidarity

HERE I SHALL ADDRESS THE TOPIC OF "MERCY AND SOLIDARITY."

Pope Francis has accorded priority in the church of Christ to mercy toward the poor. This is good; but his idea of mercy toward the poor goes back to the "preferential option for the poor" of the Latin American bishops' meeting in Medellin in 1968. Is that enough? Must not solidarity be added to mercy? Is not the personal act of mercy toward those who are in need of help generated by the profound feeling of solidarity with them? Does not the act of mercy create an enduring community of solidarity with the poor? Mercy is a personal emotion, and the act of mercy is a spontaneous intervention; solidarity is enduring and institutional, with rights and obligations. Solidarity makes the "failure to render assistance" punishable and gives the one who is needy entitlements to social security benefits.

I shall seek to identify a fruitful link between mercy and solidarity. In the first part, about mercy, I shall take up the community of human solidarity, and in the second part, about solidarity, I shall take up the religion of mercy.

From mercy to solidarity

1

In the Hebrew language that leaves its imprint on both the Old Testament and the New, the act of mercy is a genuine "gut feeling."

Rachamim is a compassion that goes so deep that the intestines tense up. The noun *rachamim* is feminine and points to the pains a mother feels at birth, the pains with which a new life is brought into the world. *Rachamim* is a feeling of being caught up by empathy and compassion: I empathize with the poor person who is suffering miserably, and I spontaneously give help. I must do so; I cannot do anything else! At the same time, *rachamim* is the creative feeling with which a new deed begins, and a life is saved or comes to birth.

In Latin, the centre of human life moves up from the diaphragm to the heart (*cor*). It is no longer the breath that makes life alive, but the bloodstream, and thus the heart becomes the centre of life. This is why the misery of the poor affects us so strongly that *misericordia* arises out of the very centre of our life. In German, *misericordia* generated the noun *Barmherzigkeit* and the verb *erbarmen*. Like the Latin noun, these words signify having a heart for the poor. Luther translated the Greek word for "having mercy" as *es jammerte ihn,* that is to say, "it made him sad," "it brought tears to his eyes," "he could no longer endure looking at it." This heartfelt mercy is a strong motivation for helping those in need, something that drives one passionately to change the situation of the poor. The word "compassion" (German: *Mitleid*) does not do justice to the original meaning of an "act of mercy."

2

The Hebrew Bible is the "sphere of truth" for the Christian New Testament and the Koran of the Islamic world. This is why we begin with the "great mercy" of God, in order to grasp the transcendental dimension of showing mercy in the world.

Mercy comes from the innermost being of God and stands over the creation and over history, over the people of Israel and the law. Mercy is God's passion for his creatures, for his people, and for the individual who prays. "His mercy is eternal" (Ps. 106:1); it "goes over the whole world" (Sir. 16:12).

God's great mercy is stronger than his anger at the wickedness of human beings and at the infidelity of his people. "For a brief moment

I abandoned you, but with great mercy I will gather you" (Is. 54:7-8). Anger and grace are not of equal value: God's anger is temporal, his grace eternal; God's judgments are temporal, his mercy eternal. God's anger is nothing other than his wounded love.

The most important fact about the great mercy is that it invalidates the law of recompense, the recompense of both "an eye for an eye, and a tooth for a tooth" and the Golden Rule: "Everything that you want people to do to you – do that to them" (Matt. 7:13). According to the law of recompense, every good action is performed in view of "reciprocity" (Confucius): "As you do to me, so I do to you." However, such an action in view of reciprocity presupposes the equality of the persons involved. This "world ethos" (to use Hans Küng's term) does not apply to the poor, the sick, the disabled, and foreigners. There is no ethical "reciprocity" for unequal persons, nor is there any demand for recompense with good things or with bad things. This is why Bavarian Catholics express their thanks by saying: *Vergelt's Gott* ("May God recompense you"). I repeat: for unequal persons, there is no ethical reciprocity, nor any demand for a response that pays the other person back. There is only the one-sided friendly act of mercy, which helps them to have life, heals them, sets them free, restores them, and gives them justice. Action on the basis of reciprocity leads to *exclusive societies.* Merciful action leads to inclusive societies.

Israel understood its history with God as the experienced expression of God's great mercy. When the people were in captivity, God came down to them and led them, in the form of his *shekhinah,* into the promised land. And after this, God led them through the terrors and opportunities of history.

3

Christ's history with God is likewise a history of God's mercy. The incarnation in Jesus Christ is also the "becoming flesh" of the divine mercy to those who were lost, to the sick and the poor, in order to find them, to heal them, and to restore them. It is not only the story of Christ's passion that is the expression of the divine mercy: the same is true of the resurrection of Christ from the dead. "By his great mercy

God has given us a new birth into a living hope through the resurrection of Jesus Christ from the dead" (1 Pet. 1:3). Through God's mercy, distress is taken away and new life is born.

4

This brings us to the well-known parable of the Good (or Merciful) Samaritan:

> "A man was going down from Jerusalem to Jericho, and fell into the hands of robbers, who stripped him, beat him, and went away, leaving him half dead. Now by chance a priest was going down that road; and when he saw him, he passed by on the other side. So also a Levite, when he came to the place and saw him, passed by on the other side. But a Samaritan while traveling came near him; and when he saw him, he was moved with pity. He went to him and bandaged his wounds . . . Then he put him on his own animal, brought him to an inn, and took care of him." [He gave the innkeeper money to continue looking after him.]
>
> Jesus asked the lawyer: "Which of these three, do you think, was a neighbor to the man who fell into the hands of the robbers?" And he replied: "The one who showed him mercy." (Luke 10:25-37)

The following points in this story are remarkable:

(a) Jesus turns around the question "Who is my neighbour?" and asks: "Whose neighbour have you been?"

(b) The lawyer was a pious Jew, while the Samaritan came from Samaria, the country of the heretics and unbelievers. When he makes the "Samaritan" the model figure, Jesus is saying: The commandment of love is universally valid. Everyone who shows mercy can become one's neighbour.

(c) We are not told whether the victim of the robbers on the road to Jericho was a Jew or a Gentile. For the act of mercy, it suffices that he has been a victim of violence. The one who shows mercy does not ask about religion, nationality, or race. His heart reacts to the distress.

(d) The priest and the Levite saw the man who was half dead, but they went on their way. This fact is an accusation against them. They cannot say: "We did not see anything, we did not hear anything, and we did not know anything" (as many Germans said when the Jews "fell into the hands of robbers").

(e) The "Merciful Samaritan" has found his way into the German penal code. §323c makes a "failure to render assistance" punishable: "One who fails to render assistance in the case of accidents and general danger or distress . . . will be punished with imprisonment for up to one year or with a financial penalty."

(f) What is mercy, and how does it happen? The Merciful Samaritan expects no reward, not even a "reward in heaven." Nor does he feel especially "good." He recognizes the distress and does what is necessary. That is enough. A genuine "Samaritan service" needs no explanation; there is no "why?" And this is precisely how the human act of showing mercy corresponds to the gratuitous mercy of God.

5

The Christian Middle Ages taught the "seven corporal works of mercy": "to feed the hungry, to give drink to the thirsty, to shelter the strangers, to clothe the naked, to care for the sick, to visit prisoners, and to bury the dead." This goes back to the story of the "last judgment" of the world in Matthew 25, where the Son of Man, the redeemer of the world, identifies himself with those in distress: "Just as you did it to one of the least of these my brothers [and sisters], so you did it to me." This elevates their dignity, and the act of mercy integrates them into the fellowship that the helpers and those who are helped both share with Christ their brother.

6

This brings us to Saint Martin of Tours. Up to this point, we have spoken only of the persons who are merciful. Now, we empathize with the situation of those in misery, since mercy must not only be given: it must also be accepted. If one is dependent on the mercy of other people, one feels humiliated, because one is unable to help oneself. Those who could provide for themselves in the past are ashamed to go to the "food bank" or soup kitchen, so that they can eat for free. Their need impels them to go there, but they do not want to be seen. How can mercy be shown in such a way that it does not humiliate and make people ashamed, harming their sense of self-respect? There are two pictures of Saint Martin of Tours. In the one picture, he stands and the beggar also stands: they are at eye level, and then he shares his cloak fraternally with the beggar. In the other picture, he sits high on his horse and the beggar kneels beneath him while he divides the cloak. The latter is top-down mercy. The first picture shows that the act of mercy must be linked to the recognition of the beggar as a brother; but the second picture humiliates the beggar twice – first through his situation of need and then through the mercy shown by the man who rides high on his horse. He could at least have gotten off the horse.

7

I now turn to mercy in Islam and Buddhism. Mercy and the act of showing mercy are praised in all the world religions. In this respect, there exists an ecumenism of the religious communities, and this must lend fruitfulness to their dialogue in view of the misery in the world. Here, we shall look only briefly at the Koran and at a Buddhist text.

"The one who has mercy on all" (*Ar-Rahman*) is one of the names of God and, together with "The one who is merciful to all" (*Ar-Rahmin*), the most frequent name of God in the Koran. The Arabic word *rahma* is related to the Hebrew word *rachamim* and is derived from the tensing up of the intestines. The two terms can be distinguished as follows: while *being merciful to all* designates God's unconditional and universal care for all creatures, *having mercy on all* is God's reaction to the suffering and the conduct of human beings. Giving alms to the poor is the fourth of the Five Pillars of Islam. In Jesus, the formulation is positive – "Blessed are the merciful, for they shall receive mercy" (Matt. 5:7) – but it is formulated negatively in an Islamic hadith: "Those who are not merciful will not receive any mercy."

One problem discussed in the Koranic schools of the past and the present is whether God's mercy is only for the believing Muslims, or for all human beings – and hence even for the unbelievers. The answer to this question determines how one behaves toward other people. If one looks at the mercy of God, the act of mercy applies to all who are in need, but if one looks at the true believers, the act of mercy applies only to the other believers who are in need. This is also discussed both in Christianity ("Let us do good to all, and especially to those of the family of faith," says Paul [Gal. 6:10]) and in Judaism, where the question takes the following form: If I am faced with two persons in need, a Jew and a Gentile, and I can help only one of them, whom should I help? My own answer to this question is that where such distinctions are drawn, there is no longer any true act of mercy that corresponds to the mercy of the Creator God.

In Buddhism, we find the figures of the merciful *bodhisattva* and the Chinese goddess of mercy, *Quan-jin* (Kannon). The former stands for compassion, the latter for the act of mercy. Mercy is called compassion, *karuna,* in Buddhism. It is one of the various forms of human connectedness, such as love, shared joy, and compassion. Karuna is not only an obligation, but also a fruit of insight, thanks to meditation and to the equanimity that is born of meditation. In his article "Karuna," Taitetsu Unno describes Buddhist mercy as follows:

In mercy, one helps and cares for those who are in need, and for helpless animals . . . Those without money are given food . . . and animals are liberated from enslavement to human beings . . .The mercy of the *Sacred Path* consists of having mercy on all that lives . . .The mercy of the *Pure Land* means helping other living beings out of compassion and a feeling of shared grief, so that they may attain Buddhahood.

In the first case, mercy is directed to distress; in the second case, it is directed to redemption through Buddhahood. In both cases, it is important for the human being to enter the force field of the "great mercy" that embraces all that lives: human beings, animals, and plants.

From Solidarity to Mercy

1

Are there structures of mercy? Up to this point, in keeping with the root meaning of *Barmherzigkeit,* we have looked at mercy only in the personal and spontaneous act of showing mercy to those in need. Does mercy function only in the personal sphere? The Brazilian Bishop Dom Hélder Câmara once said: "When I showed mercy to the poor, people praised me and called me a saint. When I asked publicly why the poor are poor, people insulted me and called me a communist."

If there exist inhuman laws and asocial structures, there also exist laws that do justice to human beings, and structures that are socially just. Accordingly, there also exist unmerciful and merciful structures. The early Christian communities certainly did not restrict their encounters with poverty to the personal sphere, like the "Merciful Samaritan." They organized the well-known early Christian *community of property,* which exists in the monastic Christianity of monks and nuns down to the present day: ". . . and there was none among them who suffered any lack" (Acts 4). Indeed, the first community in Jerusalem appointed "the seven men who cared for the poor" (Acts 6), who looked after the "widows and orphans" who were without rights and protection. It is clear that some communities cared not only for their own poor members, but also (as admiring contemporaries noted) for the "widows and orphans" of the entire city. In these two structures, we can discern the Christian roots of solidarity, which can be seen here to mean fidelity to the community: we do not allow any of us to fall by the wayside, but care for each one who belongs to us. At the same time, we see an open solidarity with all the hardships of the city or the society.

There were always many beggars who sat at the doors of the mediaeval churches, so that the pious churchgoers could perform the "good works" of mercy to them and gather for themselves a "treasure in heaven." Besides this, "confraternities" were formed to perform the "seven works of mercy" in the mediaeval societies. Even if modern people no longer believe in heaven, they feel "good" when they are "charitable" and make a donation to church services that help the poor. Since the Reformation, there are no longer any beggars outside Protestant churches. Are Protestant Christians unmerciful, because they believe in justification "by faith alone," and not by "good works"? No, the Reformation was not only a church reform in the cities, but also a social reform. After the Reformation, the deacons took on the task of helping the poor and caring for the sick, thereby preparing society for the welfare state. Bismarck's social legislation was oriented to the "Elberfeld" model, which had its origin in the Dutch Reformed community. It was Baron von der Heydt who mediated these initial approaches to the welfare state in Germany. Max Weber's thesis that Calvinism inspired capitalism is historically false. One could just as well say that Calvinism inspired socialism through the ministry of the deacons, and that it inspired democracy through its presbyterial-synodal church order.

The personal act of showing mercy leads logically to structures of mercy. Both churches supported the cooperative movement in the German territories in the 19th century, and they themselves founded many cooperatives in the countryside and in the towns, in order to combat poverty and unemployment. When people voluntarily come together in cooperatives, they become strong. The alternative to poverty is not wealth. The alternative to poverty and wealth is – community!

2

Is there mercy without humiliation? When we hear the word "mercy," we tend to think of the one who is merciful, not of the one who is in a wretched condition. How do poor persons, who are dependent on the good gifts of merciful persons, feel? How do unemployed and home-less persons, who are dependent on the "food banks" and the warm parish halls, feel? If mercy comes down from above, they feel doubly humiliated. Giving is good, but receiving is more difficult. This is why the act of mercy always also involves the recognition of the human dignity of those who are in need, and respect for their self-esteem. The best help is the "help for self-help."

The Latin American "preferential option for the poor" (Medellin 1968) is good for those who are not poor, but it is not an "option of the poor," because the poor have not opted to become poor. They are held fast in poverty, and they look for a path out of poverty into a good life shared with others. The poor are "poor" only in comparison with the rich. They are not poor per se and in other relationships. Rather, they possess their own gifts and energies, which only wait to be awakened and mobilized. "Poor" people, like all of us, do not want to be told about the things they do not possess; they want to be recognized in what they are. This is why they need, not only mercy, but also human solidarity, and they experience this in a human community of solidarity.

3

What is a human community of solidarity, and how does it function? Mercy (*Barmherzigkeit*) comes "from the heart (*von Herzen*)" and, as the parable of the "Merciful Samaritan" shows, it is personal, spontaneous, and momentary. Solidarity, on the other hand, means a sense of community and fidelity to the community; it is social, institutional, and enduring. In a community of solidarity, there is a public participation on the part of everyone, and a share for each one in what is common property. Trust and reliability, laws and obligations determine life. The archetypical Christian image is not the Merciful Samaritan, but the early Christian community of property. The modern European welfare state is a consequence of the organized solidarity between the strong and the weak, the healthy and the sick, the young and the old. The welfare state changes the poor, the sick, and the old from objects of an act of mercy to subjects of rights and entitlements: social security, medical insurance, a retirement pension. All this is more than "structural mercy" (to use Wolfgang Thierse's term). It is based on the universal human rights of citizens and is thus rather a *structural solidarity*. The modern welfare state is concerned not only for those who "fall into the hands of robbers." It also endeavours to abolish robbery and murder and to socialize the "robbers." And if the modern welfare state is also ecological, it can organize mercy and solidarity with the animals and plants, and with the earth as a whole. The more we employ renewable energies, and industry moves from a waste-making industry to a recycling industry, the better will be the situation of the total ecological system of the earth, which is the home of us all.

4

Does this make mercy and acts of mercy superfluous? No! Mercy is the soul of social justice. Without a culture of mercy, the motivation for social legislation is lost. The ethic of showing mercy to the weak, the sick, and the old must be defended today against the societal coldness of neoliberalism, for it is only a universal ethic of showing mercy that can justify the social laws and make the "failure to render assistance" not merely something that individuals can lament, but something that is punishable by the courts.

Personal mercy is necessary even in welfare states. The charitable services of the Catholic and Protestant churches in Germany are indispensable. It is true that the state's network of social security covers the greatest needs, but there are nevertheless many unemployed and homeless persons, sick and elderly persons, about whom no one cares. As experience shows, social legislation always has gaps, because life cannot be completely regulated. In the social welfare agencies, there is often a climate of suspicion of cheating rather than a respect for the human dignity of those who are in need.

Mercy opens up the community of solidarity in the nation state to the persecuted and the refugees, as far as this is possible and reasonable. That is why Pope Francis was on Lampedusa. We could say that mercy is the missionary apex of the open welfare state.

Mercy is also a source of international help. This goes without saying in the case of natural catastrophes, earthquakes, and tsunamis, as we saw several years ago in Haiti. This is more difficult for what the United Nations calls the "community of nations" in political catastrophes, as in Syria and Iraq, in civil wars and failing states. The United

Nations must intervene in cases of "genocide." Entire peoples, ethnic groups and minorities can "fall into the hands of robbers," as the human catastrophe in Rwanda and Burundi shows.

The community of solidarity and the social welfare state function only as long as the moral world is determined by solidarity and mercy rather than by the capitalistic ideology – greed, avarice, and egomania.

5

Finally, the personal act of mercy is not only necessary, but also good and beautiful. It is the translation of the mercy of God into the way we human beings behave toward each other. Our little act of mercy sanctifies this life and is a response to the great mercy of God. The personal act of mercy is unconditional and immediate in the care of the other. It is generous, not calculating. The personal act of mercy is self-evident and self-forgetting.

The personal act of mercy is present also in the indignation at the inhumanity of situations and the mercilessness of human beings.

The personal act of mercy is a happy life in the broad space of the mercy of God.

Chapter 5

The Unfinished World:
Nature, Time, and the Future

FOR ME, SCIENCE IS A "PARADISE LOST." I WANTED TO STUDY mathematics and physics. But in 1943, just while I was reading Louis de Broglie's book *Matière et Lumière*,[1] I was called up and conscripted into the German army. At the end of five years of war and captivity, I came back as a theologian. The question about God had become more important to me, but the question about scientific truth has remained with me ever since.

I have felt the invitation to this Robert Boyle Lecture[2] to be a reminder of the lost dream of my youth. Robert Boyle founded the lecture "for the defense of faith." According to my own experiences in the border zone between theology and science, when faith encounters serious science, it requires no defense but only interest and curiosity.

The question about God and the question of "what holds nature together in its innermost being" (as Goethe put it) are not wholly divergent questions. They are not controversial. According to Plato, wonder is the beginning of all knowledge. According to the Jewish-Christian tradition, the fear of God is the beginning of all wisdom. Do not these two things belong together? If wonder over the phenomena of nature converges with reverence before the great mystery of the whole, the outcome is the humble search for truth, and joy in its discoveries.[3]

Theologians and scientists encounter each other with respect and consideration. So I can understand the annoyed reaction of scientists, who think in a precise manner, when they are confronted with pseudo-scientific "creationism," and you will understand the critical reactions of theologians who take up cudgels against the new naturalistic atheism. Ideologies spring up as a result of the reduction of complex forms of life, or because of totalizations of individual aspects. Scientists and theologians dislike ideologies of this kind, because they distort the view of truth and serve irrelevant interests.

And yet, how many theologians read scientific books in order to understand God's activity in nature? And how many scientists turn to theological books, except, it may be, in order to understand their personal faith, but scarcely for scientific reasons?

The logical systems of theology and the sciences can be compared as a way of stimulating each other mutually to new ways of thinking, for example, the interrelationality in the Christian doctrine of the Trinity and in nuclear physics,[4] or the wave-particle complementarity and the person-energy complementarity of God's Spirit in human experience.

But it is also possible to work on common topics in the reality in which we live and think. In this lecture I should like to try to do this with regard to the concept of nature, the concept of time, and the idea of a world open to the future. Theology does not call into question the results of scientific research, but it does set these results in the context of wider horizons of interpretation, because it has different questions.

In the ancient world, physics, according to Aristotle, required a metaphysics in order to explain the presuppositions which it had not itself created but continually applied. Similarly, the modern sciences too must open themselves to new metaphysical questions if they do not want merely to register facts but to interpret signs as well. We know more from year to year about natural processes, but do we also understand what we perceive? Science is a hermeneutics of nature as well, if it does not merely aim to know nature, but also wants to understand what it perceives. In the sphere of hermeneutics, scientists and theologians meet.[5]

In this Boyle lecture, I should like to talk about the interactions between theology and the sciences. I am interested here in the influence of the Jewish-Christian doctrine of creation on the modern concept of nature and time, and in the influence of the modern sciences on the new theological concept of a creation that is open to the future.

The Readability of the World

The initial premise of all science is the knowability of nature.[6] However initial and fragmentary our knowledge may be, there is a correspondence between our reason and the reasonableness of the world. In describing modern genetic researches, a metaphor often used is "the book of life."[7] In its genetic structures, life becomes "readable." In the gene sequences, we learn "the spelling of life": the human genome is a "dictionary of the human being," the base pairs are like the "letters," and the genes are like "the words" of life. President Clinton called the sequences of the decoded human genome "the language in which God created life." The other metaphor about the "genetic code" makes the genetic understandable as signals or signs of an encoded message. Both metaphors present nature as a sign-cosmos of meanings which have to be understood.

The idea of the "readability of the world" is derived from the theological tradition of the "two books." There is "the Book of Books" and there is "the book of nature," said the Cappadocians.[8] Basil the Great believed that our reason has been so perfectly created by God that "we can read the wisdom of God through the beauties of created things as if they were letters and words of God's wisdom." For Augustine, only the person who has learnt to read can read the Bible, but even someone who is illiterate can understand the book of nature. John Scotus Erigena thought that the two books were two theophanies, the one given through letters, the other through forms. According to Nicholas of Cusa, "things are the books of the senses. In them the will of the divine reason is described in sensory images." However, from Keppler and Galileo onwards, the view came to prevail that "the book of nature" is written not with letters but in numbers. The cosmic wisdom speaks to the human intelligence through mathematics. That was the famous *reductio scientiae ad mathematicam* with which the scientific revolution of modern times began.

But how does human reason relate to the reasonableness of the world? With the beginning of modern times, this was described as the relation between subject and object. Through science and technology, human beings become what Descartes called "the lords and possessors of nature." Kant maintained that human reason has insight only into what it produces according to a design of its own; it constrains nature to give an answer to its own questions. And it is in this sense that applied science is pursued even today: knowledge is power.[9]

But it is possible to see the relationship in reverse as well: human beings do not merely confront nature; in the first place, they are part of it. So through the human being's perception, nature arrives at the perception of itself.[10] That does not mean that the modern relationship between nature and human being is restricted, but it is set in the wider association of nature–human being. Human knowledge of nature is also a natural process. Seen in this light, the sciences enter into their ecological age, for it cannot be in the interest of nature to destroy itself through human knowledge and through whatever human beings make of this knowledge. Knowledge is wisdom.

The Creation of Nature

In the ancient world, when people talked about the *natura rerum* they meant the essence of things. Like the Greek word *physis*, the Latin *natura* can mean both the nature of things and their coming into being, although the essentialist concept predominates. According to Plato's *Timaeus*, the *Ideas* reveal the eternal nature of temporal things; according to Aristotle, "all nature" is the essence of reality as a whole and is itself divine; that is to say, it is always identical with itself and is everywhere the same.[11]

How do we perceive the nature of things? By contemplating them – what we today call meditation. We must look through the change-able, sensory appearances of a flower in order to grasp the flower's typical nature. We see the blossom and grasp the timeless idea of blossoming. "The nature of anything" means its *noumenon*, the thing as it is in itself, not its *phainomenon*, as it is seen by the senses.

The modern empirical concept of nature no longer has any connection with the metaphysical concept of essence. In order to know something, one must observe it exactly, measure it, weigh it, and calculate it according to its inherent laws. Once we know the laws of nature, we can grasp things and control them.

How did this transformation in the concept of nature come about? It has been convincingly shown that historically, the transformation took place through the influence of the Jewish-Christian concept of nature as God's creation.[12] Let me describe this briefly:

In the ancient Greek concept of *physis* and in the Latin concept of *natura*, there was no distinction between the divine and the worldly. *Physis*, as the power to bring forth, is itself divine, just as the nature of the universe is divine. Our common image of the globe or sphere is derived from this metaphysics, for the sphere is the image of spatial perfection. As a sphere, the universe is founded in itself, is self-sufficing, perfect, displays all divine attributes, and is a self-enclosed system.

If, in contrast, creation is interpreted as God's creation, then it cannot itself be divine; it must therefore be understood as worldly. Belief in creation introduces into the experience of reality the fundamental distinction between God and world. Nature is not divine, but worldly; it is finite, not infinite; temporal, not eternal; contingent, not necessary; eccentrically based in something other, not concentrically in itself. Figuratively speaking, its form is not that of the sphere. It is an open system of signs which point beyond themselves. It holds within itself the principle of beginning and is open to the emergence of the new.

As creation, nature is derived not from God's essential being but from God's will. God did not have to create the world. It was created by God's free will. Yet it is not a product of God's caprice. God does not throw dice. The world comes into being out of God's love. It is the self-communication of the Good. To put it simply: God in his freedom brings into being a creation which corresponds to God, to God's goodness and beauty. Difference and community characterize the relationship between God and the world.

Community in the fundamental difference is experienced as the presence of the divine Spirit in all things. It is understood as God's indwelling (*Shekinah*) in a world that corresponds to him, and as the incarnation of the eternal Logos. In their essential difference, God and creation are seen to be so intertwined that we can talk about God in creation, and creation in God (*perichoresis*).[13]

The difference in the community is determined by the divine self-limitation (*kenosis*): the relative can co-exist with the Absolute to the extent to which the Absolute withdraws itself. Creation acquires its space, its time, and its potentialities for free development from God's self-limitation.[14] Only God can limit God. God is not "the all-determining reality," but in himself, God's power is so great that he concedes to those he has created space, time, and liberty in order that he may have an independent counterpart. In Max Jammer's book *Concepts of Space* (1953), to which Albert Einstein wrote the foreword, Jammer also discovered the insight into this divine mystery of creation in the Jewish-kabbalistic doctrine of *zim-zum or tzimtzum*.

To sum up

If the reality of the world is contingent, it cannot be deduced from eternal principles but has to be perceived from precise observation. The theological reason for the modern empirical concept of nature is to be found in the distinction between God's essential nature and God's will. The empirical concept of nature corresponds to the theological concept of creation and does not contradict it, although this is what some fundamentalists and some scientists seem to assume when they consider the modern sciences to be in principle "atheistic."

In classical physics, the natural laws were thought to be timeless, unalterable, always and everywhere the same, like the Platonic Ideas. Does this then mean that they are eternal orders for temporal happening, or are they themselves part of temporal happening? In the theological perspectives described, they belong to creation and, as the theologian Thomas Torrance emphatically put it, are "contingent orders for contingent happening."[15] Like time, they are created together with creation. It is not just that the processes in nature proceed according to natural laws; natural laws themselves are part of nature too. Consequently, one may justifiably ask whether natural laws are alterable (Paul Dirac), or whether they have developed in the more complex forms of life as "habits of nature" (Rupert Sheldrake).[16] This, of course, also raises the question of the constancy of "natural constants." Are they constant only temporarily, or were they always constant, and will they always be so? The theologian is concerned with the contingency of the orders of nature not just because of his belief in the Creator, but also as a way of being able to conceive of the new creation of the world.

The Discovery of Time

Very early concepts of time are derived from the recognition of "the eternal return of the same thing" (M. Eliade): summer and winter, seedtime and harvest, the return of the sun in the morning, and the "circular motion" of the stars. In many early civilizations, the circle was taken as an image of time. This is the image of reversible time. Circularity is a reflection of eternity. Its quantitative endlessness corresponds to the qualitative infinity of the eternal. In "the eternal return of the same thing," the symmetries are dominant.

In the so-called Abrahamic religions, time is experienced differently. The root experience of these religions of history is the experience of God in the Exodus out of a known present into an unknown future. The person who sets out with the divine promise given to Abraham and Sarah leaves behind a past that will never return and seeks a future that does not yet exist. This future is greater than the past: at the beginning, there is only Abraham and Sarah; and at the end, all generations on earth. This experience of God divides the times into a past that cannot be brought back and a future that has not yet been reached. This is the discovery of irreversible time. The arrow of time pierces and breaks through the circle of time.

In irreversible time, we distinguish between two modes of time, for in every moment which divides past from future, there is a before and an after. If we enter past and future along a temporal line, then the present is the point that distinguishes and joins the times. Consequently, time always begins and ends in the present. But "present" is not a temporal concept: it is a spatial one. The person who experiences time is present, not absent.[17]

If we enter these modes of time on an undirected parameter, the measurable movements are symmetrical and reversible, as the equations of movement in classical physics show. Newtonian physics presents the picture of a stable world order, with a world clock that can run forwards and backwards.

In principle, however, the Second Law of thermodynamics introduced into physics the concept of irreversible time. Entropy is not merely a measure for the irretrievable dissemination of energy; it is also a measure for the irreversibility of processes.

The result, for Ilya Prigogine, is "the paradox of time."[18] Do we have to reckon with both forms of time, the reversible and the irreversible, or can it be shown that the simple ideas about a reversible time are abstractions of the more complex processes which take their course according to irreversible time? If, ever since the Big Bang, the universe has been involved in a history of expansion, then the "paradox of time" is resolved in favour of irreversible time. The concept of a "history of nature" (C.F. von Weizsacker)[19] corresponds to the experience of history in the Abrahamic religions.

The new metaphysics no longer takes its starting point, like mediaeval metaphysics, in a supreme being, so as to distinguish between being and non-being. It proceeds from the fundamental potentiality for being that distinguishes the actual from the possible. If we relate the temporal modes "past" and "future" to the modalities of being "actuality" and "potentiality," then the potential corresponds to the future and the actual to the past.[20] Inherent in the present is the creative force for realizing the potential. All actuality is realized potentiality, just as every past is a "past future." The driving force is the potentiality. Here too, irreversibility rules. Potentiality becomes reality, but reality never again becomes possibility. "Higher than actuality stands possibility" in Heidegger's ontology in *Being and Time*.[21]

If "the future is the time for the potential,"[22] then the times "past" and "future" are not equal, because potential and actual being are different. Consequently, the way we deal with them differs. The remembered past is something different from the expected future, for what is past is fixed and cannot be changed, while the future is open. So our expectations are less certain than our remembrances. But in saying this, I have, of course, already introduced the subject who experiences the times.[23]

Remembrances and expectations are constituted by subjects who are present. That is pre-eminently true of the creative dealings of human beings with the times, both time's realities and its potentialities. But in principle, all self-referential forms of life perceive the times in this way and can distinguish between past and future.

Is the World Unfinished?

Right down to the present day, theology has assumed that in the beginning God created a finished and perfect world and that history is merely a story of paradise lost and paradise regained. Sin distorts the good creation, while grace restores it.[24] The original creation is the *status integritatis*. This view makes the Jewish-Christian belief in creation captive to the religious myth of origin and remembrance. This is shown, for example, by the German word for creation, *Schöpfung*, for its final syllable, *ung*, means the concluded process of creating and its result.[25]

The notion of the finished and perfected world also dominated classical physics at the time of Robert Boyle and Sir Isaac Newton. Boyle even proposed talking about "mechanism" instead of nature. Once it is produced, a mechanism functions by itself. The mechanistic worldview of deism developed out of this idea. God is the architect of a perfect world structure, or the Creator whose genius has brought about a perfect world machine. This world mechanism is so perfect that it requires no further divine interventions. God would contradict his own perfection, if he were obliged to correct his perfect work.

This theological idea is called "Deism," and it is generally rejected as being the beginning of atheism, for – as Laplace already said – one no longer needs a God in order to explain the mechanism of the world. But this is not entirely true: is not deism the world picture we also find on the seventh day of creation, when, according to Genesis 2:2, God "rested" from all the works he had made? Seen in this light,

17th-century deism would in fact be Sabbath theology. This fits that baroque era, which in its church architecture and its music was able to extol the glory of God in contemplation of "the best of all possible worlds." God was seen, not as the subject of a continuing creative process, but as the abiding object of worship, so that the goal of created being is "to glorify God and enjoy him forever," as the Westminster Confession says. Natural theology, which perceives in the inherent laws of nature the wisdom and beauty of God, serves the glorification and enjoyment of the divine which is present, abiding in itself.

The modern sciences have broken down this picture of a perfect and finished world. If we look at the overall history of the cosmos, we recognize today that ever since the Big Bang, the universe has expanded and is involved in a singular history open to the future. "The cosmos is an unfinished process which does not know its own future."[26] The time of the cosmos is irreversible. Its reality proceeds from a potentiality which we can term a field of expectation, in which the cosmic events emerge. The overall history of life in the creative living space of the earth is no different. As far as we know, the evolution of life is also singular and open to the future. Its time too is irreversible. New forms of life emerge from a potentiality for life which can be understood as its field of expectation. Evolution too is an unfinished process which does not know its own future. Life in its creativity is an unfinished process.

In the light of these recognitions of an unfinished nature, theologians read their scriptures with new eyes. If, for once, we read the Bible not from the beginning but from the end, it at once becomes clear that what is meant by the creation stories "in the beginning" is not a finished, perfect, primal state, but only the first act of a creation process which reaches far into the future.[27] Creation "in the beginning" opens up the prospect of history, which arrives at its goal only in the new creation of all things. The perfected creation does not lie behind us in a primal state, but ahead of us in a final one. We await the consummated creation and, together with the cosmos, we are now existing in its prehistory.

"In the beginning, God created the heavens and the earth." Where is the consummating goal of this beginning? We find the final vision in the prophets:

"Behold, I will create a new heaven and a new earth," we read in Isaiah (65:17), and the visionary John writes: "And I saw a new heaven and a new earth" (Rev. 21:1). What is to be new in the new creation of all things? "Behold, the dwelling place of God is among human beings." God will "indwell" his creation on earth as in heaven and, in the presence of the eternally living God, death will be no more; all things will participate in the eternal aliveness and righteousness of God.

In this eschatological perspective, nature can be seen to exist within a history open to the future. The phenomena of continuity and discontinuity, stability and the emergence of the new, are interpreted theologically as signs of God's faithfulness and God's anticipating creation. Let me briefly mention elements in this continuous creation process:

Preservation. This does not consist of the sovereign rule of the creator and the creator's direct interventions in its creation, as Jonathan Edwards maintained, in opposition to the mechanists of his time. It means that the creator "sustains" creation, just as in Greek philosophy the *hypokeimenon* sustains all things. God does not rule from above, but sustains from below. That is how Israel's Exodus story describes it: "You have seen how I bore you on eagles' wings" (Ex. 19:4). There is a feminine image for this patient and purposeful sustaining: "As a mother carries her child at her breast" (Num. 11:12); and a masculine one too: "As a man bears his son on his shoulders" (Deut. 1:31). According to the New Testament, God "upholds all things through his word of power (*Logos*, Heb. 1:3). It is God's patient sustaining that provides the scope for the self-creations and self-organizations of all the living, but for their self-destructions as well. For these too, Israel's wanderings through the wilderness offer vivid pictures.

The creating of the new. "Remember not the former things, nor consider the things of old. Behold, I am doing a new thing; now it springs forth, do you not perceive it?" (Is. 43:18-19). The singular Hebrew word for create (*bara*) is used more frequently for the process of creation in the present than for creation in the beginning. This process is not a creation out of nothing; it is a renewing creation out of the old one, a renewal, a heightening and a giving of new form to what is already there: "And thou renewest the face of the earth" (Ps. 104:30).[28] We perceive signs of this innovative creating in the opening up of new possibilities and in the self-transcendence of living things. We perceive them too in the emergence of new wholes which cannot be explained by the characteristics of their parts and by the sum of them.

In closing, I come back to the concept of the two books, the book of the divine promises and the book of nature. One who delights in reading them both is fortunate, since the world of such a person is richer than the world of people who want to know only one of the two books and ignore the other. But how do the two books relate to each other?

In Robert Boyle's time, religion still counted as the interpreter of the world's phenomena. "The Book of Scripture is the interpreter of the book of nature," claimed Jonathan Edwards, "because it is illuminating of those spiritual mysteries that are signified in the constitution of the natural world.[29] At that time, scientists freed themselves from the domination of this religious interpretation through the *reductio scientiae ad mathematicam*.

Today, we recognize the limitations of this reduction and are trying to find new perspectives for the richer realities and the always mysterious potentialities in the world process. "The book of divine promises" offers only one of these new perspectives on the enigmatic book of nature. That book was not written in order to save its readers from making their own investigations into the book of nature; on the contrary, it stimulates them to scientific research because it awakens their curiosity about God's presence in all things.

But perhaps there is still more to be read in the library of this world than in these two books alone.

Chapter 6

Terrorism and Political Theology

Political Theology and Anarchism:
Carl Schmitt and Michael Bakunin

The modern concept of a "political theology" was introduced into a discussion that today has become worldwide by Carl Schmitt, German constitutional lawyer and Prussian Councilor of State, in his celebrated book *Politische Theologie: Vier Kapitel zur Lehre von der Souveränität* (1922, 1934, 1970).[1] Leo Strauss in Chicago became his American partner. Schmitt adopted this concept for his theory of political authority not from the Stoic philosophy of classical antiquity, but from the Russian anarchist Michael Bakunin and his book *God and the State,* with its famous (or infamous) rallying cry: "Neither God nor state – *ni Dieu – ni maître.*"[2]

Bakunin condemned every rule by human beings over other human beings. He wanted to replace the state with an "association in which the free development of each is the condition for the free development of all," as the closing lines of the Communist Manifesto put it. Bakunin proclaimed that his cooperative socialism would be liberation from divine and human authority: "If God is, man is a slave; now man can and must be free; then, God does not exist." For Bakunin, Satan was the first anarchist, freethinker, and liberator of the world, because, according to the biblical story of paradise, he persuaded the human beings not to obey God. And "God admitted that Satan was right," and found that the disobedient human being had "become as of the Gods." Bakunin draws the following consequence from the biblical myth of original sin: human beings have liberated themselves, and will liberate themselves, "by rebellion and by thought." How does liberation from God occur? Through making oneself god: Anything one attributes to God is taken away from the human being, and hence it is also true, *e contra,* that anything that one attributes to the human being must be taken away from God. Atheism is the true basis of human autonomy. Like Ludwig Feuerbach, Bakunin held that God and the human being are consubstantial, so that what one gives to the one must necessarily have been taken away from the other. But if God and the human being are not consubstantial, this atheistic logic does not function.

Bakunin's "rebellion" was certainly meant in a political sense. He lived in the Holy Russia of the autocratic Czars and the Orthodox state church: "Slaves of God, men must also be slaves of Church and State, in so far as the State is consecrated by the Church." The only God he knew was the *state god,* and his rebellion aimed at human freedom: "Ni Dieu – ni maître." Politically speaking, he was right. Bakunin used the expression "political theology" as a casual remark, in order to defame the Italian bourgeois revolutionary Mazzini, who wanted "a free church in a free state."

However, Carl Schmitt saw Bakunin and his atheistic socialism as the arch-enemy of God and of the authority of the state. As Heinrich Meier writes, "What Bakunin denies in the name of Satan, Schmitt asserts in the name of God . . . What the atheistic anarchist regards as nothing more than human-made fiction, the political theologian regards as God-given reality."[3] Like Thomas Hobbes, Carl Schmitt employed the biblical doctrine of original sin to justify the authoritarian power of the state: it is only by the absolute power of the state that the "fight of each one against all" can be suppressed. The close of Schmitt's *Political Theology* shows the extent to which he resembles his bogeyman Bakunin: "In the greatest anarchist of the 19th century, Bakunin, we find the remarkable paradox that he had to become, in theory, the theologian of the anti-theological and, in practice, the dictator of his anti-dictatorship."

Carl Schmitt's theological-political theses can be boiled down to two:

(1) "The incisive concepts of modern constitutional theory are all secularized theological concepts."

(2) "It is the one who decides about the state of emergency who is sovereign."

He followed the Catholic constitutional philosophers of the counterrevolution against the spirit of the French Revolution: there is no middle term between Catholicism and atheism, and thus also no middle term between authority and anarchy. In the second thesis, he has in mind the "dictatorship of the president" according to Article 48 of the Weimar Constitution. In the "state of emergency," which Carl Schmitt appropriately compares to the theological concept of "miracle," "absolute" decisions are taken. This is the "absolute decision that does not justify itself, and is thus taken *ex nihilo*."[4] This is the divine decision, since it possesses all the characteristics of the absolute. Dictatorship is the state god. In 1934, Schmitt defended the Nazi dictatorship as an act of political dictatorship in a state of emergency: "The will of the Führer is law." This, however, means that it is not truth and justice that make the laws, but the absolute authority that is not obliged to give an account of itself.

Schmitt saw the conflict between the sovereignty of the state and the atheistic anarchy against the background of an apocalyptic ending of human history: because the final battle between God and Satan will come, we are already involved in a permanent civil war here and now. Schmitt proclaimed the "category of friend and foe" – "Whoever is not for us, is against us" – as the true "political category," because it is the existential category. But the archetype of this alternative between friend and foe is the dualism between God and Satan, that is to say, between good and evil.

Carl Schmitt and Michael Bakunin are mirror images of each other – and Carl Schmitt was aware of this. Both men rejected "law and justice" as well as parliamentary democracy. Schmitt's ideal sovereign rules with absolute decision, and Bakunin's rebel revolts with absolute freedom. In modern terms, the one is a terrorist from above and the other a terrorist from below. Both believe that "God" and "freedom" are alternatives, although this need not be the case. Schmitt's "political theology" is a faithful counterpart of Bakunin's anarchistic atheism, and thus ultimately its justification, because there are no other political options than this one.

Terrorism and the Modern Security State

We can distinguish between three forms of terrorism: first, the terrorism from above, in the murderous dictatorships of Stalin and Hitler in the 20th century; second, the private terror of warlords and their militias in states that are falling apart, such as Somalia, Syria, and Libya; and third, the Islamist terror, with a religious motivation and a theological justification, in the Muslim world and against the Western world.

The modern security state against private and religious terrorism increasingly resembles Carl Schmitt's ideas of a transcendental state authority and the "absolute decision." American politics reacted in 2001 to the 9/11 terror with a permanent "state of emergency." When President George W. Bush declared that "America is at war," he partially introduced martial law and suspended civil freedoms in the Patriot Act of 2001, with the right to pre-emptive strikes, with the illegitimate prison in Guantanamo, with the uncontrolled surveillance of the world by the National Security Agency, and with the killing of real or supposed terrorists with drones.

Unfortunately, President Barack Obama changed little in this area. In the Iraq War (an "undeclared war," like the USA's Vietnam War, whereas in the 20th century, Hitler had had the good manners to "declare war" on Poland, France, and England, and on the USA in 1943), President Bush assembled a "coalition of the willing" under the motto "Whoever is not for us, is against us" – as if no other options had existed. The absolute decision – that is to say, a decision that is not obliged to give an account of itself – is always justified in politics on the grounds that there is "no alternative" to it.

Modern democracy is based on the sovereignty of the people: "All state authority is derived from people" (Article 20.2 of the German Federal Constitution), or, as Abraham Lincoln declared in his Gettysburg address, "A government of the people, by the people, for the people." The modern anti-terrorist security state restricts the democratic rights of the people and proclaims "security" as the highest good. In the fight against terrorism, "absolute decisions" are justified if they promote security, even if they are not covered by law and the constitution. This brings one sphere of political decisions outside democratic control. Objectively speaking, it does not promote security to any great extent, since counter-terror generates new terrorists. The modern religious terror comes into being in the hearts and minds of human beings, and it is there, at the root, that it must be overcome. It is, of course, necessary for the police to thwart acts of terror, but this does not extinguish the terrorism in hearts and minds.

I believe that today's Islamist terror has two components.

First, there is the Islamic dualism. On the one side are the believers, on the other side the unbelievers; on the one side, those who obey God, on the other hand, the enemies of God. The decisive element here is the apocalyptic picture of the judgment of God, in which the believers enter paradise and the unbelievers land in hell. The misunderstood obedience of faith consists in anticipating this judgment of God and in linking the absolute decision of faith with the absolute separation of the believers from the unbelievers and with the annihilation of the latter.

Secondly, the jihadists worship death as they go into the murderous battle. Mullah Omar explained the mentality of his Taliban to Western journalists as follows: "Your young people love life. Our young people love death." It is a question of killing and being killed, and one cannot inflict the death penalty on mass murderers who commit suicide thereby. They are absolute. To declare that these mass murderers, whether in New York, Madrid, London, or elsewhere, are "martyrs" is blasphemy. Their god is not Allah, "the all-merciful." Their god is death.

What Happens to Democracy?

Is the suspending of democracy through the "state of emergency" the only thing that can be done in the struggle against terrorism? No. Parliamentary democracy was hard-won, through the civil Revolution in France against the absolutism of the state power and its deification, and through the War of Independence in the United States of America. These Western democracies successfully defended themselves against the fascisms of Europe and Japan in the Second World War, and against the Stalinist rule of terror in the Cold War. These three state gods fell. This is why it is good to look once more at the fundamental principles of the democracies.

First, the basis of democracy is the sovereignty of the people, which is the foundation of the modern constitutional state. The old Western name for constitution was the covenant, the covenant of the free citizens. This was based, on the model of the Old Testament, on the covenant of the people with God. God makes a covenant with the people: "You are to be my people, and I will be your God" (Ex. 19). Next, the people makes its covenant with a king and entrusts its sovereignty to him. If the ruler breaks the people's covenant with God, it is necessary to resist the ruler in the name of God. The people's covenant with God is divine, and hence absolute; the covenant of the people with the ruler is human, and hence relative. Government must be conducted within the laws of the covenant with God. It is easy to see how the traces of this covenantal theology are still at work in the modern constitutional state. In the constitution of the Federal Republic of Germany, the basic rights of the constitution take priority over the positive parliamentary legislation. They cannot be abolished by any government or any parliament. This means that the basic rights (Art. 1–4) are "absolute" and belong to the category "before God," as the preamble says. According to art. 79.3, it is "inadmissible" to alter Article 1 on human dignity and Article 20 on the democratic state under the rule of law. This gives the basic rights in the constitution a kind of "guarantee of perpetuity."

Secondly, the form of the modern democratic constitutional state is that of the separation of powers in the legislative, the executive, and the judicial powers, which means that the government's executive power is bound to the constitution. The governmental power is also limited temporally by elections. Every government must give an account to the people. These two fundamental principles exclude a deification of the state power through its absolute "decision," that is to say, its "not being bound to give an account of itself." Modern democracy does not tolerate any state god on earth. Its very being is political iconoclasm. As John Milton said, "The crown sitteth not on the head of any man, but on the constitution of free citizens."

The Threats to the State's Monopoly on the Use of Force

States fall because they cannot hold onto their monopoly on the use of force. The state's monopoly on the use of force is threatened by the privatization of force, which is promoted both by international terrorism and by the commercialization of "security."

The legal system and the police keep watch over the state's monopoly on force. When the state power, with the police and the military, is no longer able to enforce its will against the drug gangs in Mexico, the state disintegrates at its peripheries. When the state power disappears in Somalia and Libya, tribal militias spread and wage war on each other. Collapsing states are breeding grounds for private and international terror. A "market of violence" expands, where weapons of every kind and mercenaries of every skin colour can be bought. In collapsing states, there is no authority that could bring accusations of injustice and ensure that justice is enforced. Some people believe, not without cynicism, that dictatorships are more tolerable than this, because they at least enforce the state monopoly on force. But "the key to every permanent solution is to be sought in the restoration of legitimacy, in the reinstatement of a public control (whether local, national, or global) of organized violence."[5]

At the same time, the state monopoly on force is threatened by the privatization of security. Security becomes a "product" offered by private security services. Those who can afford to do so withdraw into gated communities and pay private security personnel to guard them: the state police are no longer needed. In rich Western countries, the number of private security personnel exceeds that of state police officers. But as E. Eppler notes, a state that expects its citizens to purchase their security on the "market of violence" does not deserve to be called a state. It loses its citizens' loyalty and becomes a disintegrating state.[6] The neoliberalism that desires this result is nothing other than political anarchy. The necessary state monopoly on force can be maintained only when all the citizens want this, campaign for this, pay taxes for this, and do not withdraw from the community.

The democratic constitutional state held its ground against the terror from above and against the cruel dictatorships of the 20th century. It will also prevail against the international and religious terror from below.

How Does an "Open Society" Cope with Its Enemies?

Before we sketch an ethics of the political "love of enemies," let us take a look at Europe.

From aggression to attraction

From the beginning of the modern period, imperialism and colonialism made their way from the European nations to the rest of the world in America, Africa, Oceania, and Asia. One European nation after the other aimed at world dominion: the Spanish world empire was followed by the British Empire and the Francophone world of France. Finally, the German Reich too wanted to have colonies in Africa and Asia, and Italy tried to establish its empire in Libya, Eritrea, and Somalia. For Africans and Asians, Europeans were victorious rulers and aggressive robbers. The last step was the division of the ancient realm of China among the European superpowers. Then came the First World War, where the European nations destroyed each other. In the Second World War, they lost their empires. Today, the imperial madness of the European nations is a thing of the past, and the colonized peoples in Africa and Asia have liberated themselves.

What happened in Europe? Through Charles de Gaulle and Konrad Adenauer, the old enmity between German and France was buried; through Willy Brandt and the treaties with the Warsaw Pact countries, Germany's aggressive hostility in East Europe was overcome. After the collapse of the imperial Soviet Union in 1990, a new Europe came into being in the European community. Europe, which had been a terror to the peoples, became a continent of hope for millions of persons. The European nations became attractive for people from Africa, the Middle East, the Balkans, and Ukraine, who were in search of work, security, and freedom. Europe became their dream of a good life. This transformation of the European nations from imperialist aggression to democratic attraction made Europe an "open society." The Europeans in Europe are not very conscious of this – they are afraid of the rising stream of refugees – but this is how people outside Europe see it. Asiatic countries like China, Japan, Korea, or Taiwan are not attractive for people who are in search of work, security, and freedom; and this applies at the present time *a fortiori* to Muslim countries. The refugee map of the United Nations Refugee Agency is proof of this. Such countries are less "open societies" than the nations that make up the European community.

Political "love of enemies"

Ever since the crucifixion of Christ by the violence of the Roman occupying power in Jerusalem, Christians have had a profound abhorrence of violence. "The one who takes the sword will perish by the sword." They have proclaimed the kingdom of Christ as the kingdom of peace that was promised by the prophets of Israel. They wanted "to make their swords into plowshares and their spears into pruning hooks . . . and no longer learn how to wage war," as the prophet Isaiah (2:4) had promised.

The behaviour of world Christianity changed only when Emperor Constantine made Christianity the imperial religion and his successors made the Roman Imperium the Holy Empire of Christ: "*In hoc signo vinces*; In this sign you will conquer": this was the cross of the Emperor's dream, and it has nothing to do with the cross of Christ on

Golgotha. Constantinian Christianity made the "swords" into Christian swords and the "spears" into Christian spears, and reflected in its political ethics on the "just war." Only monastic Christianity, which was called into life in Egypt by Antony and Pachomius, refused to go along with this.

The non-Constantinian Christianity in Syria, Persia, and Mesopotamia did not share in this development, since it was outside the walls (*extra muros*) of the Christian Imperium. Today, a new non-Constantinian Christianity has come into being in Africa and Asia. In Europe too, Constantinian Christianity is nearing its end, and a post-Constantinian Christianity is awakening to life, with the "just peace," not the "just war," on its agenda. If this is to be realized, "swords must be made into plowshares." In other words, the industry of war must become an industry of peace, and the armies must become forces that make peace. This, however, demands a new way of dealing with one's enemies.

The love of enemies that Jesus teaches in his Sermon on the Mount is not a love of enmity, as in the perverted dualistic thinking that sees only either friends or foes. Rather, it is a path to overcome enmity. When one encounters enmity in private life or in politics, this generates a spontaneous desire for revenge: "I will do to you what you are doing to me." One thus becomes the enemy of one's enemies and succumbs to enmity. In an ethic of reciprocity, this is the only possible reaction to enmity.

There are three possibilities of coping with enmity: first, submission; second, thinking in terms of friends and foes; and third, overcoming the enmity. The first possibility leads to self-destruction. The second leads to the destruction of the enemy and of one's own self. The third leads to life in common. "But I say to you, Love your enemies and pray for those who persecute you, so that you may be children of your Father in heaven; for he makes his sun rise on the evil and on the good, and sends rain on the righteous and on the unrighteous" (Matt. 5:45-46).

It is not the enemy who provides the orientation for one's feeling and acting. One refuses to let the enmity be forced upon oneself. It is God who provides the orientation for his children, and God loves life – both one's own and that of the enemies. Accordingly, God sends sun and rain to everyone. If we do not react to enmity with hostility, we open up for our enemies the possibility of abandoning their own hostility and committing themselves to life in common.

This has been discussed in recent Christian ethics under the rubric of the "intelligent love of enemies." How can one overcome enmity and respect one's enemies as human beings? The first step is to refuse to let enmity be forced upon oneself. The second step leads to recognition of the other person: "Love your neighbor as yourself, because he is like you" – and, I should like to add, "you are like him" (M. Buber). And recognizing oneself in the other also means recognizing the other in oneself. The third step must lead to the recognition of the reasons for the enmity. Since aggressions are often generated by private or collective insults, it is helpful to study the history of the sufferings of hostile persons or peoples and to seek a healing for memories that make people ill. The love of enemies is not an "ethics of attitude" (as Max Weber supposed), but an ethics of responsibility. We accept responsibility, not only for our own life and for the life of those who are under our care, but also for the lives of our enemies and of those who are under their care, just as the sun and the rain create all life on earth. In this sense, the love of enemies is not only a reaction to enmity, but a creative, imaginative commitment to life in common.

Do not be overcome by evil,
but overcome evil with good. (Rom. 12:21)

Chapter 7

Is the City a Place of Hope?
The Urbanization of Humankind –
A Challenge for Christianity

WITH THE BEGINNING OF THE INDUSTRIAL AGE, A GENERAL movement toward urbanization took hold of humankind. Today, more than 50 percent of human beings live in cities, and month after month millions are added. Everywhere around the globe, villages are growing into cities, cities are growing together, and unlimited urban areas emerge. A city with more than ten million inhabitants is counted as a "world city." In Asia and Africa, cities emerge whose names were unknown in old Europe.

Today the city seems to be the hope of millions of humans for freedom from nature and for economic opportunities and social relationships. But has the city itself a future? What kind of future do we imagine for our own city and for humankind in general?

Is "the brave new world" already beginning in Mexico City, São Paulo, or Chongqing? Or is the ecological catastrophe of our planet earth beginning in those monster cities? Is the megalopolis a hope for the good life, or is it the apocalypse of the self-inflicted downfall of humankind? To speak in mythical terms: When we build such modern mega-cities and want to live in the urban possibilities, are we working in "Babylon" on behalf of our own prison or are we anticipating the "heavenly Jerusalem"?

The German word for town, *stadt*, with its well-known pre-industrial romantic allusions, doesn't satisfy anymore. The American "city" is already different. A European *stadt* has a centre with a marketplace, town hall, and church, whereas an American "city" has a "main street" or "a broadway" or no centre at all, like Los Angeles. The modern Asian mega-city, like Shanghai or Seoul, is in the eyes of European visitors a conglomerate of skyscrapers. The African megalopolis has vast slum areas – as soon as one is cleaned up, new ones emerge. One must see the differences between a *stadt* like Tübingen, a central European *stadt* like Berlin or Paris, and new global world cities such as Seoul, Manila, or Lagos.

The City in Antiquity

Why did cities come into being at all, and how were they organized? In the centre of ancient cities, we find the temple of the city gods, the castle or palace of the rulers, the market, and the harbour for trade.

The temple was built in the "centre of the world," the *axis mundi*. The temple offered an "opening above" – a "door to heaven"; it also had an "opening below" and was a door to the world of the ancestors. The temple was an image of the known cosmos: *imago mundi*. The temple also stood at the centre in the passing of time: at midsummer and in midwinter, certain sunbeams were reflected at its centre. The temple represented an image of the three-fold world: heaven – earth – and the underworld. It created order in the chaos of history, and peace in the catastrophes of nature, and it brought the human world into harmony with the divine world. Accordingly, the order of the ancient cities reflected the order of the central temple. In the liturgy of the temple, the cultures of the city and the land were sanctified.

The political power was closely connected with the religious power, because the kings were at the same time the high priests of their city or country. The Roman emperor was the *pontifex maximus* of the Roman empire. The Chinese "son of heaven" celebrated rituals at the "altar of heaven" and the "altar of the earth" in Beijing, the "centre of the world." The secular and the religious powers were undivided. The emperor was sanctified, and the gods of the fatherland took care of the welfare of the people – as long as the people offered the required sacrifices.

The first cities – and we believe that Uruk in Mesopotamia and Jericho in Palestine were among the first – created new forms of organization of the citizens. Families and clans lived in the villages, while the citizen was born in the city. Certainly, family-clans also lived in the ancient cities, just as they do today, but all citizens had to be organized for defense against danger from outside. Different nationalities lived in separate quarters. Different classes emerged: here the poor plebeians, there the rich patricians. Some cities had city tyrants, but it was also in cities that the beginnings of democracy developed, as for example in Athens.

Together with the temple and the castle, the markets for trade and goods developed in the cities. The city-dwellers were dependent on the products of the those who dwelled in farming lands. Markets were the commercial centres of cities. Cities at the crossroads of long-range trade routes – for example, the Silk Road to China or the incense road in Arabia – or at harbours became very rich.

The Modern Industrial Town

Industrialization created a new city: villages became city quarters, and the old cities grew rapidly into immigrant towns. American cities were immigrant towns from the beginning. But migrant people do not like to exist in a "lonely crowd"; they form neighbourhoods of the same origin and language. We find the Italian quarter, the Polish and the Caribbean quarter, and, of course, "Chinatown."

Industrialization not only changed traditional cities but also developed the typical industrial town. We see this in the German Ruhrgebiet, or in England between Manchester and Birmingham. A whole area becomes a network of industrial towns. The industrial town has no lasting centre: factories and manufacturing plants are erected and deserted. The industrial town is dependent on economic trends. People don't work in order to live there, but live there because they find work there. In the early years, industrialists and owners of coal mines took responsibility for the settlements of their workers in order to have a loyal working class, but since profit has become the only orientation, workers are obliged to take care of themselves. Their living quarters in skyscrapers are like "pigeon cages"; the streets where people met and talked were replaced by highways for traffic. Good neighbourhood is extremely difficult to find in living quarters like these. Ghost cities emerge with a high suicide rate. In modern industrial townships, the power is no longer political or religious, but lies in the financial and commercial districts.

Democratization of the Capitalistic Town

The socialistic city – commanded by Stalin and built from Vladivostok to Berlin and from Riga to Bucharest – failed. One can still see the remains of the dreary buildings that degraded human beings. Those are sad remnants of Stalinism.

Does the capitalistic city have a better future? Cities are capitalistic whether you live in a modern world city or in an old university town like Tübingen. If you have to leave your apartment because you can no longer pay the rent, you know this. I believe, then, that our task today is to democratize the capitalistic city, to realize "freedom – equality – brotherhood" (*liberté – égalité – fraternité*) in order to live in the city with human dignity, in peace with nature, and open to the future. Democracy was born in the city. The implementation of human rights and citizen rights is the urban form and style of life.

To democratize the capitalistic city and its possibilities, we need visions for the future: "Where there are no visions, the people perish" (Prov. 29:18). When hope dies, the resistance against injustice and corruption wanes, and the people become apathetic.

One of these visions of a city of justice is deeply rooted in the consciousness of the Christian people: The vision of the heavenly city Jerusalem coming down on earth to connect heaven and earth so that God may dwell with humankind and human beings may dwell with God. The God-history of the world began in a garden called Eden, in Greek "paradise," and ends in a city: the heavenly Jerusalem on earth.

The heavenly Jerusalem on earth is a garden-city, a unity of culture and nature. The trees of life are on both sides of the river with the water of eternal life. This city does not close its gates at night: it is secure and open and hospitable. This city has no temple, because the glory of God is the light and enlightens all inhabitants. This is a messianic vision of peace, embracing God, human beings, and nature in an abundance of life: the city of God.

The civil revolution that began simultaneously with the industrial revolution called this peace "brotherhood": "All human beings become brothers," as Schiller said in his "Hymn to Joy" (the sisters joined in on their own). This meant, not an enlarged family life, but human friendship in a friendly world. In the city, hospitality is found, as well as good neighbourhood, mutual help, and "open heaven." It is the city of justice and of solidarity: the city of humanity.

We shall try to demonstrate this by looking now at special problems that are raised by the capitalistic city. I am speaking as an attentive citizen, not as a specialist. So don't expect solutions to these global problems of the mega-city.

Anyone who has to leave their apartment because they can no longer pay the rent knows how capitalism governs our cities. Housing has become a commodity and is subject to the logic of the market: profit maximizing! The city has become a business with its own marketing, producing a climate for investments. Those who can't pay the rent must leave for poorer quarters. This produces ghettoes of the rich, the middle class, and the poor.

Does there exist a human right to housing and to city life? If equality is an essential part of democracy, housing must not be left exclusively to the market. It would be inhuman if the cost of rent determined who I must live with in a neighbourhood. The cities must take care of social housing and must not change social housing into luxury apartments in order to take in higher rents.

There is a disproportion in capitalistic cities between private property and common property. Private property is protected by the law and is privately cared for, while common property is difficult to protect and receives little respect. However, one type of common property cannot be privatized, because it is vital for everyone. These are the "global commons": the air we breathe, the water we drink, the ground on which we walk, the light through which we see, the security that lets us live.

To illustrate these "global commons," I tell a story: When Chile's dictator Pinochet sold the water rights of Patagonia to the Italian firm Benetton, a clever citizen of Santiago had the idea of buying a park together with the air above it in order to make users of the park pay not only an entrance fee but also a breathing fee. He did not actually realize this idea, but it shows the limits of the privatization of the global commons. It is not only the citizens of Beijing and Tokyo who pray, "Give us this day our daily air."

In America, the results of the privatization of security are seen, on the one hand, in the gated communities of the rich with private security personnel, and, on the other hand, in the slums and favelas with their gang wars. In the one, private guards replace the police and in the other, no police officer dares to enter at night. Only the monopoly on the use of force in the hands of the government can guarantee a minimum security. The government must never hand over this monopoly on the use of force to gated communities or give it up in slums.

Freedom also means mobility, but I have seen big cities where cars blocked the entire city and the inner city became inaccessible. The good ideas of a car-friendly city or a city-friendly car are dead. One can make driving so expensive that only the rich can enter (for example, in London), or can allow only cars with even numbers to drive on certain days, and those with uneven numbers on others. One can promote car-sharing and rent-a-car, or can recommend bicycling and let the buses drive free of charge and without tickets. But the solution to the conflict of "car versus city" is not yet at hand, and is perhaps never to be found. While 100 human beings can live on a few square metres if one constructs tall buildings, 100 cars cannot do so: they need streets.

The City and Ecology

The growth of the city is accompanied by increasing pollution of the environment. The growing city needs more and more land, and concrete houses stand in nature like an "army in foreign land" (Ernst Bloch). Industry and traffic disseminate a smog so thick that on some days people cannot see the sun anymore, and the groundwater sinks considerably under the big city.

It is not only external nature that is changing: the internal nature of human beings is changing in the big city too. City dwellers lose the natural cycles of day and night, summer and winter, to which body and soul are adjusted. Urban life promises freedom from nature, and requires this freedom. "Health" is no longer natural, and "fitness" is what counts: fitness for work.

The problem of how city culture and the nature of the land and in human beings can be brought into livable harmony is as old as the city itself. This is why there have been so many experiments:

The most radical idea is decentralization, with the catchphrase "Small is beautiful." This idea has failed because of the consumption of land. Another idea is to place parks in the inner city, such as Hyde Park in London, Central Park in New York, or the Tiergarten in Berlin. This park becomes the "green lung" of the city. It is remarkable how successfully defended this "common good" has been against privatization and construction. Even the Copacabana beach in Rio is free.

When, at the start of the 20th century, the German "Youth Movement" went out from the "grey walls of the city" to find pure air and original life on the land, the idea of the "garden city" spread and the concept of allotments for the poor was born. These can still be seen in Germany along the railroad tracks: small gardens with little huts in long or large colonies.

Today we hear of "city gardening" and the "greening of the city" in the USA. Chicago and New York already look impressively "green." This is, however, only nature consisting of plants and trees; the city has lost contact with the animal kingdom. This was replaced by the zoo, where you can see animals in prison. But some wild animals return: we find city foxes in London, coyotes in New York, and wild boars that lay waste to gardens in Berlin.

Global City Culture

When the railroads were constructed in the 19th century, the same stations were built everywhere, from Victoria Station in London to the Lehrter Bahnhof in Berlin. Today, airports in all countries look very much alike. We arrive in a place, but we do not recognize it; then similar taxis drive us to similar hotels, where we sleep in similar beds. These are global hotel chains. New buildings in cities are much the same everywhere, built by international star architects. In the department stores, international firms like Armani, Vuitton, Boss, and Max Mara repress local products. And in discotheques, you can hear the same music everywhere. A uniform world culture has emerged, and the local cultural traditions are relegated to "folklore": dance groups and singing clubs entertaining the tourists.

In the big city, everything must be available all the time. The seasons no longer count: strawberries at Christmas and apples at Easter. The freedom of urbanized people requires everything to be possible – albeit for those who can afford it. On the streets we find all the restaurants of the peoples of the world. We can eat Italian food in Seoul and drink Bavarian beer in Beijing. The globalized city promises unlimited possibilities.

We can, however, live according to nature even in the big city if we want to: "Think globally – eat and drink locally." The globalized uniform world culture must not suppress local cultural traditions, but can arrange them to meet each other for intercultural exchange. One must only want this. Local cultural traditions can act with a new self-consciousness vis-à-vis the boring uniform world culture.

Today some cities gain their identity and give their citizens self-respect by means of festivals: Munich with the Oktoberfest, New York with the city marathon, and Rio de Janeiro with the Brazilian carnival. These festivals are like the special "melody of the city." Citizens identify with their city and feel proud and at home there. In many places, the local football clubs provide this identity and pride. In Germany, the Protestant Church organizes a Kirchentag every second year in one of the big cities, with 150,000 participants over four days and nights. The Catholic Church too has a nationwide presence. In Korea, "Evangelization" may be the Christian festival for the city.

Big cities do not celebrate the natural seasons, but they carry the memorial culture of history, as revealed by the many monuments we see when we visit them.

The City as a Challenge to Christianity

Some 40 years ago, Harvey Cox presented the thesis that the secularization of modern men and women is caused by their urbanization: The "Secular City has no temple." Some 15 years ago, he corrected himself by writing the book "Religion in the Secular City." He is right. Religion didn't just disappear with urbanization. Religion has changed with the change of humans, and urbanization in mega-cities is a great change of life.

The city per se is no special challenge to Christianity. Early Christianity was a city religion. Christianity did not emerge from a natural religion of rural people, but from the city of Jerusalem, and it spread around the Mediterranean Sea in harbours and central cities, as the letters of the apostle Paul show. People did not come to the Christian faith through reverence of the powers of nature; the rural people were then called pagans. The Reformation was to a large extent effective in cities like Zurich, Geneva, and Strasbourg. Protestantism was called a city dweller's religion, while Catholicism was strong in rural areas. In early industrialization in England, the free churches, especially the Methodists, grew up among homeless workers. And the latest awakening of Pentecostal churches began in the Azusa Street Revival in Los Angeles as a typical big-city phenomenon. Even today, Pentecostals are still worshipping in empty factories.

During the migrations into the industrial areas, the personal decision of faith replaced the traditional belonging to a church. The voluntary congregation replaced the old town church. In the big cities, the individual freedom of choice is growing, and traditions are fading away. People become mobile, changing their living quarters frequently. The Christian churches ought to take the crisis of traditions as a chance for new missionary communities that extend an invitation to others.

Let me explain this further:

Some are asking whether the mega-city is calling for the mega-church, while others see the promise more in small Christian communities, such as the house churches. I do not see this as a contradiction: every living congregation consists of many small communities. These were and still are the Christian families, these are and will be more and more the house churches, small communities of one's own choice.

Forming a house church requires Christian hospitality, and hospitality presupposes good neighbourhood. I recently encountered a "meet your neighbour" movement, whereas in earlier times, this was a matter of course. In those days, if you moved in, you visited your neighbours and the neighbours welcomed you. In modern skyscrapers, people don't know their next-door neighbours, let alone those on other floors. They do not care for one another or provide help in emergencies. Again and again we hear of people who have died who are discovered only weeks later. Good neighbourhood is necessary for a good life, and it is from good neighbourhood that the house churches emerge.

An open Christian congregation is also the place where "before God" all people are equal. Wealth and poverty are not the essential point here. Men and women, black and white, those with disabilities and those without are accepted in the same human dignity before God. Modern competitive society isolates people, but the Christian community unites them. Coming into a Christian church, one must feel: "With you it is not so . . ." The alternative to poverty is not wealth; rather, the alternative to both wealth and poverty is – community.

For many city churches, community building and social work in the quarter belong together. On the one hand, Christians participate in citizen initiatives to improve social conditions, and on the other hand, churches provide soup kitchens for the hungry, shelter for the homeless, free medical care and legal advisory boards, practical help, and hospices for the dying. A lively congregation has so many gifts and energies of the divine Spirit that everyone can find a place where they are needed. The larger church bodies participate in the politics of the city and the nation. We have not only church theology but also public theology, and both are parts of the kingdom-of-God theology on earth.

In ancient times, the temple's task was to keep the heavens "open" over the city or country. The Chinese "son of heaven" sacrificed in the name of the Chinese people to the state gods and cared for the welfare of the country. Modern states no longer have state religion – it was replaced by the "freedom of religion" of all citizens. Is heaven now closed, privatized? The answer is no. Religion keeps "open" the transcendent dimension of individual life, common life, and the life of the city and state. Christian worship is a "gateway to heaven," just as Jacob gave the name Beth-el to the place where he saw "heaven's ladder" in his dream (Gen. 26:19). With the resurrection of Christ, heaven is opened for the whole suffering creation, as the martyr Stephen declared: "Behold, I see the heavens open" (Acts 7:58). This is why the prayer for the city and the blessing *urbi et orbi,* to the city and the whole earth, belong to every place of worship, not only in Rome. "Seek the best of the city."

In conclusion: The big city is at the moment the great hope of humankind. But does this mega-city itself have a future? Can the big city keep its promise of freedom and unlimited possibilities of life?

We don't know the answer to this, but we do know that only the big city has a future, that is, an unknown and most dangerous future. Only the city, not the countryside, has memories and expectations, because the city lives in the permanent difference between past and future. This is why cities are continually reconstructed.

For many people, to speak today about the future awakens fear and anxiety instead of hopeful expectations. There is a reason for this: People want the present to endure forever. Why? The urbanization of humankind is part of the great project of modern times. Because the end is uncertain, urbanization is a dangerous project. If this experiment fails, only a few people will survive to become the wiser for it. It is a unique, and perhaps the final, experiment of humankind. It is an experiment we can undertake only once. How might urbanization fail? The older ones among us may remember the destruction of big cities in the firestorms of the Second World War: Hiroshima and Nagasaki. The younger ones may fear the climate catastrophe that is descending upon all of us.

We may win the future of the big city, but we may also fail. The future may bring progress that leads to a better life, but it may also bring the destruction of all human life. We need the audacity of hope to decide for life. Christianity anticipates the success of the big-city experiment, as long as the churches disseminate the hope of God for humankind and see our future and the future of the earth in the coming of the City of God "on earth as it is in heaven."

PART TWO

Learning from the Past

Chapter 8

God and the Soul, God and the Senses

"I DESIRE TO KNOW GOD AND THE SOUL. NOTHING ELSE? ABSOLUTELY nothing" (*Deum et animam scire cupio. Nihilne plus? Nihil omnino*), wrote Augustine in his *Soliloquies* (1.2.7), thereby creating the paradigm that has guided Western Christian theology down to the present day. The knowledge of God and the knowledge of self are related reciprocally, and so closely that every affirmation about God contains a self-affirmation, and every self-affirmation contains an affirmation about God, as in an ellipse with the two focal points "God" and "the soul." "God and the soul" has dominated Western spirituality too: the path to God is the path inwards: "That I may know myself – that I may know you" (*noverim me, noverim te*). "Return into your own self: it is in the inner human being that the truth dwells."

I will present this theological principle at prominent points of the history of Western theology: in Augustine himself, in mediaeval mysticism, in the Reformation theology of Luther and Calvin, and not least in the modern theologians Schleiermacher and Bultmann. The corresponding philosophical tradition from Descartes to the existential philosophy of Karl Jaspers will be mentioned. After a personal dialogue with Augustine, I will then present the alternative: God and the body. I shall complement the Augustinian principle of "God and the soul" by means of the new principle of "God and the senses." My intention is to open up Western subjectivity to a psychosomatic and ecological spirituality.

God and the Soul

Augustine: God and the soul

The soul as subject

After the Bible, the *Confessions* of Augustine, written in 397/98 CE, is the most widely read book of the Western world.[1] It has left a deep imprint on Western psychology and mystical spirituality. "The human being himself is immensely deep" (*Grande profundum est ipse homo,* 4.14.77). There is something in human beings that not even the spirit within them knows of. This deep dimension of the soul emerges because Augustine no longer understands the soul as an intellectual substance in the human being, but as the reflexive self-understanding of the human being. This is why his psychology is found in his "confessions," and his confessions offer a pure introspection of the "I" that gets to the bottom of itself. The substance of the soul and the "I" are identical: "When the spirit knows itself, it knows its substance, and when it reaches certainty about itself, it is certain about its substance" (*De trin.* 10.10.16). What is involved is thus the psychological analysis of the consciousness of the "I." One might remark critically that, since the reflecting "I" can never completely objectify itself, never completely "get behind" itself, it would indeed be unfathomably deep – were it not for the presence in the soul of the transcendental depth that is designated as the relationship to God. "But you were more interior than my innermost dimension" (*interior intimo meo,* 3.6.11). This is why the innermost dimension of the human being is in the closest proximity to God. "You are the life of the souls, the life of the lives. As such, you live from your own self and do not change, you who are the life of my soul" (*tu vita es animarum, vita vitarum, vivens te ipsa et non mutaris, vita animae meae,* 3.6.10). The Augustinian soul is in the place *ubi nullus sexus ist*: it is transsexually the same in men and in women. The human being who is devoted to God – not in order to attain to goods outside of God, but for the sake of God – is superior to everything and is unconquerable.

The soul as the image of God

But why does the soul have a special relationship to God in its depths? Augustine writes: "You are going astray by rushing around: return!

But whither? To the Lord. He is there at once. Return into your heart first of all . . . Return into your heart and see what you experience there from God. In the inner human being Christ dwells; in the inner human being you will be renewed in accordance with the image of God. In his image, recognize the author."[2] The image of God is the bond between God and the soul, the divine form of the soul, its interior self-transcendence. William of Saint-Thierry, a 12th-century mystic, has God say to the soul: "Know yourself, because you are my image. Thus you will also know me, whose image you are, and you will find me in yourself."[3] Self-knowledge leads to knowledge of the inner condition of being the image of God, and thereby to the knowledge of God; and the knowledge of God leads to self-knowledge in the image of God. Through their senses, human beings recognize in the world "traces of God," and through the soul one knows God in the mirror of one's own condition of being God's image. "The excellent and primary mirror in which we see God is our rational soul, provided that it finds itself."[4] Self-knowledge is more infallible than knowledge of the world. Augustine thus anticipates Descartes' argument: "If I am mistaken, I exist. For one who does exist cannot be mistaken. And thus I exist, since I make mistakes" (*De civ. Dei* 1.C). It is only the soul, as the subject of self-knowledge, that is distinguished by being the image of God; the body of the human person, like nature, bears only the "traces of God." Self-consciousness is immediate and needs no mediations via the senses. This is why it is closest to God. The immanence of the infinite God in the soul calls forth the endless self-transcendence of the soul.

The restless heart

Augustine can also call this self-transcendence of the soul the restlessness of the heart:

> *You yourself stir us up,*
> *so that we may delight in praising you,*
> *because you have made us for yourself,*
> *and our heart is restless until it rests in you.*

Tu excitas, ut laudare te delectet,
quia fecisti nos ad te,
et inquietum est cor nostrum,
donec requiescat in te. (Conf. 1.1)

This anthropological principle has left a deep mark on the Christian soul in the West: here, we have the homelessness of the Western soul, its Faustian drive, its unquenchable desire, its unending yearning, and its torment.[5] Every comparison with East Asian mentalities shows that this "restlessness of the heart" is typically Western. We should note that, for Augustine, this does not have its origin in the paradise that was lost through the fall. It is something that is created along with the human being, something in which the dependence on the human being on God, his or her being the image of God, asserts itself. Unlike other creatures on earth, human beings are not tied to one particular environment; they are endowed or stricken with openness to the world. It has been affirmed that it is in this openness to the world that their openness to God is stimulated.[6] They cannot find rest anywhere in the world, but only in God. The human being who seeks God is the response to the God who seeks the human being. The *imago Dei* is not a quality of the human being, but the relationship of God to the human being and the relationship of the latter to God. This is why the soul would not seek God, if God did not draw it to himself. Max Scheler speaks of an "emptiness of the heart" that longs for the infinite God.[7] In psychological terms, one can speak of an excessive drive in the human constitution that remains unfulfilled in the world and finds no satisfaction there. In theological terms, the "restless heart" is undeniably unambiguous: it can express the love of God, but it can also express the human desire to be like God.

With his anthropology of the "restless heart," Augustine had a lasting influence on the Christian world, which became the Western world before it secularized itself into the modern world. Even in a world without God, hearts remain "restless" and find no peace. Every cultural comparison shows that this is a Christian-Western-occidental anthropology, not in the least a universal anthropology. It is the Westerner who feels, thinks, and lives in this way, because he or she has this restlessness in the heart: always curious, always discovering and conquering, never at peace with oneself, both one who seeks God and at the same time a "monster without respite and rest." People in other regions of the world and at other historical periods have lived differently. Up to now, we possess only historical anthropologies that are limited both spatially and temporally. We have no universal anthropology. Anthropologies that are put forward with a claim to universality are mostly imperialist anthropologies. A universal anthropology would have to find its fulfilment in the universal sphere; the Declarations of Human Rights and the Earth Charter point in the direction of a future anthropology of this kind.

The mystical uniting of the soul with God

The mediaeval theology of mystical experience developed out of the Augustinian concentration on "God and the soul." Here, we shall look only at two images: the mystical wedding of the soul with God in Mechthild of Magdeburg and the birth of God in the soul in Meister Eckhart.

Mystical theology seeks to be a "wisdom of experience," not a wisdom of doctrine.[8] Mystics are masters of life, not masters of doctrine. Mystical theology speaks of the path inwards, of the pilgrimage of the soul to God, of the ladder of love that leads to God, of an outward journey with no return (Dorothee Sölle). The mystical *sapientia experientialis* is always both ethical and mystical, a teaching about virtues and an experience of God, an art of living and an ecstasy. Life is a drama of love, of the love for God that is unhappy, that despairs, that is liberated, that makes one happy, and that is blissful: everyone is an erotic being who seeks God. The infinite God kindles this unquenchable passion in the one who is God's image. This is why measurelessness is the measure of the love of God. Mystical theology often describes the story of love between God and the soul with words from the Song of Songs, the love song in the Old Testament. But this will sound merely mawkish, if one forgets that unhappy love is the most terrible thing that human beings can suffer.

Hugh of Saint Victor has given the best description of the goal of mediaeval mysticism:

> Rising up to God means entering into oneself, and not merely entering, but stepping out beyond oneself in one's innermost dimension, in a manner that cannot be put into words. One who thus enters most intimately into his own self, penetrates himself in his inner dimension, and rises up above himself, truly raises himself up to God.[9]

The mystical marriage

Mechthild of Magdeburg, a Beguine who lived from ca. 1207 to 1282, wrote the book *The Flowing Light of the Godhead* around 1250. This has been called a "fragment of an inner biography." Its title brings together the "outpouring" of the Spirit and the "light" of life, and places the soul that seeks God in the light that flows from the Godhead:

> *O pouring God in your gift,*
> *O flowing God in your love,*
> *O burning God in your desire,*
> *O melting God in the uniting with your beloved.*[10]

God comes into the soul like "dew onto the flower." God comes to rest in the soul, and the soul loses itself in being taken into God. It is because of this goal of the mystical marriage with God that the human soul is "mortal, measureless, and incessant." It purifies itself on seven steps of true love, via the pain of repentance, the torment of confession, the labour of penitence, against the love of the world and the temptations of the devil, the insatiability of the flesh and the accursed self-will, until the soul becomes a pure act of desiring God.

> *Lord, now I am a naked soul*
> *and you in yourself a God*
> *in great glory.*
> *The union of us two is eternal life without death.*[11]

After this, the mystical silence begins. God gives himself to the soul, and the soul gives itself to God. The "path of love" has reached its goal. What takes place in this uniting of the soul with God is dark, unknowable, and indescribable. Since it can be experienced only with the entire soul or not at all, the soul can neither become conscious of it nor describe this uniting. The *silentium mysticum* takes over.

The birth of God in the soul

Meister Eckhart is too rich to be quoted in a few words, and we must therefore be content with two indications. He takes up the idea of the image of God as a mirror in the ground of the soul: in God's image, God knows himself. Those who know themselves in this image know themselves in God, just as God knows himself in them. God's self-knowledge and the soul's self-knowledge are one and the same: "The eye in which I see God is the same eye in which God sees me; my eye and God's eye, that is one eye and one seeing and one knowing and one loving."[12] In his sermon *Beati pauperes spiritu*, he describes the soul's path to God as the successive abolition of all mediations between God and the soul: "The human being ought to be so empty of all things and all works, both internally and externally, that he could be a place in which God is able to work." He then goes on to say that even this "place" must be abolished:

> So then, we say that the human being must stand there in such poverty as if he were no place, nor had any place, in which God could work. Where the human being still retains a place in himself, he still retains differentness. It is only when the human being stands empty of God and of all his works that God, if he is to work in the soul, is himself the place in which he wishes to work . . . in this way God accomplishes his own work, and the human being in this way endures God in himself.[13]

In his sermon *Qui audit me*, he coins the celebrated formula for this detachment and divestiture of the soul: "To leave God for the sake of God."[14]

In positive terms, when the ground of the soul becomes one with the being of God, this means the "birth of God" in the soul. This is not a metaphor, but touches on the inner-trinitarian life of God: just as the Father in eternity begets the Son, and the Son proceeds from the self-knowing of the Father, and the Father creates all things for the sake of the Son and through him, so too the Son brings all created being back into the uncreated being of the Father. This eternal process is repeated in the soul of the "noble person," which takes on the form of God and itself becomes the "Son of God." This presupposes the Augustinian idea that the soul itself has a trinitarian structure. Is this a theory of divinization? The answer to this question depends on whether the "ground of the soul," the *scintilla animae,* is thought of as created or uncreated.[15] Does it correspond to God himself as the image of God, or is the ground of the soul itself by nature divine? If "equal can be known only by equal" – as Eckhart holds, when he says: "The righteous person is one with God. Equality is loved. Love continuously loves that which is equal; that is why God loves the righteous person as one who is equal to God himself" – then the ground of the soul is divine by nature. But if the love of God is thought of as creative, it loves precisely that which is unequal, in order to make it correspond to his own self. In that case, however, it need not involve only the "soul" of the human being: it encompasses body and soul, human society, and the natural world on earth.

"God and the soul" in Reformation theology

Martin Luther

We begin with Luther's early Reformation treatise *On the Freedom of a Christian* (1520), and then turn to his formulation of the *articulus stantis* and *cadentis ecclesiae,* the "first and primary article" of the justification of the "sinful human being by the gracious God." We shall attempt to show how Luther breaks out of the Augustinian circle around "God and the soul," yet still remains tied to it.[16]

Luther begins his treatise on freedom with the two natures of every Christian: the spiritual inner nature and the bodily external nature. In accordance with their souls, human beings in faith become "spiritual, new, interior human being[s]"; but in accordance with flesh and blood, they remain "bodily, old, and external human being[s]." Luther takes up this Platonic dualism of body and soul in order to affirm that nothing external can either take human beings captive in their interior or set them free: "None of these things reaches to the soul, in order to set it free or to take it captive, to make it pious or wicked." It is only the word of God that can reach the soul and make it free and pious. Where the soul possesses the word of God, it is free and blessed. Luther takes the principle of "God and the soul" to a deeper level through the medium of this union: namely, the word of God and the faith of the soul. Where the word creates faith, a reciprocity between God and the soul arises: "When God then sees that the soul grants that he is true, and thus honors him through its faith, he in turn honors it and regards it as pious and truthful." The soul justifies God through its faith, and God justifies the soul through God's grace. This reciprocity generates a unity between God and the soul: "The soul of one who adheres to the word with right faith is so completely and utterly united to God that all the virtues of the word become the soul's own possession, so that the soul becomes a child of God." But for Luther, the true medium between God and the soul is Christ. He takes over from mediaeval mysticism the image of the wedding of the soul with its heavenly bridegroom, and interprets it in terms of the theology of the cross: that which Christ has, becomes the possession of the soul, and that which the soul has, Christ takes upon himself. This is the "joyful exchange": Christ takes on himself the sins, the damnation, and the sadnesses of the soul and gives it his own righteousness and blessedness.[17] This exchange takes place, not in a mystical moment in the apex of the soul, but in the faith that justifies: in his suffering and dying on the cross, Christ takes the sins of the world upon himself, in order to give believers the freedom of his resurrection and the full-ness of his life. Luther takes over here the Augustinian theology of the soul and puts it at the service of the knowledge of Christ in faith. The "Christian of the future" need not be a "mystic" (as Karl Rahner demanded); he or she will be a believer. All the burden of guilt and sadness will leave him; in faith in Christ, he will become "good, whole, and beautiful."[18]

However, the limits of the Augustinian bracket around "God and the soul" become clear when Luther reduces justification in faith to the forgiveness of sins, and draws a distinction between the spiritual world of faith and the external, physical, and public world. The doctrine of justification is indeed the "core of Reformation theology"; but is it also its "limit"? According to Luther, the object of theology (*subjectum theologiae*) is not God *per se*, nor the doxology of the triune God, but

> *Homo peccati reus ac perditus et*
> *Deus justificans ac salvator hominis peccatoris.*
> *Quicquid extra hoc subjectum in Theologia*
> *quaeritur aut disputatur, est error et venenum.*[19]

Ernst Wolf comments: "The 'object' of theology is not a metaphysical being, but a concrete historical event, God's salvific dealings with the sinful human being."[20] I believe that this does not exhaust the content of the event of justification: we have the justification of the sinners, but what about justice for the victims? After the forgiveness of sins, what about the new light of righteousness and the bestowal on the children of God of the right to inherit the coming kingdom of God? The righteousness of God, which justifies and creates justice, includes also "the new earth on which righteousness dwells." The hope of the justified human being embraces not only the spiritual realm, but also the secular realm; not only the soul, but also the body; not only the individual person, but also human society; not only humankind, but also this earth. "God and the soul": this may be a beginning, but ultimately it is a question of God and the earth, as the great promises of Revelation 21 affirm.

John Calvin

The compulsion to conform to the paradigm of "God and the soul" proves even stronger in Calvin than in Luther. Calvin begins his dogmatics, the celebrated *Institutio christianae religionis*, with the following affirmations: "All our wisdom – provided that it truly deserves the name of wisdom and is true and reliable – encompasses basically two things: the knowledge of God and our self-knowledge. These two are connected in many ways, and this is why it is not so simple to say which of them comes first and begets the other from itself" (I, 1, 1).[21] Astonishingly enough, Calvin here treats theology and anthropology on the same level. Indeed, he actually begins with human self-knowledge: "First of all, no one can contemplate himself without at once directing his senses to look at God, in whom he 'lives and moves' (Acts 17:28). . . . Our very existence as human beings consists in our possessing our being in the only God." And elsewhere, "One who knows himself is not only inspired thereby to seek God, but is, so to speak, led by the hand to find God." Self-knowledge and the knowledge of God are reciprocally related to each other in such a way that they condition each other, and that one cannot have the one without the other: "On the other hand, the human being certainly cannot come to know himself truly unless he has first seen the face of God, and then passes from this act of seeing to look at himself" (I, 1, 2). He closes the introductory chapter by explaining how he will proceed: "Doubtless, the knowledge of God and self-knowledge are firmly linked together. But the right order in doctrine demands that we treat first the knowledge of God, and then self-knowledge" (I, 1, 3).

One would have expected stronger reasons than merely "the right order in love" for the priority of the knowledge of God vis-à-vis self-knowledge. Above all, however, it is striking that Calvin does not begin here with the knowledge of Christ, which otherwise is central in his eyes for both the knowledge of God and self-knowledge. His words may seem to assert that the knowledge of God and self-knowledge are linked directly, but this is not the case: they are linked to each other through Christ. For the Christian faith, the mirror in which one may see God and oneself is the face of the crucified Christ. Blaise Pascal put this better than Calvin: "The knowledge of God without the knowledge of our wretchedness generates arrogance. The knowledge of our wretchedness without the knowledge of God generates despair. The knowledge of Jesus Christ creates the midpoint, because in him we find both God and our wretchedness."[22]

The soul as subject and as self-relation

From the philosophy of the modern period, we look at only two trans-formations of the concept of soul, in Descartes and Kierkegaard, in order to demonstrate the intensifications or dead ends that we encounter in the modern period.

René Descartes

Descartes held "that the two questions about God and the soul are the most important of the questions that are to be discussed with the aid both of philosophy and of theology," as he wrote in the dedicatory text of his *Meditations*.[23] He completed the transition (which began with Augustine) from the Platonic conception of the soul as an immortal substance in which the mortal body of the human being shares until death, to the true subject in the human body as in the world of things. The old body-soul dualism gave way to the subject–object dichotomy of the modern period. The human subject becomes conscious of his or her self through thinking, not through sensory perception. The human body, with its sensory perceptions and sensations, thus enters into the realm of objective things. Although the thinking "I" is united to its body – Descartes was not clear about how this took place; his bet was the pineal gland – a non-extended, thinking thing coexists with a non-thinking, extended thing in the human body. Descartes pushed this distinction so far that he held that he was "truly distinct from my body" and "could exist without it."[24] As a non-thinking, extended thing, the body with its senses is like a machine that is subject to the laws of nature. Nothing remains of the Aristotelian–Thomist view: *anima forma corporis*. The soul that thinks itself lifts itself up, superior to its own body. I am a thinking subject, and I have a body. When soul and body are defined by means of mutual exclusions (thinking – non-thinking, not-extended – extended), it is no longer possible to think of a "linking" (*complexio*). This does justice neither to the subjectivity of the soul nor to the objectivity of the body. The body, reduced to "extension," no longer has any sensory perceptions and sensations. The "soul" as subject, reduced to thinking, is held fast in self-certainty. The certainty of God can be perceived only in self-certainty. This is the modern variant of the Augustinian paradigm of "God and the soul." The psychosomatic unity of the human being is dissolved, and the ecological home of the human being in nature is abandoned. The human being becomes the "lord and possessor of nature," as Descartes puts it in his *Discourse on the Method*. It is not too much to say that we see here the intellectual foundations of the self-destruction of modern people and of their destruction of nature. *"L'Homme machine"* – the title that Descartes' pupil, the physician Lamettrie, gave to his book – is not a vision that promotes life, whether for the human being or for the earth.

Søren Kierkegaard

In his *Philosophische Weltorientierung* (1932), Karl Jaspers translated the Augustinian paradigm of "God and the soul" into the philosophy of "existence and transcendence," thereby translating his psychology into existential philosophy. "Existence" here does not in the least mean what the term means in colloquial speech, namely, what people build up as their physical, external, and economic "existence" in the struggle for survival; rather, "existence is that which relates to itself, and therein to its transcendence." "That which is called 'soul' and 'God' in a mythological mode of expression, and 'existence' and 'transcendence' in a philosophical language, is not world."[25] This is what makes the modern philosophical and theological concept of existence so unrealistic. According to this concept, other living beings and the things of the world cannot "exist"; only self-conscious human beings "exist." Like Descartes, Karl Jaspers drew a distinction between "being object" and "being 'I'," and he reserved the concept of existence for "being 'I'."

Søren Kierkegaard had translated the Augustinian "soul" by the "self" of the human being:

> The human being is spirit. What is spirit? Spirit is the self. What is the self? The self is a relationship that relates to itself . . . A relationship that relates to itself, a self, must either have posited itself or have been posited by something else. If the relationship that relates to itself is posited by something else, the relationship is doubtless the *tertium*, but this relationship, the *tertium*, is in turn

also a relationship and relates to that which has posited the entire relationship.[26]

Kierkegaard calls this self the "self before God" or the "theological self": "The more the idea of God, the more the self; the more the self, the more the idea of God."[27] The human self thereby becomes an "infinite self."

The soul as self-consciousness

We close this review of the history of theology by looking briefly at two representatives of the Augustinian paradigm in modern Protestantism: Friedrich Schleiermacher in the 19th century and Rudolf Bultmann in the 20th.

Friedrich Schleiermacher

In his influential *Glaubenslehre* (Doctrine of the faith, 1821, 1830), Schleiermacher seeks to elaborate a modern theology of consciousness, and this is why he begins with the "immediate self-consciousness."[28] A self-consciousness is "immediate" when is needs no sensory or social mediations. This is the "highest stage of the human self-consciousness," and exists in reality only together with lower stages mediated by the senses. At every moment, however, the immediate self-consciousness accompanies the forms of the mediate consciousness. It does not exist on its own, but only linked to something else. However, all the forms of consciousness are linked to our immediate self-consciousness. The "piety," today called "spirituality," from which all ecclesial communities live, is a determination of the immediate self-consciousness: namely, "that we are conscious of being absolutely dependent or – to say the same thing with different words – of being in relationship to God."[29] The immediate self-consciousness and the consciousness of absolute dependence constitute the "pious self-consciousness." The theological ellipse unites the two focal points of the immediate self and the absolute God. Self-consciousness and the consciousness of God belong together and form an inseparable unity. Christ is the prototype of the human being with the "constant powerful consciousness of God" that is the source of his redemptive deeds.

The problem here is the idea of an "immediate" self-consciousness: in order to get a consciousness of oneself, a subject must be able to distinguish itself from itself, and to make itself the object of its consciousness. It is in this differentness that it can arrive at an identification. Both of these, however, take place only via mediations. Immediateness and self-consciousness are mutually exclusive. An immediate self-consciousness is an ahistorical self-consciousness, a self-consciousness without a memory. Schleiermacher's "immediate self-consciousness" is a postulate, and cannot be distinguished from a self-forgetting, mystical unconsciousness. This is why he also calls it "the highest stage of self-consciousness."

Rudolf Bultmann

It is easy to recognize the Augustinian schema in Bultmann's existentialist theology: "The object of theology is God, and theology speaks of God by speaking of the human being as he stands before God, that is to say, on the basis of faith."[30]

In his essay "*Welchen Sinn hat es, von Gott zu reden?*" (What does it mean to speak of God? 1925), he states plainly that talking about God does not belong to the universal, objective truths, but must always be related to the existential situation of the one who speaks. "If one wants to talk about God, it is obvious that one must talk about oneself."[31] He regards it as "a remarkable matter" that we cannot really talk about God and our own existence, since neither of these is at our disposal. All we can do is to speak "out of" our existence and "out of" God. "We cannot speak about our existence, since we cannot speak about God; and we cannot speak about God, since we cannot speak about our existence. We can only do the one together with the other. If we could speak out of God about God, we could also speak about our existence, and *vice versa*." "We never know about God; we never know about our own reality: we have both only in faith in the grace of God."[32] There is clearly a mystery that enfolds God and human existence, and this is why Bultmann calls it "a remarkable matter." He sees faith as the possibility of speaking authentically out of God and out of one's own existence. One could ask, with Augustine: "Nothing else?" And one would receive the Augustinian answer: "Absolutely nothing."

Rudolf Bultmann was an objective New Testament scholar, but his hermeneutic was the subjective, existential methodology. He had written at an earlier date that the exposition of a text must correspond to the self-exposition of the interpreter who understands it: "The text then makes it possible for me in each case to open up to myself anew an understanding of myself on the basis of the text. It is not the 'source' for something that existed in the past. Instead, it speaks by speaking of my existence."[33] He later called this the existential interpretation. The demythologization of the New Testament, which made him both celebrated and controversial, is only the other side of the coin of this existential hermeneutic.

Both are late effects of the limits of the Augustinian paradigm that focuses on "God and the soul" and that consequently is incapable of breaking out either to the doxology of God for his own sake or to the world that discloses itself to our senses.

God and the Senses

What do I love, when I love God?

One evening, I read in Augustine's *Confessions* (10.6, 8):

> But what do I love when I love my God? Not material beauty or beauty of a temporal order; not the brilliance of earthly light, so welcome to our eyes; not the sweet melody of harmony and song; not the fragrance of flowers, perfumes, and spices; not manna or honey; not limbs such as the body delights to embrace. It is not these that I love when I love my God. And yet, when I love him, it is true that I love a light of a certain kind, a voice, a perfume, a food, an embrace; but they are of the kind that I love in my inner self, when my soul is bathed in light that is not bound by space; when it listens to sound that never dies away; when it breathes fragrance that is not borne away on the wind; when it tastes food that is never consumed by the eating; when it clings to an embrace from which

it is not severed by fulfilment of desire. This is what I love when I love my God.

A little later on, he writes: "I have learnt to love you late, Beauty at once so ancient and so new! I have learnt to love you late! You were within me, and I was in the world outside myself. . . . You were with me, but I was not with you" (10.27). And I answered him that same night:

> When I love God, I love the beauty of bodies, the rhythm of move-ments, the brightness of eyes that shine, the embraces of love, the feelings, the sounds, the smells, of this colorful, wonderful creation. I want to embrace the whole world, when I love you, my God. I love you with all my senses in the creatures of your love. I know that you await me in all the things that come to meet me.
>
> For a long time, I sought you in myself and hid myself away in the snail shell of my soul and protected myself with armor of untouchability. I was inside, in myself, but you were outside. I was not with you, I refused your invitation to life. But you surrounded me from all sides, and enticed me out of the loneliness of my heart into the broad space of your beloved life. And so I emerged from myself and placed my soul in my senses, and discovered in the Other that which is my own. I love you with all my senses. My mortal body yearns for you. The more I love you, the living God, the more do I love life.[34]

The Spirit of God and human spirituality

As the word "spirituality" itself states, what is involved here is the taking hold of the human being by the Spirit of God. Spirituality develops where the Spirit of God is experienced. When "the love of God is poured out into our hearts through the Holy Spirit, who is bestowed on us" (Rom. 5:5), a spirituality of the heart comes into being. When the Holy Spirit is "poured out on all flesh," a spirituality of life comes into being. When the Spirit is present everywhere and sustains all things in heaven and on earth, keeping them together and orienting them to their future, a cosmic spirituality comes into being. The spirituality of the soul and of the interior human being that I have presented above was a one-sided perception of the holy in the human soul, a perception gained by turning away from the external world and from the human senses. But if the soul is defined through turning away and an ascetic denial of the body and of the senses, narrow boundaries are set for the Spirit of God, and the result is a spirituality that is hostile to the body. The Holy Spirit becomes a Spirit "removed from the world. This was the spirituality of the ascetics in the Egyptian desert, and the monastic spirituality and the spirituality of celibate priests. But it is also the spirituality of the captives who have nothing left but the "inner life."[35]

> Close the windows of your senses,
> otherwise the spirit of the world will take hold of you;
> and pay attention to how God draws you from within,
> the God who loves to keep you recollected.

> Soul, close the eyes from this circling of the earth;
> fall away gently and quietly from yourself,
> and from place and time;
> in the now of eternity
> God can be seen.

These are the words of the 17th-century Protestant mystic poet Gerhard Teersteegen. He sought God not only "within," but also immediately, without his creation, in order to dissolve his soul in the sea of the Godhead: "I want God in pure form; away with you, creature! My flesh and my heart do naught but pine."[36]

According to the biblical traditions, the Holy Spirit is not the Spirit of this age of the world that is passing away, but the dawning of the morning of the coming new world of God. This, however, does not mean that the Spirit of God works in a manner that is hostile to the body, unworldly, or non-sensuous. The Spirit of God makes the earth holy, makes life come alive, and awakens all the senses. The Spirit of the resurrection comes as in waves of "living water" into hearts, into the society that shatters all the boundaries of races, genders, classes, and peoples, into the emergent energies and forms of the creatures in heaven and on earth. It is necessary today to open up the narrowness of the schema of "God and the soul" for God and the body, and for God and the senses. The "soul's salvation" of the Augustinian tradition must be opened up to the salvation of society and the salvation of the sighing nature of the world. We need a spirituality of the world, a piety of the daily life that sustains the world and renews life.

God and the body

God created the human being in God's own image, "as man and woman he created them" (Gen. 1:22). This means that the entire human being, in the psychosomatic form as man or woman, and human beings in their social relationships to one another, are God's image on earth. We cannot speak here of a priority of the soul, and there is no trace in the anthropology of the Old Testament of a higher appreciation of the soul, thanks to its relationship to God, and a depreciation of the body.[37]

Nor is there in Paul any defensive ring around "God and the soul."[38] On the contrary, it is the body that is a temple of the Holy Spirit: "The body is meant for the Lord, and the Lord for the body . . . For you were bought with a price; therefore glorify God in your body" (1 Cor. 6:13-20). He says of the apostles of Jesus: "always carrying in our body the death of Jesus, so that the life of Jesus may also be made visible in our bodies" (2 Cor. 4:10). What is the reason for this striking emphasis on the relationship of the body to God? For Plato, it is the *meditatio mortis* that makes the immortality of the soul certain; for Paul, it is the bodily resurrection of Jesus that makes certain the "resurrection of the flesh" (as we said in the older translation of the Apostles' Creed): "Moreover my flesh will live in hope" (Acts 2:26). If the body is seen as the temple of the Holy Spirit, this means that God dwells, not in a separated apex of the soul, but in the whole of the bodiliness that is open to the senses and to society. Physical life is sanctified and affirmed. It is not the unlived life of asceticism, but the lived life of love that unites one to the living God. The soul of the human being manifests itself in the animate body, not in a bodiless inner dimension.

The human being always appears before the presence of God as a psychosomatic and social totality. One can also say that it is only "before the presence of God" that human beings appear in their totality – that is to say, in the entire history of their lives, since in the presence of eternity, all the times that we experience as a sequence are contemporary.

In his consciousness, the human being experiences himself and his bodiliness in a dialectical form: Helmut Plessner has accurately described the eccentric position of the human being as both being a body (*Leib*) and having a body (*Körper*).[39] This is based on the spontaneous *and* the reflective self-experience of the human being. If I act spontaneously, I am united with myself in direct living; if I reflect on myself, I distinguish myself from myself and I become my own vis-à-vis. These two forms of consciousness must be set in relation to each other; they must not be separated, for otherwise a human being will become sick. If I act and react only spontaneously, I am like an animal; if I continuously reflect on myself, I become schizophrenic. In lived life, what matters is to maintain the equilibrium, or to seek again and again to establish a balance. This finds expression when busy people say: "I need a pause, I must rest, I have to stop, I have to find myself again." But in an over-organized, over-reflective society, the other side is equally important: the new spontaneity, the adventure of life. As the strong woman says in the film *Antonia's Line,* "You have to live!"

"I am, but I do not have myself. This is why we are only in process of becoming." Ernst Bloch wrote these words in 1930 in his book *Spuren.* He points here to the social "we"-relationship, in which the dialectic of "being myself" and "having myself" finds its concrete, social, and future forms.[40]

The Spirit of the living God is the "Spirit of life," who is experienced in the lived life and in the love of life. Where God is present, this love is experienced; and God "dwells" where this love makes life alive:

Ubi caritas et amor,
ibi Deus est.
Where there is love and loving-kindness,
God is there.

God and the cosmos

In the Christian understanding, the creation of the cosmos is a trinitarian operation: God the Father creates the world through his eternal Logos in the energies of the Holy Spirit. The world is a non-divine reality, but one that is permeated by the Spirit of God. If all things are created by God, through God, and in God, they also exist by God, through God, and in God.

The consequence of this trinitarian understanding of the creation is the idea of a cosmos that is the work of the Spirit. This is how Hildegard of Bingen in the Middle Ages saw and experienced the world:

The Holy Spirit is life-giving life,
mover of the universe and root of all created being.
He purifies the universe from impurity, he takes away guilt and
anoints the wounds.
Thus he is shining life, worthy of praise, raising up and reawak-
ening the universe.[41]

We find a similar aphorism in the Reformation period, in John Calvin:

For the Spirit is present everywhere and sustains, nourishes,
and gives life to all things in heaven and on earth.
The fact that he pours his power into everything
and thereby promises being, life, and movement to all things:
this is clearly divine.[42]

This is not a pantheism that equates God with nature; nor is it a panentheism that sees all things in God. Instead, it corresponds to the Old Testament–Jewish thinking about the *shekhinah*, whereby the

Spirit of God "dwells in" all things. The God who decides to make a covenant with his people also wants to "dwell in the midst of the Israelites."[43] When, one day, all the lands are full of God's glory (Is. 6:3), the temple in which God "dwells" will be his creation, brought to perfection. The New Testament affirmations about the Holy Spirit correspond to the ideas about the *shekhinah* in the Old Testament: *inhabitatio Spiritus Sancti.*

When we think of the cosmos, we look upward to the starry sky, but the world that is closer to us is the earth. Modern theology has seen the earth merely as that which the human being is to "subdue" to himself (as the first creation narrative says). But this is one-sided and false. The earth is created and permeated by the divine Spirit: "When you send forth your spirit, they are created; / and you renew the face of the earth" (Ps. 104:30). At Sirach 40:1, the earth is called "our mother," as is the case among most peoples. Can one "subdue" one's own mother, exploit her and sell her off? The starting point for the new ecological theology is that the earth is our "home." "Humanity is part of a vast evolving universe. Earth, our home, is alive with a unique community of life. . . . The protection of earth's vitality, diversity, and beauty is a sacred trust."[44] This way of seeing the earth corresponds to the biblical reverence for life on the earth better than the objectification and subjugation of the earth by the omnipotent human being. As the Old Testament sees it, the earth is

> *a unique creative creature, because it brings forth life (Gen. 1:24);*
> *a covenant partner with God (Gen. 9:13);*
> *a creature that celebrates the Sabbath of God (Lev. 25:4);*
> *full of the divine life-force (Ps. 104:30);*
> *containing within itself the salvific mystery of the Messiah*
> *(Is. 4:2) and of the righteousness of God (Is. 45:8).*

In the Christian understanding, God has "reconciled" the cosmos (2 Cor. 5:17). The exalted Christ is the head of everything in heaven and on earth (Eph. 1:10; Col. 1:20). The cosmic Christ is the Christ who is to come and who will judge in righteousness, not only the living and the dead, but also the earth. This means that Christians do not live in a hostile world, nor in a paradisiac world; they live in a "reconciled world." And this creates confidence in the world, despite many catastrophes in nature in the world. This generates a cosmic spirituality, such as Francis of Assisi expressed in his famous "Canticle of the Sun."[45] If we are a "part of the universe," we will respect all things for their own sake, independently of their usefulness for human beings, and we will encounter all our "fellow creatures" with reverence for life. We will seek union with the Spirit of God through the sensory perceptions of the world. We will not only retreat into ourselves in order to seek God; we will also go out from ourselves, in order to experience the presence of God with all our senses in the outside world. "You awaken all my senses. . . ."

A spirituality of the senses

Spirituality is the work of the divine Spirit, whom human beings seek and experience. In the biblical creation narrative, God "breathed into the nostrils of the human being the breath of life; and the man became a living being" (Gen. 2:7). This passage vividly depicts how the Spirit of God, God's "breath," becomes the vital force of the human being. Accordingly, people feel the divine Spirit with their senses in their own vitality. Spirituality and vitality are not antithetical. One who seeks God must want to live; one who finds God awakens to the fullness of life. When the divine Spirit takes hold of someone, it opens that person's senses to the miracle of life. We become attentive and alert.[46]

We have five senses, but which is the most original sense, that out of which the others have come into being? From ancient times onward, the sense of touch has been called the original sense. We touch and feel with the nerve cells in the skin. Our skin unites and separates our outside world and our inside world: we feel and develop feelings, we taste and develop taste. We "feel comfortable in our own skin"; some are "thick-skinned," while others are particularly "thin-skinned." What our skin feels becomes a metaphor for our inner life. Out of the skin that encloses the body, sensitive special organs have developed: taste cells in the mouth, olfactory cells in the nose, hearing organs in the ears, and the eyes. The brain with which we process the sensory impressions developed out of coils of skin.

We distinguish between "close-up senses" and "remote senses." With the close-up senses (touching, tasting, and smelling), we make immediate contact with objects. The remote senses (hearing and seeing) need the mediation of sound and light.

All sensory impressions have an influence on our wellbeing, just as our wellbeing has an influence on our senses. Our senses are extinguished in deep grief; we no longer register anything, we feel nothing any more, apart from our pain, and our senses are paralyzed. We no longer react to sensory impressions. They leave us cold, because nothing matters to us. A life subject to routine and program makes us insensitive. Our *joie de vivre* disappears, and our senses are put to sleep; our actions and reactions are repetitive, and we perceive nothing new.

On the other hand, the vital force of love makes us come alive, and opens our senses. We know each other and feel that we are known; we speak to each other and listen to each other; we feel each other, and feelings awaken in us. Life in its fullness pulsates in our veins. Love awakens all our senses and fills us with interest in the life of other people and in the life that we share. The love of life makes us capable both of happiness and of suffering. We sense the vitality of life, but also the deadliness of death.

The vital force of hope directs our senses toward the life that is fulfilled. We wait in suspense for hitherto unknown experiences of life. We open our senses for what is coming toward us. Thanks to hope, we do not abandon ourselves in the face of the powers of death, of disappointment, or of humiliation. Hope of the fullness of life awakens our senses every morning.

Finally, the spirituality of the sensuous life also means that one can rest and let the sensory impressions work on us. In rest lies strength, as we often say. The biblical Sabbath precept teaches us to rest on the seventh day and to leave the world around us in peace. The mystics sought this rest in God by entering into the interior life of the soul. They sought the divine rest in the ground of the soul or on the seventh stage of the "mountain of the soul." All they were doing thereby was to transport the Sabbath precept from the experience of time into the inner experience of the soul. It is much simpler and more natural to take the seventh day for this purpose.[47]

But coming to rest is something that we need to learn; it does not happen automatically. We need time to loosen the tensions, to liberate ourselves from cares and expectations, and to let go of the things that hold us fast; to become "free and empty" of all things, as the mystics said, to stop regarding one's own self and all things in terms of goals and uses, and instead to perceive with all our senses the goodness and beauty of existence. Perhaps it is only in the Sabbath rest that we perceive nature as God's beloved creation, rather than as "our environment." The Sabbath rest is the *kairos* for natural theology – not in order to take nature as the starting point for knowing God, but rather to take God as the starting point for knowing nature.

A healthy person possesses a total of five senses, but they are not all equally powerful. The senses need to be trained. We need a school of the senses. We can indeed see, but often we discern nothing; we can indeed hear and perceive noises, but often we fail to listen. Modern people can indeed smell and taste, but their sense of smell is atrophied, and a good sense of taste needs to be trained.

Our sensuousness is determined not only by our wellbeing and our attitudes to life, but also by the culture in which we live, which invites certain senses and subdues others. The media of the modern world – radio, television, telephone, fax, email, internet, etc. – invite our remote senses: one must be able to see and hear, in order to participate. The modern means of transport are steered by our eyes and ears. We react with great attention to signals in light and sound, and we can remain awake for hours on end. People from other cultural areas cannot do so; but they know the signals of the wood and the sea that we do not know.

But what has happened to our close-up senses? If we live in big cities – and more than 50 percent of us live in mega-cities, while the trend to urbanization shows no signs of slowing down – we no longer smell very much, because the exhaust fumes on the streets and the fine dust have paralyzed our sense of smell. We need a strong perfume, if we are to be able to smell anything at all. Life in big cities has become a hurried life. People find their nourishment at McDonald's or Burger King, and ruin their sense of taste. They gulp down Coca-Cola, and can no longer tell the difference between one drink and another. We see even small children who have no great ability to distinguish one thing from another by touching and feeling. Our sense of touch is underdeveloped. In comparison to the indigenous inhabitants of Papua New Guinea, modern people are masters of their remote senses and sick in their close-up senses. We see and hear almost everything, but we smell, taste, and feel less and less.

If one is to live and work, one must not only use one's senses: one must also teach them and train them. We see much with our eyes, but we discern only little. One needs time, in order to learn how to look properly. It is only when we look properly that we perceive things for their own sake. It is only when we open ourselves to the impression made by our senses that we perceive things and human beings as they are. *Tantum cognoscitur, quantum diligitur,* said Augustine: "We know to the extent that we love."

We hear the noises of the external world, but usually we do not listen. Listening too is something that must be learnt, as every music teacher can testify. Judaism and Christianity are religions of hearing: "Hear, Israel." At the birth and the resurrection of Christ, human beings "heard" the voice of the angels. There is not only a hearing with the ears, but also a "hearing with the heart" and a deep hearing with the whole of one's body.

God breathes throughout his entire creation. When God's Spirit of life takes hold of us, an undreamt-of love awakens to life in us, and our senses open up. Rabanus Maurus prays as follows in his Pentecost hymn:

Accende lumen sensibus,
infunde amorem cordibus.
Kindle light for the senses,
pour love into the hearts.

In order to resist cynicism and indifference in the face of the modern destructions of the life of the earth, we need to elaborate a new ecological spirituality. Those who begin to love life, the life that we share, and the life of the earth, because they love God, will resist the killing of human beings and the destruction of the earth. This new spirituality regards the earth as a sacrament, because it conceals in itself the mystery of the presence of God. This makes universally true what is proclaimed in the Lord's supper or eucharist: "Taste and see that the Lord is good." Holy communion addresses the remote sense of seeing and the close-up sense of tasting, and thereby addresses the human being as a whole. Ecological spirituality invites us to live with all our senses in God's creation, which is filled with God's Spirit.

Chapter 9

The Unfinished Reformation: Ecumenical Answers to Unresolved Problems

From Disputation to Dialogue

I begin with some remarks about the culture of dispute in the Reformation period, which has disappeared, and about the modern culture of dialogue.[1]

When I studied theology in Göttingen in 1948, the generation who had experienced the "church struggle" under National Socialism was still dominant. Ernst Wolf and Ernst Käsemann represented the "Reformation theology," and I was its passionate adherent. We learned theology in the mode of conflict that had been exemplified by the Theological Declaration of Barmen of the Confessing Church (1934): "We confess" and "We reject." As far as I know, there were no "dialogues" between the National Socialist "German Christians" and the Confessing Church. In the wake of the German church struggle, we thought in categories of "friend or foe," and we sang: "Hot or cold, yes or no, we never want to be lukewarm." My teachers were gifted with determination, but not with openness to discussion, since they regarded every compromise with Luther as "rotten." They followed the Reformation culture of dispute.

Many in my generation wanted to break out of this inner-church dimension, which threatened with time to become sterile, and to attempt a "theology with its face to the world" (to use Johann Baptist Metz's term). And so, with a political theology, we came into conflict with the political ideologies of the "world," and a dispute became necessary when a concrete need existed. These were the "Christian–Marxist dialogues" in the 1960s in Salzburg, Herrenchiemsee, and Marienbad, whose participants included Karl Rahner, Ernst Bloch, Roger Garaudy, Machovec and Gardarsky, and Metz and me. "If we do not talk with one another now, we will one day shoot at each other." In the divided world of the Cold War, the external situation made dialogue necessary. And this was a dangerous dialogue: in August 1968, Soviet tanks put an end to the "socialism with a human face" in Prague. All our Czech dialogue partners were persecuted. Twenty-one years later, the Soviet Union was exhausted.

The second dialogue became necessary "after Auschwitz." The Jewish–Christian dialogue sought to overcome the centuries-old Christian anti-Judaism of the churches and the Christian states. This dialogue began with conferences in the USA about the Holocaust, and it continued in Bible studies at the Protestant and Catholic church conferences in Germany and in today's declarations by the Protestant Church in Germany (EKD) and the Catholic Bishops' Conference about the permanent election of Israel.

Today, we face an inflation of dialogues. There is a desire to "get into conversation" with as many people as possible. Theology must be relational and communicative. The subject about which we are speaking is not so important; the relationship into which we enter in the dialogue is more important. The dialogue of our own day serves, not truth, but community. These dialogues in search of community go from one church to another, from one religious community to another. At the same time, disputes in search of truth arise in all the churches, and in all the religions, between conservatives and progressives, between fundamentalists and modernists. Why are the dialogues in search of community and the disputes in search of truth separate? Why do community and truth not go together?

Public theological disputations were held in the Reformation period. Afterwards, the municipal authorities of a city or the prince of the region decided in favour of the new or the old faith, and mostly in favour of the new faith. In parliaments, there are discussions, followed by a vote. A trial includes a plea, and at the end the judge pronounces a verdict. A discussion is at the service of agreement, and an appointment to meet is at the service of action in common.

It is only in modern "dialogues" that there is no goal, since the path is goal enough. In modern television talk shows, all the participants speak at cross purposes, interrupt each other, or speak for as long as they possibly can. A result is not intended.

There is a stale joke about the modern philosophy of communication: A traveler is in a foreign city and asks someone who encounters him: "Do you know the way to the railway station?" The other replies: "I don't know either, but I am happy that we have gotten into conversation with each other." It is not surprising that theology has fallen silent. I still remember the vigorous disputes about "demythologization" or "feminist theology" (to mention only two examples). Today, theologians have become peaceful. There is scarcely any conflict nowadays, and the public sphere takes scarcely any notice now. "Academic theology" has abandoned the churches and concentrates on gaining recognition in the house of the sciences. Dogmatics turns into the philosophy of religion. In earlier times, people complained about the argumentativeness of the theologians, the *rabies theologorum.* Today, theology has become a harmless matter. Is that not a good thing?

No! We must once again learn to say yes or no. A conflict can contain more truth than a tolerant dialogue. We need a theological culture of dispute, with resoluteness and respect. Why? For the sake of God's truth!

In 1948, the World Council of Churches (WCC) declared in Amsterdam: "Let us ask God to teach us with each other how to speak a genuine *no* and a genuine *yes.* A no to all that contradicts the love of Christ. A yes to all that conforms to the love of Christ, to all who establish justice, to all who make peace, to all who reach out for a new heaven and a new earth in which righteousness dwells." Martin Luther cultivated an uncultivated culture of dispute in the age of "ruffianliness." He called his adversary Schwenkfeld "Stenkfeld" ("stinking field") and, according to legend, he cut through a tablecloth between himself and Zwingli. Luther valued the truth of God more highly than friendship or respect. Theological truth is worth a heated conflict, especially among friends. Theology without confession is worthless.

Without yes and no, the theological dialogue degenerates into a mere exchange of opinions.

The Unity of the Church, Or: The Universal Papacy of All Believers[2]

The churches of the Reformation broke away from Rome because they were excommunicated by Rome, and they became state churches. Luther burned the Roman bull of excommunication outside the city gates of Wittenberg. The state church was the state religion: *cujus regio – ejus religio*. In the aftermath of their terrible experiences with the German Nazi state, the Protestant churches changed their name in 1945: they no longer understood themselves as the "Deutsche Evangelische Kirche" ("German Protestant Church," DEK), but as the "Evangelische Kirche in Deutschland" ("Protestant Church in Germany, EKD). This was a big step on the path to the autonomy of the Protestant Church: "German" was no longer the sign that qualified the nature of the church, but the place where the one worldwide church existed. First comes the gospel ("Evangelische" from "Evangelium," "Gospel"), and only then comes Germany. But since we believe, in the words of the Nicene Creed, in "the one, holy, catholic, and apostolic church," we must ask: Where is the "service of unity" in the Protestant Church?

"Unity" is a gift and a task of every church in the name of the triune God. From Martin Luther onwards, Protestant theologians have taught the "universal" – or, as I would prefer to say, the common – "priesthood of all believers." Luther affirmed: "The one who comes crawling out of baptism has thus been consecrated a priest, bishop, and pope." This means that it is high time to put into practice the universal papacy of all believers. The "service of the unity" of the church is the task of every believer and of every church. Despite the further diversification and pluralization of the non–Roman Catholic churches into numerous denominations, we nevertheless believe in the "one church of Christ," and we recall in the ecumenical movement Jesus' high-priestly prayer "that all may be one" (John 17:21). Protestant churches too are the "one catholic church." But although we believe this, we do not act accordingly, since we distance ourselves from others. The Reformation was intended, theologically speaking, as the renewal of the entire one catholic church, on the basis of its origin. It was a Catholic Reformation. It became a "Protestant Reformation" only in 1530 in Augsburg, when the princes made their churches their own possession. The ecumenical movement of our own days reminds us "Protestants" of our Catholic character.

The political aspect of the Roman papacy – as the head of state of the Vatican City state – belongs only historically, not essentially, to the "service of unity." It is not only Protestant Christians who wish a return to the papacy as it was before the time of Constantine, for then Protestant churches too could accept the "service of unity" of the bishop of Rome. However, the universal and communal "service of unity" in every church, in every parish community, and in every family is more important. Ultimately, the Roman Catholic churches and parish communities are also churches and parish communities of the gospel; in other words, we acknowledge them as "churches of the gospel." "We are the church!" How does this work? We have all had the same experience in the ecumenical movement:

> *The closer we come to Christ,*
> *the closer we come to each other.*

What is the relationship between the unity of the church and its catholicity?

Are they one and the same thing? I do not think so. They are different qualities of the church of Christ. When we speak of "unity," we have in mind the inner unity of the church, while the catholicity of the church envisages its external universal horizon: the word "catholic" (*kath' holon*) means "all-embracing." But it is only the kingdom of God that is all-embracing; this does not yet apply to the church, which therefore understands itself as the anticipation and the beginning of the kingdom of God in this world. The church acknowledges that Israel is the first anticipation of the kingdom in history. Israel, taken as a whole, is not one "church people" in the church that embraces all peoples, but a "kingdom people" of the messianic kingdom. This means that there is no mission to the Jews; rather, Judaism must be stimulated to realize the "principle of hope" of its great prophets.

The word "catholic" can also have another meaning today, an ecological meaning: "so that everything might be gathered together in Christ, in heaven and on earth" (Eph. 1:10). *Restitutio omnium in Christo*: this is the Christian faith's universal hope for the reconciled cosmos. Christ is not only the head of his body, the church. He is also the head of the reconciled cosmos.

For the sake of the "unity" in which we believe, it is right that the remembrance of the fifth centenary of the Reformation should be celebrated not only in a Lutheran spirit, but above all in an ecumenical spirit. We should not glorify Martin Luther "the German" in a political-national spirit (or demon) as was done in 1817 and 1917. The date of 31 October is neither Luther's birthday nor the day of his death, but the Reformation Day of "the one and catholic church."

Reformation "by Faith Alone": The Baptists[3]

Who were the "Baptists," and why were they cruelly persecuted by both Catholics and Protestants? Luther called them "Enthusiasts," and historians speak of the "left wing of the Reformation." I believe that they were the only Reformation movement "by faith alone." They called themselves "children of God." I am speaking here of the peaceful Baptists, not of the struggle for control of Münster in 1534.

How did the Reformation come about? After sermons about the Reformation and the approval of the people, the magistrates of the cities or the regional princes implemented the Reformation of the churches and schools, thereby asserting their sovereignty over the church. These Reformations took place within the framework of the laws and traditions of the "Holy Roman Empire of the German Nation." Christianity is the imperial religion, and the *Sacrum Imperium* is the "thousand years' reign" of Christ. The Reformers remained within this tradition of the *Corpus Christianum*. It was only the Baptists who rejected the very foundations of the Christian state religion, namely, infant baptism and military service. They refused to serve with the sword, because "Jesus forbids the power of the sword." They refused to take oaths, "because Jesus forbids those who belong to him to swear any oaths." They refused to assume any role of secular authority, "because it cannot be fitting for a Christian to be part of the authorities." These appeals to Jesus and to his Sermon on the Mount are found in the Schleitheim Confession of 1527, which Michael Sattler drew up in the form of "seven articles concerning the fraternal union of some of God's children." This meant that the Baptists rejected the Christian state religion and the "Holy Empire." They were persecuted by both Catholic and Protestant authorities in accordance with the imperial law and were regarded as heretics in terms of faith and as enemies of the Empire. When Michael Sattler was interrogated in Rottenburg, and said, "If the Turk comes, one ought not to offer him any resistance, since it is written: 'You shall not kill'," it became clear how extremely dangerous the peaceful Baptists were – for they were attracting many of the people. This was why Michael Sattler's execution in Rottenburg was public, and especially cruel: they cut out his tongue, welded him to a cart, tore the flesh from his body with glowing tongs, and burned him alive on the gallows hill outside the city on 20 May 1527. His wife Margaretha rejected every attempt to save her life, and she was drowned in the river Neckar a few days later.

Michael Sattler had been the prior of the celebrated monastery of Saint Peter's in the Black Forest, a man who had received an excellent theological and humanist education. He had been with the peasant rebels in Memmingen in 1525. Afterwards, he joined the Baptists in Zurich and did missionary work in Upper Swabia. He made many adherents in Horb and the surrounding district and baptized them in the Neckar. His mission was the following:

The Christians are left all alone
and trust in their Father in heaven
without any external secular armament.

Like Michael Sattler, the Baptists were the martyrs of the Reformation period. One of their hymns begins: "How lovely is death to those who are saints." Menno Simons and the "Mennonites" sustained this Reformation movement in the past and continue to do so today.

Let me offer some remarks about this:

First, several years ago, the Lutheran World Federation asked the Mennonites to forgive the condemnations and persecutions of the Reformation period. This gesture cannot remain without consequences: We must revise article 16 of the Augsburg Confession of 1530, or decide to make an official comment that we no longer uphold the condemnations: for otherwise, no Lutheran candidate can be ordained on the basis of the Augsburg Confession. After all, we no longer call them "Enthusiasts," but rather "Historic Peace Churches"!

Secondly, we read in Isaiah 2:4:

> *They shall beat their swords into plowshares,*
> *and their spears into pruning hooks;*
> *nation shall not lift up sword against nation,*
> *neither shall they learn war anymore.*

The Lutherans turned the swords into "Christian swords," in order to wage "just" wars (CA 16). The Baptists withdrew to the farms of their brotherhood and wanted to busy themselves exclusively with "plowshares." And who turns the swords into plowshares? Who transforms the industry of war into an industry of peace and turns steel helmets into cooking pots, as we did in 1945? The kingdom of Christ is not only a peaceable kingdom, but is first and foremost a peacemaking kingdom. It is not the "peaceable" whom Jesus declares blessed, but the "peacemakers" (*hoi eirênopoioi,* Matt. 5:9).

Justification of the Perpetrators of Sin – Justification of the Victims of Sin[4]

There is something missing in the centre of Reformation theology, which is the doctrine of justification. This has been brought to light in Germany by the cases of sexual abuse in the Catholic Church and in the Odenwald School: up to now, we know in the church and in the public sphere how we ought to deal with the perpetrators, but the misery of the victims leaves us perplexed. In the case of the perpetrators, we ask how they came to perform their disgusting actions; but in the case of the victims, we do not look for ways that would allow them to emerge from their shame and disgrace. In the church and in the public sphere, we are oriented to the perpetrators and we forget the victims.

The Reformation doctrine of justification has its origin in the mediaeval sacrament of confession. The power of evil is given the name of "sin." We speak of the "forgiveness of sins exclusively through the grace of God in faith." This is correct, and important; but it is only half the truth, since the sinner is the perpetrator of evil, and where are the victims of his sins? We pray: "Forgive us our trespasses," and where are the victims of our guilty trespasses? The sacrament of penance has a one-sided orientation to the perpetrator. The doctrine of justification, the very heart of Reformation theology, forgets the victims. Here, there is a gaping lacuna in the Christian doctrine of grace.

This can already be seen in the apostle Paul's doctrine of sin. In Romans 7:19-20, he writes honestly and self-critically: "For I do not do the good I want, but the evil I do not want is what I do. Now if I do what I do not want, it is no longer I that do it, but sin that dwells within me." Why does he not direct his gaze on those to whom he has done evil, those to whom he has failed to good? Why is he concerned only with his own self? If we compare his doctrine of sin with the Jesus of the synoptic gospels, we are struck by the fact that Jesus sees not the perpetrators of sin, but its victims: "When he saw the crowds, he had compassion for them" (Matt. 9:36). He sees the victims of injustice and violence. He brings them the message of the kingdom of God and heals them. He includes them in his fellowship with God.

In the Old Testament Psalms, we find God's righteousness not only in the forgiveness of sins ("In your righteousness deliver me and rescue me," Ps. 71:2), but also on the side of the poor and the weak, of the victims of sins: "The Lord works vindication and justice for all who are oppressed" (Ps. 103:6; 146:7-9; 82:3-4). God's righteousness is not merely a righteousness that declares good and evil. Nor is it a righteousness that repays good with good and evil with evil. It is a creative righteousness. It is a righteousness that creates justice for the victims of sin. For the perpetrators of sin, it is a righteousness that brings restoration.

Let us examine this more closely with regard to the perpetrators and the victims. For the perpetrators, there exists the ancient and well-tried ritual of penance; for the victims, we still have the task of finding a corresponding ritual for their justification.

The perpetrators of evil are restored through the forgiveness of their sins, in penance. This entails three steps:

First comes the *confessio oris,* the confession of the evil that they have committed. The first step is the step out of the darkness, where things are suppressed and kept silent, into the light of the truth. This is not easy, because the confession of guilt is always linked with self-abasement. As the South African Truth Commission has shown, this is almost impossible for the perpetrators of extreme wrongs, for torturers and murderers. They need a protective space. This can be the confessional and a pastor's seal of confession, but it must at any rate be a social place in which the hope of forgiveness is already present. With trust in God's mercy, sinners can confess their guilt without destroying themselves. This is a good Protestant insight: through the Law of God, we recognize our sins and confess them in the light of the gospel. Since those who perpetrate evil and fail to do good always have a short memory – if, indeed, they have a memory at all – they are dependent on the memory of their victims. They must see themselves with the eyes of their victims, in order to reach a true self-knowledge. The "After Auschwitz" conferences have shown us this.

The second step is the *contritio cordis,* the change of heart, repentance: "turning away" from the paths that led one to commit an evil deed or to fail to do what is good, and "turning around" (the literal meaning of the word "conversion") to life and to the good. These words are to be taken personally. The personal is important, even today, because only human beings who themselves have been transformed can transform bad situations into something better. Today, this also involves the breach with political and societal systems of injustice that produce so much violence and injustice. These are not only the dictatorships and the systems of political terror, but also societal systems that produce poverty and industrial systems that ruin the earth.

A third point: the perpetrators enter into a new community with the victims only when they do everything possible to remove the damage they have wrought. This is called the *satisfactio operum,* "reparation," although we know that it cannot make undone any evil that has taken place, nor offer any "compensation." But every "reparation" is a beginning of a new community between perpetrators and victims, as happened (for example) in 1948 between the Federal Republic of Germany and Israel. In penal law, this is called the "victim-offender mediation."

What could the vindication of the victims look like? I offer a suggestion.

The first step resembles the sacrament of penance: the *confessio oris,* the step into the light of the truth. The victims of injustice and violence must not only emerge from their suffering: it is even more necessary for them to emerge from their mental humiliation, which closes their mouths. In the case of sexual violence, an additional factor is shame at the desecration they have suffered. They need a free space where their suffering is acknowledged, in order that they can scream their pains out. They need ears into which they can pour their story, in order that they can regain their self-respect. The perpetrators' confession of their guilt can help them here, but the victims need not wait for this, because they must also be freed from their fixation on the perpetrators: they need not be "victims" forever. In the God who "creates justice for those who suffer violence," they rediscover their dignity as persons. They also need the protective space of a community in which they feel accepted: "Shatter the fetters of your shame! What you suffered has not touched your soul!" Telling their story to sympathetic people is the first step into the truth. Only the truth can set the victims free. The oppressive silence often lasted for 30 years in the victims of sexual abuse, before the first words came from their lips, and people listened to them.

The second step is the raising up of the victims from their humiliation, so that they lift up their heads to God. The victims too need to "turn around." This is the "conversion" from self-pity and self-hatred into the broad space of a loving affirmation of their lives. This is the presupposition for the third step.

It is not revenge, but forgiveness that sets one free. Everyone who suffers injustice or is insulted has dreams of vengeance; this is perfectly natural. But when evil is answered with evil, no justice is achieved. On the contrary, the evil is only doubled. Paul rightly says: "Do not be overcome by evil" (Rom. 12:21) – and not by the evil that pays back evil in its own coin. One who murders a murderer is likewise a murderer. When we forgive our debtors, we do good not only to them, but also to our own selves: we overcome the evil that has made its way into us. Forgiveness is also an act whereby the victims heal themselves.

Celebrating the Lord's Supper Together – Going to Communion Together

A silent but effective eucharistic movement has occurred in the last 50 years. Lutherans, Reformed, United churches, including the Bohemian Brethren, the Waldensians, and the Old Catholics, signed the Leuenberg Agreement in 1973; and the Protestant Church in Germany and the Anglican Communion reached an agreement in Meissen. In 1982, the World Council of Churches, with the collaboration of Catholic and Orthodox theologians, adopted the Lima Document on baptism, eucharist, and ministry. This means that unity is now possible.

On the level of Protestant parishes, the Lord's supper, as *the* meal of the community, has come to have a central position in worship, and in Catholic parishes, the chalice is once again regularly given to the laity (as I hope). The fixation on guilt and death in Protestant parishes has been balanced by the festive outlook on the kingdom of God. We stand in a circle and pass the bread and wine to each other; we bless each other, holding our hands. Fewer people come to church, but the eucharistic community of the parish has grown. The church has thus lost "Christendom," but has gained the living parish community.[5] My own experience of the Lord's supper goes back more than 75 years, three-quarters of a century, and I can attest that something has changed for the better.

The Reformation in the 16th century aimed at the reformation of the one church of Christ and was intended as a catholic reformation.

This is why it remains imperfect and incomplete, as long as the division into Protestant churches and the Catholic Church lasts. Since the church divisions have their origin in excommunications from eucharistic fellowship, the fellowship at the table of Christ is the goal of the Reformation and of all ecumenical endeavours.

The fellowship of faith comes about when Christians – whatever church they belong to – hear Christ's invitation and come together to the table where the crucified and risen Christ waits for them. Over the bread and wine, I see the outstretched arms of the crucified Lord. Whether we speak in Catholic terminology of the "eucharist," in Protestant terminology of the "Lord's supper," or in ecumenical terminology of "holy communion," the only thing that matters is what happens there: "Christ's blood, shed for you" and "Christ's body, given for you."

We do not celebrate the eucharist or Lord's supper in our own name or in the name of our churches, but in the name of Christ. I believe that it is not the meal of the church, but Christ's meal. Even when we understand our church as the "body of Christ," the Lord's supper, the eucharist, belongs together with the cross on which Christ's gift of himself for us and for many is accomplished. This is why, ultimately, Catholics will not be counted off against Protestants here, or married persons against unmarried. Here, sinners are made righteous, victims are raised up, sad people are consoled, and the despairing are filled with hope.

In the face of the Christ who was crucified for us and for many, how can we continue to uphold our separations and excommunications? We are celebrating the "primal sacrament" of the one church: Jesus Christ.

Let me offer a practical suggestion.

After receiving communion, we ought to remain sitting at the table and talk about how we understand what we have just experienced. In the Lord's supper, the priority truly belongs to the praxis of Christ; our theology comes in second place. One who demands that we must first agree on a theological theory about what happens there is interrupting the Christ who invites us! That means preventing the shared experience of Christ! It is easier to talk after eating and drinking than to do so beforehand with a hungry and thirsty soul.

I have gone to communion in every church in which I have heard the voice of Christ that invites me, and I have never been rejected.

The reformation of the one church takes place first of all in the eucharistic fellowship of the Lord's supper. I would like to see a eucharistic movement from community to community.

The closer we come to Christ,
the closer we come to each other.

Reformation of Faith – Formation of Hope

It is important to recognize the boundaries of the 16th-century Reformation in order to take the ecumenical step beyond these boundaries. Let me mention three boundaries:

First, the Reformation occurred only in the Latin church of the West. The Orthodox churches of the East remained untouched by the ideas of the Reformation.

Second, the Reformation took place only in the conditions and the traditions of the "Holy Roman Empire." The Reformers remained within this *Corpus Christianum,* while the Baptists went beyond this boundary.

Third, as the name states, the Reformation of the 16th century referred to a Christianity that already existed, not to a Christianity that belonged to the future. It was a reformation of faith, not a mission of hope. It was a re-formation, not a new formation of the mission of the church in the world for the kingdom and the righteousness of God. While Luther and Melanchthon were teaching Reformation doctrine in Wittenberg, Francis Xavier was carrying out missionary work in Asia among the newly discovered peoples, and Bartholomew de Las Casas was defending the American Indians against exploitation by his fellow Spaniards. The discovery of the peoples of America and Asia occurred only 25 years before Luther published his 95 theses in Wittenberg. In terms of world politics, the Reformation was a limited, intra-European event.

What expectations about the future did Luther and Melanchthon have in Wittenberg in their days?[6]

Luther and Melanchthon remained within the laws of the *Sacrum Imperium*, and this is why they also shared the picture of this empire in world history and its apocalyptic, as people saw it at that time. The picture of world history resembles a revelation of God's plan of salvation. This picture is the result of transposing the six days of creation onto the six ages of world history. A passage from the Talmud played an important role for the Christian world chroniclers and apocalyptists:

> *In Elijah's school it is taught:*
> *The world will endure for six thousand years:*
> *two thousand years of chaos,*
> *two thousand years of Torah,*
> *two thousand years of the messianic age,*
> *but because of our many sins,*
> *some of these years have already elapsed.*

Luther prefaced his last book, *Supputatio annorum mundi* (The calculation of the years of the world, 1545), with this adage, which is also found at the beginning of the celebrated world chronicle by the Wittenberg physician Carion (the *Chronicon Carionis*), who translates into Lutheran concepts this computation of the ages of world history:

> *Two thousand years ante legem,*
> *two thousand years sub lege,*
> *two thousand years sub gratia.*

This means that the end of the world is near. When the Turks besieged Vienna in 1529, they were interpreted in Wittenberg as the biblical peoples "Gog and Magog." According to Revelation 20:8, Satan will be set free after the thousand years' reign of Christ, and Gog and Magog will rush down upon "the camp of the saints and the beloved city" (Jerusalem). Here, the important point is not the apocalyptic, but the identification of the "Holy Roman Empire of the German Nation" with the thousand years' reign of Christ. Those who live at the end of the thousand years' reign of Christ see nothing else before them than the end of the world and the judgment of the world.

Why did the men of Wittenberg hold fast to this abstract doctrine of the ages of the world and its apocalyptic? Why did they not (like the apostle Paul) see the future that belongs to God in the light of the resurrection of Christ? I suspect that this was due to the Augustinian restriction of theology to God and the soul, in the form of "the gracious God and the sinful soul." This leads to a doctrine of two kingdoms, in which the kingdom of the world is going toward its end, in keeping with the doctrine of the ages of the world. It is also important to note that Luther took the theology of the incarnation, which was the preferential theology of the West, one stage deeper, to become the theology of the cross. The result in the Lutheran tradition was that Good Friday became the highest festival day – not Easter with the resurrection of Christ.

Every Christian hope begins with the rising of the crucified Christ and sees the end of this world in the light of the beginning of God's new world.

Faith owes its existence not only to the present grace of God, but also to the promise of the coming kingdom of God. It is a "rebirth to a living hope." "Faith is the assurance of things hoped for" (Heb. 11:1). The kingdom of God is not only God's rule, but also fullness of life. Jesus did not found any new religion: he brought new life, eternal, divine life, into the world.

A formation of this hope will follow the re-formation of faith today.

Out of the disintegration of the Christian world, a new church will arise, autonomous, peaceable, ecumenically united, inviting, and trustful.

This is my hope for the completion of the Reformation. But may it be the case that reformations are never completed?

Chapter 10

Persevering in Faith:
Roots of a Theology of Hope[1]

The Question of the Continuity of Faith

It seems to be a particularly long-lasting experience of our generation that all the contents of life, values, virtues, obligations, and hopes – everything that is capable of giving a person support and stability – are subject to history and to its changes. This leads to a very elementary question: Does faith exist in history only in the risk, in the leap, in the decision that is taken ever anew, only in the specificity of existing in history from one moment to the next? Does the believer stand continuously between certainty and uncertainty; between the certainty that is disclosed in the moment, through the word that goes forth, and the dark uncertainty about whether one may lose oneself and faith in the very next moment?

In view of our experience of the historicity of human existing, an experience conditioned by many catastrophes – as Wilhelm Dilthey put it, "everything flowing in the process, nothing remaining" – it appears at first sight impossible to refute the view that faith is an act that must be posited again and again. Where everything that is solid and enduring changes, where human beings in the "maelstrom of time" cannot be today what they promised to be yesterday, and do not achieve tomorrow what they are resolved upon today, how then is faith to be preserved in unchanging sameness, in a timeless monotony? After all, faith concerns the real existence of the human being, not some pious consciousness that he or she has acquired, nor the perennial tradition from ecclesiastical institutions. Rilke rightly observed, "What shuts itself down and remains is at once congealed." Here, it seems that we should follow the insights of the philosophy of life: life is alive only in becoming, in transformation, in the abrupt departure; and faith too is alive only in this way, existing "between the times." "Faith as an historical act is always the concrete decision in the moment. In other words, faith never exists otherwise than in overcoming unbelief."[2] Human beings are wholly present at every moment only when they break down the bridges to the past out of which they have come, tear apart the dreams about the future that blind them, and entrust themselves totally to the unrepeatability and uniqueness of what is happening in the present moment. In that case, faith must be an uncertain risk that is new each time. Faith is a struggle and a daily repentance; it exists for human beings only in the act of coming into existence (*in statu nascendi*), and they therefore need continuous contestation (*Anfechtung*) as its dark and mysterious fellow-travellers, just as existence in decision needs the stimulus of danger and of adventure.

When, however, the New Testament looks ahead to the future of the community in time – and that means to persecution, to contestation, and to the suffering of the last days – it does not speak of risk, of a basic decision that must be taken anew again and again, or of the necessity of a daily repentance. On the contrary, it speaks very pointedly of a hope that is certain, of "patience" and of "remaining," of "preservation" and "standing the test": in other words, of the *perseverantia sanctorum*. "But the one who endures to the end will be saved" (Matt. 10:22; 24:13). The one who "holds the word fast" brings rich fruit (Luke 8:15). A faith that does not become patience is useless (James 1:2ff.). "Fidelity" is already an intrinsic element of faith (*pistis*), which in the coming contestation will take on the form of *hyponomê*, "patience," of the acceptance of suffering for the sake of Christ, of enduring in fidelity and in the confession, and in sharing in the "patience of Christ" (Heb. 10:32; 12:2; 12:7; James 1:4; 5:11; Rev. 1:9; 2:2; 13:10, etc.): in other words, as *perseverantia*, as *patientia*, and as *tolerantia crucis*. For faith is hope in God in view of the things to come (Rom. 5:5), and this certain hope gives faith the character of a waiting that is patient and at the same time rushes toward the Lord who is coming (Rom. 8:25; 12:12). The "patience of hope" (as the beautiful formulation in 1 Thess. 1:3 calls it) belongs to the totality of the fellowship of those who believe in Christ. In the gospel and the letters of John, faith is primarily a matter of "abiding": an abiding in the word of Jesus, an abiding in him, which finds its solid inner ground in "the abiding of Jesus in those who are his": "I give them eternal life, and they will never perish. No one will snatch them out of my hand" (John 10:27). Only trust in something that deserves trust can justify a relationship of absolute certainty to the future (Martin Buber). Since faith is called into life by God's eschatological promise, it finds in this word the certainty of its own future. It entrusts itself to the fidelity of God, who does not abandon the work of his hands (as the Psalms say), and who "will bring to completion by the day of Jesus Christ the good work that he began" (Phil. 1:6).[3]

Hope and Persevering in Faith

It is precisely this future perspective of faith that shapes the whole of John Calvin's theology. This is why he has been called "the theologian of hope" among the Reformers. Faith is *"meditatio vitae futurae,"* a striving for the life to come, a passionate expectation of the fidelity of God, which generates the power to stand firm and to remain standing in the temporal contestations. This is the firm hope in God's fidelity, with which he will fulfil the promise that awakens faith.

For the scholastic and Tridentine doctrine of certainty, the question of the subjective assurance of salvation was posed only with regard to the degree of sanctification that the individual Christian had attained (and that was never anything other than imperfect). Calvin orients this question to the objective reliability of the divine promise. It is a central Reformation insight that in the preached word of scripture, God's own and ultimate word encounters the human being in the midst of history. In other words, it is not only a fragmentary, and hence ultimately uncertain, human knowledge of God that makes its voice heard in the word of scripture and in preaching, but the *Deus loquens*, the God who speaks.[4] God's truthfulness excludes every doubt and all uncertainty. This word, in which the "speaking God" encounters the human being, creates, nourishes, and sustains faith and justifies the solid certainty of faith.

Faith is born of the word of God and is therefore "of the same nature" as the word. If the word of God is trustworthy, faith cannot remain in uncertainty. If the word of God remains forever – that is to say, until the end of time – then faith too remains where the word remains.[5] Faith is the "yes," the signature, the confession, and the human trust that is the response to God's truthfulness (*veracitas*). Since the word is stable in God's fidelity, there is no risk that the faith of the human being will become precarious. "The relationship of faith to the Word is permanent; faith can no more be detached from the Word than the sunrays from the sun from which they go forth."[6]

Calvin's concept of faith is always determined by the certainty of hope. "Since it is certain that God does not deceive us in our hopes, hope must not be full of doubt. . . . It is certain that God cannot do otherwise than correspond to our hopes, which are based on his own Word." This is why faith and hope are reciprocally related. Faith believes that eternal life is given to us. It takes hold of the present mercy of God in God's word. Hope expects that what we are now in a hidden manner, through God's word, will one day be fulfilled and revealed.

> Faith believes in the truthful God, and hope expects that he will display his truthfulness when the time and occasion are right. Faith believes that God is our Father, and hope expects that he will always behave as such towards us. Faith believes that eternal life is given to us, but hope expects that this will one day be revealed. Faith is the foundation on which hope rests, but it is hope that keeps faith upright and alive.[7]

This is why Calvin draws the following conclusion:

> How foolish it is to limit the certainty of faith to one moment (*punctum temporis*), since faith of its very nature transcends the barriers of this life and reaches out to the future immortality. One may

concede, at the most, that it is possible to arrive at a judgment about God's grace on the basis of the present state of our righteousness;[8] but it is asserted that we cannot know anything definitive about our perseverance until the end.[9] All that we would have would be a glorious confidence in salvation, if a "moral supposition"[10] leads to hold that we are in grace before God at the present moment, but have no idea of what can happen tomorrow (Rom 8:39!) . . . It will be objected that he [Paul] often terrifies us with a reference to our weakness and inconstancy, for he says: "Let the one who thinks that he stands take care lest he fall" (1 Cor 10:12). This is correct, but it is not a terror that casts us down to the ground. Rather, it is meant to teach us to humble ourselves under the hand of God, as Peter explains (1 Pet 5:6).[11]

In the temporal sphere, this hope bestows on faith a special character that Calvin terms the *perseverantia sanctorum,* which is manifested and accomplished in the constancy of faith (*constantia fidei*) and in bearing the cross (*tolerantia crucis*). The latter imprints the form of Jesus Christ on the believer, who grows into *conformitas* with the suffering and crucified Christ.[12] The hope that is certain always generates patience and constancy, since hope itself is nothing other than the *perseverantia fidei.* Calvin can call the firm constancy of the heart, which is acquired in hope, the "noblest part of faith": "Now that we believe in the Word of God, the task that remains is to hold out until the accomplishment of all things."[13]

But this standing firm and abiding in faith, nourished and supported by hope, would necessarily be uncertain and frail, had not Christ given those who belong to him the certainty that their election is irrevocable and permanent. Calvin always saw perseverance in faith as based on the absolutely steadfast election by God. He writes already in the *Institutio* of 1536: "God has given his elect into the care and protection of his Son, Christ, so that he may not lose any of them, but may raise them all up again on the Last Day (Jn 6:39). Under such a good guardian, they can indeed go astray and slip, but they certainly cannot get lost."[14] In these words, Calvin complements the idea of election in the historical calling with the idea of the preservation in the temporal sphere of those who have once been called. He develops this idea in the *Institutio* of 1559:

> If we want to know whether God is concerned about our salvation, we must ask whether he has entrusted our salvation to Christ, for he has installed him as the only one who brings blessedness to all who belong to him. If, however, we doubt whether we have been taken by Christ into his fidelity and care, he himself counters such a doubt by freely offering himself as our shepherd and telling us that we are included in the number of his sheep, when we hear his voice. . . . Sometimes, however, we are overcome by fear about our future state. For, as Paul teaches, it is only those who first are chosen who then are called. And Christ shows that although many are called, only a few are chosen. Indeed, Paul himself warns in another passage against feeling certain (1 Cor 10:12). . . . Finally, experience teaches sufficiently that calling and grace have little value in the absence of perseverance, which is not given to all. But Christ has set us free from cares of this kind, for his words are truly promises for the future, when he says: "Everything that my Father gives me comes to me, and I shall not drive away the one who comes to me" (Jn 6:37). . . . This is also the source of Paul's confident boasting in the face of life and death, things present and things to come (Rom 8:38), since such a boasting must have its root in the gift of perseverance. . . . There can be no doubt that when Christ prays for all the elect, he asks for them what he once asked for Peter, namely, that their faith may not fail (Lk 22:32). The inference we draw is that there is no danger at all that they may fall away, because the Son of God has prayed for the constancy of their fear of God. And his prayer has not been rejected.[15]

For Calvin, persistence in faith is founded in the fidelity of God, or more precisely, in the narrative of the Father that is not revoked, and in the sacrifice, the prayer, and the rule of Christ that preserve us; his working in these three offices is invincible. Persisting in faith is not an achievement or a virtue of the human being. It is not something that simply happens to be present. The presupposition, the beginning, middle, and end of persistence in faith is preservation by God, which is a work of God's grace and is therefore indestructible. In all the contestations that have their origin in the believer's own weakness, there is a constant consolation in the fact that no human failure will lead God to alter fidelity with regard to election and preservation in Christ. But the promise of persistence in faith, the promise that one will not fall out of God's gracious hand even when one falls, even in contestation and in sins, is not a proposition drawn from experience that would offer the believer certainty. It is a proposition drawn from faith, which allows the believer to experience what it says and to overcome contestations.

This found a confessional expression in the history of Calvinism. For example, Christoph Pezel speaks in the Consensus Bremensis (1595) of the "four immovable columns of the certainty of faith":

> Moreover, sacred Scripture sets up four immovable columns for the true faith against the fear of apostasy, of despair, and of eternal repudiation because of the sins we have committed. Faith rests, certain and sure until the end, on these four columns: 1. the invincible power of Christ's sacrifice; 2. the perpetual intercession of Christ for all believers; 3. the omnipotent power and governance of Christ; 4. God's eternal love and the election by his grace, through which he has chosen us in Christ. He never in all eternity alters this love and the election by his grace.[16]

Just as God's fidelity is of its very nature always "eternal fidelity," so too the persistence in faith is of its very nature "persistence to the end," both to the end of one's life (*perseverantia usque ad mortem*) and to the end of all things (*usque ad finem*). It thereby goes beyond the boundaries of possible human experience, just as, for Calvin, the hope that is born of faith transcends such boundaries. When considered in the light of its goal, this hope lies beyond anything that human experience and reflection can demonstrate. It becomes manifest finally and definitively in the last judgment and in the resurrection. It is therefore related to the *eschaton* of history, which comes to the human being only from God and can be realized only by God. It is therefore impossible to agree with O. Ritschl that what Calvin says about "faith in the temporal dimension and persisting faith" "inevitably stimulated people to observe other Christians and to assess whether they belonged to the chosen, or perhaps rather to those who believe in the temporal sphere."[17] The question about the certainty of election and perseverance is not in the least a question about other people; it is about the certainty of the one who asks.[18] With regard to one's fellow human beings, two principles are important for the one who believes here in the temporal sphere. First, one judges with love and with hope, as Calvin teaches, in full accord with Luther and Augustine:[19] *bene sperandum est de omnibus*. And second, one judges in awareness of one's human limitations. This judgment is an important criterion with regard to membership in the community, once one has inquired into the question of the profession of faith, sacramental fellowship, and the example of a Christian lifestyle.[20] But for the one who is appointed, addressed, and called, "It is the Holy Spirit alone who is the unique, faithful, and certain witness of his election, and on this election his perseverance depends."[21] One cannot combine these two questions to make one single question, for that means the destruction either of certainty or of love.

The doctrine of persistence in faith is nothing less than the reverse side of Calvin's doctrine of predestination. His doctrine of election remains exposed to misunderstandings as long as we fail to see how it becomes a demonstration of the fidelity of God and of the perseverance of faith. We can surely say that Calvin's doctrine of election always reaches its culmination in view of the *perseverantia sanctorum*, in keeping with Karl Barth's affirmation: "The whole Gospel shines out only when this doctrine shines out."[22]

Remaining in Faith under the Word and the Spirit

Persistence in faith becomes visible only at the end of history, as a concluding manifestation and fulfilment of the election by grace. The historical realization of the election and the historical demonstration of God's fidelity take place in the sermon, "which leads people to faith and maintains them in perseverance in an uninterrupted onward journey."[23] The historical "remaining" of the believer thus takes place in continuous relatedness to the *cursus praedicationis*. This is not primarily a persistence of individual believers in their decision of faith, but their calling into the community and remaining under the word (*perpetuitas doctrinae*). Calvin thus envisages the continuity of faith in an emphatically ecclesiological manner. The remaining is not the achievement of human beings' personal steadfastness. Rather, the new situation created by Christ, in which the believers themselves become new, remains.

In this word, which proclaims God's gracious election, God's fidelity takes on the character of an event. And with this word, the "seed of God" (1 John 3:9; 1 Pet. 1:23) descends into the heart of the one who is truly called. The word brings about faith and forms it. Those who are called are sealed with the Holy Spirit, and Calvin holds that this sealing or indwelling of the Holy Spirit is every bit as indestructible as the word of God itself: "We must hold fast to this: faith may indeed be very small and very weak in the elect, but once its testimony is entrenched in in their hearts, it can never again be torn out of them, since the Holy Spirit is for them the certain pledge and seal of their being children (*adoptio*)."[24] "God alone renews the elect continuously out of an indestructible seed, so that the seed of life (*samen vitae*) can never be completely lost in their hearts."[25]

Calvin speaks here not only of a preservation (*conservatio*) of the faithful that is theologically and Christologically grounded, but also of a subjective continuity of faith itself, which is pneumatologically grounded. He speaks not only of a "once and for all" of the possibility of salvation that is offered to the human being in Christ, but also of the uniqueness and unrepeatability of the effective reality of salvation, which cannot be lost. This reality is brought about in the elect and the believers through the Spirit. The grace of the endowment with the Spirit and of faith is given once and for all and therefore cannot be lost, since it is not a historical and transitory gift, but a historical and eschatological gift. Those who are chosen cannot fall out of the faith that they have attained when they were called by God. They can indeed make the Holy Spirit sad, but they can never lose the Holy Spirit definitively. But this "never again" is not based on human beings' own steadfastness; it is nothing other than the fidelity and truthfulness of God the Holy Spirit, who never abandons his word and his work. This is what Calvin means when he says that even in sins, and even when faith is completely obscured, the "seed of the Holy Spirit" remains in those who are elect and called.

When the perseverance in faith is given this pneumatological grounding, this, of course, immediately triggers all the reservations about false security that arise from the doctrine of justification. However, one can certainly speak legitimately not only of a constancy and reliability of "God with us," but also of a constancy and reliability of "God in us," without thereby fatally confusing the divine and the human; for otherwise, this would mean that human beings in their despair would have to take their own weaknesses more seriously than the work that God has begun in them. God has promised – with the inner necessity of his fidelity to his own self – that he will fulfil this work. Even when human beings consider their own weakness, they may trust in the triumph of the Spirit of God. The testimony to the eternal purpose of God takes away all contingency from the event of faith, and the testimony to God's constant fidelity takes away all precariousness from the continued existence of faith.

Precisely at this point, however, it is absolutely necessary to note that the promise of the enduring indwelling of the Spirit cannot be understood as an analytical proposition about something that exists in the human soul, something that the believer can also attain in self-reflection. Rather, this is exclusively a kerygmatic promise that awakens its hope even where there is nothing to be hoped for: namely, the promise that the Holy Spirit intercedes for the believer with unutterable sighs (Rom. 8:26f.). According to Augustine, Calvin, and the Calvinists Zanchi and Perkins, the certainty of perseverance is nothing other than the certainty of the prayer: "and lead us not into temptation." It was only in orthodox Calvinism and in early Pietism that the doctrine of the hidden and abiding "pledge of the Spirit" was detached from the framework of covenant theology and eschatology in which Calvin speaks of this matter, and was translated into the idea of a mental *habitus* of faith that could not be lost.

The "Remaining" of Faith in Contestation and Grave Sins

If one seeks the existential *locus* of Calvin's doctrine of election, one encounters first of all the idea of the division of human beings into the classes of the elect and the rejected; but the idea of the certainty of perseverance repeatedly comes into the foreground as the pastoral and ethical praxis of the doctrine of election.

Luther and Melanchthon, following Gabriel Biel, speak of the following two contestations: first, the *tentatio de indignitate,* the anguish caused by one's own unworthiness, which arises when one is accused by the law; and second, the *tentatio de particularitate,* which arises when God is preached as one who elects only a few and rejects many.[26] Calvin and the Reformed theologians follow Augustine by speaking of a third contestation, the *tentatio de infirmitate fidei,* the horror at the weakness of one's faith when confronted by the severity of persecution and temptation. Like Luther and Melanchthon, they see the answer to the *tentatio de particularitate* as the gospel of Jesus Christ: if you want to be certain of your election, do not begin with the hidden counsel of God or with the depths of your own soul, but listen to the voice of the gospel. Christ is the only mirror of election. These theologians find the answer to the *tentatio de infirmitate fidei* in the doctrine of election. If you want to know how firm your faith is, you must draw the following inference: it is because God has chosen me for salvation that I believe. The fact that I believe is God's own work. But God will be faithful eternally, and will not abandon the work of his hands. One should also counter this contestation with the consolation of the utterly steadfast election by God's grace. God's fidelity promises perseverance.[27]

Calvin is far from asserting that this certainty exempts faith from struggle, unrest, and contestation. On the contrary, the continuous struggle against sin and the unrest caused to the conscience by one's own lack of trust are a genuine evidence of the presence of God's Spirit in the human being. But there is no doubt about the outcome of this struggle of the spirit against the flesh that erupts when one is called, a struggle in which the human being is caught up, because this struggle is carried on in the certainty of Christ's victory. "God equips us with the power of his Spirit in all struggles, so that we are never conquered or destroyed."[28] This presence of the invincible power of the Spirit is a divine promise and, as such, it is operative in the struggle of faith. Believers are not invincible in themselves, but only in the fellowship with Christ and with the Holy Spirit. The bond of this fellowship between God and those who belong to God is unbreakable. Because we are held fast in faith, Calvin can say not only "But in all the attacks that seek to disturb [the mind of the pious person], he nevertheless emerges again and again from the abyss of the contestations and remains at his post,"[29] but also "No matter how many their fears may be, we deny that they ever fall away or deviate from the certain confidence that they have gained by the mercy of God."[30]

> The root of faith will never (*numquam*) be torn out of a pious heart.
> It remains hanging down in the very depths, no matter how much
> it seems to be stricken and to bend to this side and that. The light
> of faith will never (*numquam*) be dimmed or quenched to such an
> extent that not even a glimmer is left under the ashes. This is a clear
> proof that the Word, which is an imperishable seed, brings forth a
> fruit similar to itself, with a shoot that never completely (*numquam
> in totum*) dries out and perishes.[31]

Accordingly, true believers will therefore never fall away *totaliter*. The faith that they have once attained can never be completely destroyed by Satan's contestations. The believer is allowed to live out of the certainty that God will grant the perseverance of faith, in the power of the Spirit, even when the believer no longer feels anything of this.

On the other hand, however, Calvin admits that faith can suffer interruptions: "Here, I do not deny . . . that our faith sometimes suffers a kind of interruption, when it is thrown about hither and thither in its weakness by the hefty attacks that oppress it. Its light is quenched in the thick darkness of the contestations. But no matter what happens, it does not desist from diligently seeking God."[32] The believers "fall under the impact of the attacks, but then they get up again. They are wounded, but not mortally. In short, they are in a hard struggle all their lives, but at the end, they retain the victory. Naturally, I do not affirm this of every stage in the struggle."[33] Calvin thus holds that the believer can, to all appearances, be completely defeated. But they can never be defeated definitively, once and for all. There are defeats in the course of the struggle, and it may even seem that the fall is complete. But there is never any doubt about the outcome of the struggle, namely, the victory of Christ and the triumph of his believers together with him.

These quotations show the form in which Calvin teaches Augustine's principle of the irresistibility of grace. This is the certainty that not even the sins into which the believers fall can separate them from the love of Christ and put an end to the indwelling of the Holy Spirit. His pupil Hieronymus Zanchi wrote:

> The holy ones are always holy before the Lord in Christ their Head, whose members they are. In themselves, however, they cease in difficult hours to be holy, although never totally, but only in part, because the seed of God remains in them, and they can never lose their faith, because God holds them in his hand even when they fall. They lose their fruits of their faith in their feelings and they lose their certainty, but God preserves their faith for the sake of Christ, so that they are never detached completely from their Head, but rather grow up to the perfect man.[34]

The great examples adduced again and again by the Reformed theologians in support of this thesis are the chosen King David in his adultery and murder and the chosen apostle Peter in his denial. Both remained chosen because the hidden root of faith was retained in their hearts. They thus do not fall completely away from faith, nor do they fall definitively into mortal sin: they come to repentance.

Precisely these examples show clearly that the perseverance in faith must not be understood to mean that an unassailable remnant of faith (*semen Dei*) is preserved in the hearts of the elect even in sin. The biblical narratives speak of a partnership or relationship with the Holy Spirit that is granted even to the sinner. For what is David without Nathan's promise, without his mysterious prophetic partner? What is

Peter in his denial of Jesus without the Christ who makes the confession on his behalf and prays for his faith when it is contested? It is only thanks to the promise made by Nathan, which continues to hold good, and thanks to the intercessory prayer of Christ, which is not rejected by God, that the mortal sins of David and Peter are not sins that lead to death and to perdition. Calvinist orthodoxy, however, immediately ceased to take account of this specific context. It spoke of the enduring root of faith in the heart of the one who was chosen, just as people spoke in the age of Idealism of a "good core" in the human being. The disregard of the relational concepts of Calvinism in this question led to emphatically habitualistic affirmations about the enduring state of faith in the one who was chosen. But perseverance in faith and protection from a total and definitive falling away can be affirmed only of the sinner's fellowship with Christ and with the Spirit. They can never be postulated of the one who is chosen independently of this fellowship.

Calvinist theology has employed the following dogmatic formula to maintain the certainty of perseverance: once the elect have come to faith, they can neither completely (*nec totaliter*) nor definitively (*nec finaliter*) sin, thanks to election by God's grace, which is not revoked, thanks to the prophetic, priestly, and kingly office of Christ, whose power triumphs over contestation, sin, and death, and finally, because of the fidelity of the Holy Spirit. This is expressed in confessional documents: in the Heidelberg Catechism, qn. 1, 31, 47, and 54; in the Gallican Confession, article 2; in the Declaration of the Synod of Dordrecht, canon 5; and in the Westminster Confession, articles 12, 17, and 18.

Calvin's Position between Luther and Bucer

With his doctrine of perseverance, Calvin stands midway between his two teachers, Martin Luther and Martin Bucer.

Luther never taught such a certainty of persistence in faith. Karl Holl proposed the well-known thesis (which has scarcely been contradicted down to the present day) that Luther "held that the certainty of election is never attainable (in the run-of-the-mill Christian), but he nevertheless taught the assurance of salvation."[35] This thesis is correct only if "the assurance of salvation" is understood as the present-day, momentary assurance of faith that comes from its encounter with the word of justification, and if "certainty of election" is understood as that assurance about persisting and being preserved constantly. In a letter sent to C. Hofmann in 1522, Luther affirms: "My principle is that we must trust in the grace of God, but must remain uncertain about the future *perseverantia* or *praedestinatio* of ourselves and of others, as Paul says: 'Let the one who stands take heed lest he fall,' although there cannot be any doubt that the apostles were certain of their salvation."[36] These words are directed polemically against the Enthusiastic theses of Karlstadt, and have obvious echoes of the teaching about certainty in Duns Scotus and of the commonly held idea in scholasticism that the apostles had received a special revelation. Although Luther always bases the certainty of faith on the reliability of the fidelity of God, who does not deny himself and will not lie, he clearly does not go as far as Augustine and Calvin in the question of perseverance. We find similar language in the Church-Postil:

> For here there is no place for fear or faltering about whether one is pious and a child of God by grace; rather, the only fear and concern here is about how one may remain constant until the end. Danger and concern exist only in this regard, for there all blessedness is certain. But it is uncertain and a source of concern whether one will be constant and retain this blessedness. Accordingly, one must walk in fear, for such a faith counts not on the work or on oneself, but only on God and his grace. This grace cannot and will not abandon him as long as this insisting continues. But one does not know how long it will last. If the contestation succeeds in driving one to such a point that this insisting ceases, grace too ceases. . . . Those who are justified and their works are in God's hand, but everything regarding the future is made uncertain, so that the human being does not know whether one is in grace or deserves disgrace. One does not say that this is uncertain at the present time, but rather that it is uncertain for the future, and that this is why one does not know whether one will remain standing against the attacks of contestation.[37]

Does this make remaining in grace dependent on the unceasingness of prayer and of faith? Lutheran orthodoxy came to hold that this perseverance might be taught only in this relationship of dependence, whereas Luther himself on various occasions extended to the question of perseverance too his basic insight of justification by faith and of the unfree will of the human being, appealing thereby to Augustine and reaching a similar conclusion to Calvin.

> The free will is of no value here, nor does the grace of the primordial state (*gratia prima*) suffice; rather, perseverance is necessary, and this is not a matter of the human being who wills, but of the God who sustains one. Pay heed to the affirmation that it is greater to remain than to begin, because those who hold firm need preservation by God's hand. For many begin, fewer continue, and only very few go through to the end, just as the Lord teaches in the Gospel about the seed that is cast into various kinds of soil. But what is perseverance, if not a continual beginning (*continua inchoatio*)?[38]

Luther underlines, no less emphatically than Calvin, that the certainty of faith depends exclusively on the trustworthy character of the word of God. God is reliable in his promise; God will not lie. God cannot deny himself. But Luther emphasizes that this certainty is "outside our own selves" (*extra nos*), that is to say, in Christ alone. This is why he distances himself from concepts that base the certainty of faith on an abiding indwelling of the Spirit. "We do not overcome the contestation because there is a place within us that is protected against temptations, a place at which God holds us fast. Rather, we overcome because the Christ who suffers and is crucified for us is beside us precisely in the bleakest hours of darkness and hopelessness."[39] Accordingly, perseverance can occur only in the movement of turning ever anew to this Christ who is for us and beside us. This means that Luther inclines to an actualistic understanding of faith, of election, and of perseverance, and the Lutheran confessional texts consistently display the thesis that the Holy Spirit can be lost through unbelief: Augsburg Confession, 12,7; Apology 4,64; Schmalkaldic Articles 3,3; *Solida declaratio* III, 26.

We must ask whether Luther's thesis that persisting in faith is nothing other than beginning ever anew in faith does not level down the uniqueness, the irreversibility, and the unrepeatability of God's history with the human being. From Luther's perspective, all the periods of the life history of a person are equally valid and equally proximate to God. But if a decision must be taken "ever anew" and is never seen as given and accomplished, something that survives and is preserved in fidelity, this means that every *de facto* decision is dissolved into a continually oscillating possibility. It is indeed true that when one persists in faith, this faith is not a state of resting in something given. On the contrary, it is a continuous struggle and a movement in hope. But it is precisely in this way that it manifests itself as fidelity to something given: namely, to the fact that one is called and chosen.

Lutheran orthodoxy immediately escaped from the various difficulties generated by Luther's theology by adopting Melanchthon's line. Continuity is supplied only by the perseverance of the church and of its means of grace, which accompany the human being and hold open the possibility of salvation. One can always fall out of faith in mortal sins, sins against one's conscience, and sins against the foundation of faith, thereby driving the Holy Spirit away. But as long as one lives, one can always turn back and acquire the Holy Spirit anew through genuine penitence. The word that calls and invites remains above every human being, immovable and universal.

The perceptive Catholic theologian Cardinal Bellarmine was therefore justified in posing this celebrated question: If even the believers can perish eternally, how then can they have a firm assurance of salvation? It was only the orthodox Lutherans around Johann Gerhard who restricted the principle that faith could be lost. They taught that although the elect among the reborn could fall totally into mortal sins, they could not do so definitively. Since they are the elect, they will at some point in their life regain faith and the indwelling of the Holy Spirit through repentance and penance. These scholars regarded being elect *and* perishing definitively as a contradiction in terms. Johann Gerhard comes close to Calvin's doctrine of perseverance when he writes: "The promise of perseverance that is given to those who are reborn is sufficiently certain, since it depends on God's omnipotence,

God's fidelity (*fidelitas*), and God's goodness."[40] Through a solid faith, we can take hold of perseverance, and we can be certain that our prayer for persistence will be heard. But in the temporal sphere, a perseverance of this kind exists only when the human being persists in hearing the word and in using the sacraments. It is not a perseverance of the Holy Spirit in the hearts of the elect directly and independently of the word and the sacraments.

Calvin's theological opponents on the other side are Martin Bucer and the Spiritualism of Strasbourg. Bucer already declared in 1530, in his exposition of Matthew, his conviction that the "seed of the Holy Spirit" is planted in the elect at their birth, so that some "seeds of piety" are already present in the elect even before they are called concretely. These "seeds" are manifested as a predisposition toward faith and the fear of God. Bucer sees the "elect" as the "good," also in a moral sense. They bear in themselves a certain "spark of the image of God," which is seen in their exemplary humanity and in their zealous love of neighbour. Thanks to this seed, they can never sin out of total enmity toward God. If they sin, they do so out of ignorance or weakness, but always with a conscience that rebukes them.[41]

Calvin's polemic against this Spiritualist teaching about the chosen person is passionate:

> In reality, the elect are not chosen directly from the mother's womb, nor are they all chosen at the same time. They are chosen as it seems good to God to distribute his grace, and they are gathered together into Christ's flock when they are called. . . . Some people dream that some kind of "seed of election" was planted in their heart from their birth, and that they are always inclined to piety and to the fear of God through this seed. But they have no support in Scripture, and experience itself refutes them. What "seed of election" was it that sprouted in the past in those who wallowed throughout their entire lives in despicable wickedness and the most abominable vices?

Nevertheless, he concedes: "The Lord saves and preserves those whom he has decided to snatch away out of this abyss, so that they may not fall into unforgivable blasphemies.[42]

Calvin thus holds strictly fast to the calling and election that take place in history through the word, and he proclaims an eschatological perseverance for the faith that is kindled in this way. This is an exclusively historical-eschatological presentation of faith and election, of hope and preservation. If Calvinist orthodoxy and Reformed Pietism had remained in this position, they would have been protected from the psychological formulae of Bucer. But in the post-Reformation period, it was no longer Calvin, but Bucer who set the standard. This can be seen very clearly in the history of Calvin's idea of the "seed of election," from the Strasbourg theologians via orthodoxy and Pietism down to the Enlightenment and the Idealism of the 19th century.

Both paths, the Lutheran and the actualism that goes beyond Luther, and Bucer's habitualism in the doctrine of faith, show the dangers between which Calvin steers his doctrine of the historical-eschatological *perseverantia sanctorum*.

A Look Ahead

We are confronted today by the same question. The only way to avoid the Scylla of the existential-theological actualism and the Charybdis of the habitualism of the pious consciousness in the doctrine of faith is to do what Calvin did: on the question of perseverance and of persisting in faith, we must listen anew to the affirmations of scripture. To take one example: in contemporary philosophy, O. F. Bollnow criticizes the existentialistic one-sided reduction of the human person to a being who exists only *in actu,* and philosophers are beginning to rediscover the relationship to fidelity that is essential if the human being is to become a human being. The consequence for theology is clear: it ought to have reflected long ago, with a completely different emphasis, on the essence of Christian existence as an existence in hope, in fidelity, and in preservation by God.

The history of the Huguenot martyrdom shows how greatly Calvin's doctrine of predestination, when it developed into the promise of perseverance for the "church under the cross," contributed to the correct knowledge of the gospel, to steadfastness, and to patience. The history of the pioneering actions of the Puritans in North America shows how greatly this assurance of being preserved in God's fidelity generated Christian freedom and joy in constructing the world. Something of the Huguenot steadfastness is echoed in the words that the orthodox Calvinist Pierre Dumoulin uttered in the period of ecclesial powerlessness after the fall of La Rochelle, the last Huguenot fortress: "There is nothing in the Christian religion that is more apt to console consciences, there is no dogma with a purity that is to be conserved with greater care, than the doctrine of the assurance of perseverance."[43]

In the present-day situation of the church, and in view of the things to come, which are hidden from us, it is important in every respect that we rediscover fidelity, patience, and perseverance in our calling and in our faith, as the brothers and sisters "who share with you in Jesus the persecution and the kingdom and the patient endurance" (Rev. 1:9).

Chapter 11

The Passibility or Impassibility of God: Answers to J. K. Mozley's "Six Necessary Questions"

THERE HAS BEEN A THEOLOGICAL DISPUTE ABOUT THE PASSIBILITY of God within Anglican theology since 1850. Some have taken the eucharist as their starting point, others metaphysics. To my knowledge, German theology took no notice of this discussion in its early stages. Only in Ernst Troeltsch could I find a reference to it, suggested to him by Baron von Hugel, who was himself an advocate for the passibility of God in that debate. Only through Dietrich Bonhoeffer, who was a minister in London from 1934 to 1936, did the idea of the "suffering of God" finally enter German theology. In his *Letters and Papers from Prison*, published in German in 1951 as *Widerstand und Ergebung*, Bonhoeffer confesses, "Only the suffering God can help," and exhorts Christians to "stand with God in his sufferings."[1]

England had already seen the publication of the extremely informative study *The Impassibility of God: A Survey of Christian Thought* by J. K. Mozley in 1926,[2] and – presented as a solution to the problem – Bertrand R. Brasnett's *The Suffering of the Impassible God* in 1928.[3] Incited by Bonhoeffer's *Letters* and my book *The Crucified God* (1972),[4] the theological dispute about the passibility of God flared up anew, now globally, with contributions from within various denominations and continents. It is within this tradition that the "radical Baptist" Paul Fiddes published his important contribution *The Creative Suffering of God.*[5] In his honour, I would like finally to respond to the "six necessary questions" posed by J. K. Mozley in the year of my birth.[6]

The First Question

The first and most important question posed by Mozley is: *What do you imply by the term "God"?*[7] The alternatives he offers are God as "the absolute," as "ultimate reality," as "the supreme element within the absolute," or "God as personal," If we regard God as the absolute, we cannot ascribe to his infinity anything finite, including passibility. This is also relevant to the unity of the universe, for in Mozley's view, God the absolute has no place in William James' "pluralistic universe."

Let us turn first to the term "absolute." Borrowed from the Latin past participle of "ab-solve," the word originally means "de-tached," i.e., independent, untouchable, unrelational and immovable. In its adjectival form, we use "absolute" as synonymous with "total," "certain," "indubitable," and "without alternative." "The absolute" is one of those terms defined by exclusion of the opposite: the absolute is not the relative, just as the infinite is not the finite. This also works in the other direction: the relative is not the absolute, the finite is not the infinite. But terms defined by mutual exclusion always remain dependent on each other. Therefore, "the absolute" can never stand absolutely alone, but always depends on the relative whose negation it is.[8]

Is "the absolute" really God? My former Tubingen colleague Joseph Ratzinger, as Pope Benedict, was locked in constant combat against the "relativism of the modern world." Why? Because he knew "absolute truth." But in so doing, he did not really fight modern relativism but, ironically, stabilized it, for in comparison to his "absolute truth," *everything* worldly seemed relative.

He should, instead, have combatted totalitarian absolutism in the modern world: the ideological absolutism of the 20th century, the Nazi-absolutism of race, the communist absolutism of the Party, and finally the 21st-century capitalist absolutism of greed for money, together with the absolutist rhetoric of some politicians, who claim that their decisions had "no alternatives."

"What do you imply by the term 'God'?" Already in Martin Luther, we find this question approached not from the perspective of metaphysics but from that of human faith:

> To whatever we look for any good thing and for refuge in every need, that is what is meant by "God"; to *have* a God is nothing else than to trust and believe in him from the heart. As I have often said, it is the trust and faith of the heart, nothing else, that make both God and an idol.[9]

The "absolute" and the "personal" in God are not opposites. Rather, we are dealing with the transition from a mediaeval metaphysics of substance to a modern metaphysics of subjectivity, i.e., from Thomas Aquinas to Hegel. The divine substance has fixed attributes such as immutability and impassibility; the divine subject engages in free actions. The divine substance is omnipotent; the divine subject is self-determining.

Today, Christian theology speaks

- of God *in relationship:*[10] we humans can know nothing of an unrelational God;
- of God *in the process of becoming:*[11] we humans can know nothing of God as a closed system;
- of God *in history:*[12] the reality in which God and human beings interact is not the perfected cosmos but the incomplete history of the world; and
- of God *as* coming:[13] his eschatological future reveals the world in becoming, in history, and in its yet unrealized possibilities.

Today, we do not analyze the nature of God, but take as our starting point God's self-identification in his revelations.[14] *Who* God is also determines *what* God is.

This is demonstrated by the Shema Israel (Deut. 6:4-5):

Hear, O Israel: The Lord is our God, the Lord alone. You shall love the Lord your God with all your heart, and with all your soul, and with all your might.

Who is "the Lord"? This is revealed in the story of the Exodus, where the first commandment says, "I am the Lord your God, who brought you out of slavery." For God, the story of the Exodus is a story of the *shekhina*; for his people, it is a story of liberation. "The Lord" is the subject; "God" is his predicate. The practice is the Passover feast.

This is also apparent in the confession of Christ:

God is "the Father of our Lord Jesus Christ" (1 Cor. 1:3).

For God, the story of Christ is the story of the incarnation, *kenosis* unto death, and resurrection unto eternal life. For all people, it is the story of salvation from sin and death. The Father, the Son, and the Spirit are the subject; "God" is the predicate. The practice is the eucharist.

The Second Question

The second question is: *What is the true doctrine of God's relationship to the world, and, especially with reference to creation?*[15]

Mozley here wants to register "God's priority to the world, as cause to effect," so as not to attribute worldly characteristics to him. He continues: "If . . . God has brought the world into being, what does this mean for God? Is it true to say that he has limited himself?"[16] He thinks that the creation and preservation of the world by God signal a dominance of God's transcendence over his immanence.

Unfortunately, Mozley does not go into detail about the act of creation and the manner of God's preservation of that creation. We do so now:

i) If God chooses to create non-divine being, then this decision concerns not only that created being, but also his own uncreated being: God determines himself as Creator. This self-determination of

God as Creator is logically prior to the act of creation, and represents a self-limitation of God.[17]

ii) If a finite world is to co-exist with the infinite Creator, then God has to limit himself in order to make space and time for his creation and to respect its freedom. This self-limitation of God, which is implied in creation, is called *tzimtzum* (contraction or self-withdrawal) in the Jewish tradition of Kabbalah. In Christian theology, God's self-limitation is seen as the first act of God's grace, his self-withdrawal as the first act of divine *kenosis*. Emil Brunner writes:

> This means, however, that God does not wish to occupy the space of his being by himself; he wishes to make space for other being. By doing so, he limits himself . . . The *kenosis* that culminates in the cross of Christ begins in the act of creation.[18]

From Nicolas of Cusa to the present day, many theologians have regarded the fact that God chooses to engage with this finite, fragile, and corruptible world as its Creator and preserver as his first act of self-abasement, which ultimately leads to his Passion as "the lamb that was slain from the foundation of the world" (Rev. 13:8). This signals the fact that God's heart contained a willingness to suffer before the world was created. Why? Because God does not create and preserve his creatures arbitrarily, but out of love.

iii) God's acts of creation and preservation cannot be regarded as a one-sided "priority of God to the world" if they are done out of love. Done out of love, they are taking and giving, speaking and hearing, creating and resting, doing and suffering – in other words, a dialogical interaction. Biblical evidence for this is found in the opening of the story of the flood in Genesis 6:5-6:

> The Lord saw that the wickedness of humankind was great in the earth, and that every inclination of the thoughts of their hearts was only evil continually. And the Lord was sorry that he had made humankind on the earth, and it grieved him to his heart.

This passage is rightly called "the pain of God": God's remorse conflicts with his faithfulness to creation. God, however, remains faithful to his stubborn human creature, and suffers the appropriate remorse.

iv) This makes clear what "preservation of the world" in spite of human evil and natural catastrophes means. It consists in bearing the world because God loves it and has hope in it. What images does the Bible use for this "bearing God" (Dietrich Bonhoeffer)? First, a feminine image:

"Carry them in your bosom, as a nurse carries a sucking child," to the land that you promised on oath to their ancestors. (Num. 11:12)

Then, a masculine image:

. . . and in the wilderness, where you saw how the Lord your God carried you, just as a man carries a child, all the way that you travelled until you reached this place. (Deut. 1:31)

Then, a comforting image for old age:

[E]ven to your old age I am he, even when you turn grey I will carry you. (Is. 46:4)

And finally, for the entirety of creation:

. . . he sustains all things by his powerful word. (Heb. 1:3)

The preserver of the world is revealed in the crucified Christ, for he "bears" the sins of the world and also the suffering of its victims. W. H. Vanstone expresses this poignantly in the last verse of his poem "Morning glory, starlit sky":

Thou art God, no monarch thou thron'd in easy state to reign.
Thou art God, whose arms of love aching, spent, the world
sustain.[19]

The world-preserving God is less like a heavenly emperor than like Atlas, bearing the globe on his strong and patient shoulders.

v) Mozley wished ultimately to describe the creation and preservation of the world by the word pair transcendence/immanence in order to make immanence "absolutely dependent" on transcendence, as Schleiermacher would say. However, since Karl Rabner, in his famous essay "Christology within an Evolutionary View of the World,"[20] coined the term "self-transcendence of the immanent spirit," transcendence and immanence have been regarded not as separate but as intertwined: the transcendent immanence of the divine Spirit is the ground of the self-transcendence of the worldly spirit.

The Third Question

The third question follows from the relationship between God's transcendence and immanence: *Can the life of God be essentially blessed and happy, as being that eternal life which cannot as such be in any way affected by the time-series and its contents, and yet also a life in which suffering finds a place, in so far as the life of God enters into the time-series and works within it?*[21]

Mozley answers this question, as is to be expected, in the following way:

a) Passibility is not an intrinsic truth of the divine nature,
b) yet it expresses a certain aspect of the condescension of the
Absolute to the contingent, of the Eternal to the things of time.[22]

God's transcendence is impassible, while God's immanence is passible. In God's essential blessedness, there is no space for suffering, but a life that contains suffering nevertheless finds space in the life of God which has entered time and this earth.

This leads us to Brasnett's solution: "the suffering of the impassible God." This solution to the problem is age-old. Bernard of Clairvaux already said, *"impassibilis est Deus, sed non incompassibilis."*[23] God cannot suffer in himself, but he can co-suffer; and God became human to be with us in our suffering. This is revealed in the passion of Christ. Thus, in all suffering we are accompanied by one who co-suffers. "Consolation is present in all suffering, the consolation of God's compassionate love – and so the star of hope arises."[24]

But how can an impassible God feel compassion? How can a God incapable of suffering love? How can God feel compassion for something he does not know? Does God perhaps only appear capable of love and suffering to us, without being so in reality? Anselm of Canterbury may have thought so when he wrote, "Thou art compassionate in terms of our experience, and not compassionate in terms of thy being."[25] Thomas Aquinas concluded, cogently: "For in God there are no passions. Now love is a passion. Therefore love is not in God or God loves without passion."[26] Friedrich Schleiermacher, too, rejected the idea of divine compassion and therefore excluded the term "divine mercy" from his doctrine of faith.[27] "The origin of absolute dependence" cannot be affected at all; it has, according to Karl Barth's critique, "no heart."[28]

This is how far one gets with Mozley's metaphysics of substance. However, if one shifts to a metaphysics of subjectivity, then God's condescension in time on this earth is his self-revelation (Karl Barth), and in God's self, there can be no distinction between an inside and an outside. God does not contradict himself; rather, the way God appears to us in his revelation "is the way he is beforehand in himself" – otherwise, the term "self-revelation" would be inappropriate.[29] God's self-revelation is also God's self-dedication, and dedication can only be rendered completely or not at all, but certainly not partially – otherwise, the term would be inadmissible. Self-revelation and self-dedication are actions of love. Love can only be ascribed to a subject, not a substance.

The Aristotelian-Thomist metaphysics of substance has its origins in the religious enlightenment of ancient Greece. It does not affect the God of Israel. Why did Aristotle call God *"apathes"*?[30] To exclude the moods and affairs of the Homeric gods. The God of Israel is not subject to such moods, but he is full of compassion for his people. This is why Abraham Heschel interpreted God's love and ability to suffer by way of his pathos.[31] The history of Israel with God, according to Hosea, is a love story. From Jesus' history with God, the early Christians deduced the unconditional love of God. God not merely loves – "God is love" (1 John 4:16). The story of Christ is the story of the Passion of God in the double sense of passion and suffering.

I wonder why Mozley insisted so strongly on a metaphysics of substance, and did not consider the doctrine of the Trinity. By means of it, he could have solved the problems of creation, transcendence and immanence, eternity and love, and not least the problem of the possibility of God – for those problems arise only from the attempt to merge the biblical traditions of God with Greek metaphysics.

The Fourth Question

In his fourth question, Mozley engages carefully with the question of human and divine "feeling," since he regards "suffering" as a special case of feeling. He thus formulates his question as follows: *How is feeling in God related to feeling in men? And is there a particular kind of feeling properly describable as suffering, and experienced as suffering by God?*[32]

Mozley thinks it is easier to ascribe reason and will to God than feeling. Thought and will can sensibly be ascribed to "God who is Spirit"; but that is not really the case with feeling. This general problem is particularly true of the negative "suffering." Mozley does not consider the mercy, joy, or anger of God. Mercy is no marginal feeling, but involves the whole person, as the Hebrew analogy of giving birth expresses so well.

It is unfortunate that Mozley is not mindful of Ephesians 4:30, where Paul exhorts the community: "Do not grieve the Holy Spirit." Paul apparently regards the Holy Spirit as receptive and capable of being grieved and saddened by human beings.

Mozley does not wish to dismiss the entire idea of a "suffering God"; rather, he offers a solution. Human beings are made in the image of God. Therefore, human feeling, integral as it is to the entirety of human life, "presumably" finds its archetypical perfection in God.[33] It is therefore truer to say "that God feels than that he does not."[34]

However, in the history of Israel with God, we find a much closer relationship than mere analogy: If God "wishes to live in the midst of Israel," he also participates in its joys and sufferings.[35] In his *shekhinah,* "the Lord" identifies with the persecutions and sufferings of his people: what happens to his people also happens to him.

The prophet Isaiah's vision of the suffering servant speaks in even stronger terms: "Surely he has borne our infirmities and carried our diseases" (Is. 53:4). This servant of God bore not only our earthly sorrows, but also our suffering vis-à-vis God: "He was wounded for our transgressions, crushed for our iniquities" (Is. 53:5). From the beginning, Christians saw in the suffering, tortured, and crucified Jesus the promised servant of God, and interpreted his sufferings in line with Isaiah's prophecies. But we are dealing here not merely with an identification of God with a human, but with God himself – with the one to whom God said, "You are my beloved Son, in whom I am well pleased," and who called God "Abba, dear Father."[36] We are therefore justified in speaking of the suffering Jesus as the "suffering God." The suffering of the Son from his abandonment by God whom he called "Father" corresponds to the suffering of the Father from the death of the Son. The night in Gethsemane preceded the day of Jesus' death and is key to the interpretation of what happened between Father and Son in the divine darkness of the cross. The God incarnate not only suffers our diseases and sorrows, but also our suffering vis-à-vis God, and is with us in the "dark night of the soul." The idea of suffering does not merely, as Mozley opines, have moral connotations; rather, the cross is the very centre of the Christian experience of God.

The Fifth Question

The fifth question can be answered more briefly, since it is already contained in the preceding questions: *Is a real religious value secured in the thought of the possibility of God?*[37]

Mozley once again distinguishes between the "nature of God" and the "grace of God." The idea that God's nature should suffer as the world suffers has no "religious value." The metaphysical attributes of glory have greater religious and devotional value. It is said that God suffers from his love for us. Yet if God suffered, man would be no better off. However, "[i]s the alternative to a suffering God an unsympathetic God?"[38]

I would like to reply as follows:

i) It is not good to introduce contradictions into God. "God remains faithful to himself; he cannot deny himself" (1 Tim. 2:13). And if "God *is* love," then this sentence describes both his nature and his work. The inner life of the Trinity is the eternal perichoresis of love.

ii) The theology of the early church only knew of one alternative: either to be subjected to suffering (as all finite beings are), or not to be subjected to suffering (as the divine substance is). The more we understand God as Trinity, the more we take note of the joys and sufferings that arise from love. As the Orthodox theologian Dumitru Staniloae wrote to me, the question of the suffering of God is answered positively in the idea of the mercy of God.

iii) That God suffers has comforting theological significance for suffering humans: they feel the proximity and solidarity of God. "Even though I walk through the darkest valley, I fear no evil; for you are with me" (Ps. 23:4). God is with us! And if they look to the Passion of Christ, they believe that God was in Christ and reconciled the world to himself: God is for us!

iv) An apathetic God unconcerned with the fate of his creatures would be a rather unsympathetic God.

The Sixth Question

The sixth and final question concerns the theology of the cross: *What is the relationship of the cross as the historic means of God's redemption of the world to that eternal background of God's love out of which the cross is given?*[39]

Mozley is of the opinion that the metaphysical question of time and eternity must be solved before the passion of the cross can be interpreted as the "historic counterpart of a Passion ever living in the heart of God."[40] I do not interpret the cross of Christ within the framework of a general metaphysics, but within that of the Christian doctrine of the Trinity.[41] I therefore cannot separate the theological significance of the death of Christ from his resurrection.

What is presented as Jesus' abandonment by God on the cross in the Gospel of Mark is interpreted in the Pauline epistles as the offering up of the Son by the Father in the Holy Spirit, and as the self-surrender of the Son (Rom. 8:32; Heb. 9:14; Gal. 2:20). This double offering is a sign of God's self-dedication to us in love, from which nothing – neither death nor life, neither powers nor dominions – can separate us (Rom. 8:39). Thus, the problem of time and eternity is solved in the sense that eternity appears in time and fulfils it.

If one separates the cross from the resurrection of Jesus, it appears as a "historical" event. The "historical Jesus," however, is the dead Jesus, for death makes life historical. The resurrection of Jesus "from the dead" means, as the phrase suggests, the anticipation of the general resurrection in this One, and the beginning of the overcoming of death in and through that One.[42] The risen Christ is the incarnate promise of a new beginning of life at the end of this world of death. This resurrection of the crucified inaugurates the new creation of the world: here in the Spirit – there in glory. Thus, the problem of time and eternity is solved through an eschatological conception of history.

The salvific significance of the cross of Christ is only apparent in the light of his resurrection from the dead. There is no salvific significance of the cross in isolation from the resurrection. In the cross, the forgiveness of sins is effected in the resurrection, the new birth to a living hope. Both belong together. The limitation of atonement theology is that it disregards the resurrection, as Mozley inadvertently shows. But there is no reconciliation through the self-dedication of Christ without a transformation of the reconciled through his resurrection. Liberation from the burdens and sins of the past is a consequence of the beginning of a new future of life.

The joy of God is greater than the suffering of God.
The joy of God remains in eternity.
The suffering of God remains as suffering that has been
overcome.
The crucified Christ bears the new, eternal creation.

Two necessary questions:
1. If God is immutable and cannot be moved, why do we pray?
2. If God is impassible, how can God feel compassion and show mercy?

Chapter 12

The Mystery of the Past

Remembering *Beginning*
Forgetting *Letting go*
Excusing *Forgiving*

The Past in Existence and in Time

Time in existence

The mystery of the past is that it does not pass away. On the contrary, it accompanies us as our past and it exists even when we no longer exist. William Faulkner was right to say: "The past is not dead, it's not even past."

No one can steal our past from us. Everything good and beautiful that has happened to us, and that we have done, remains. It is unassailable. No one can relieve us of our past. Everything bad and ugly that has happened to us, and that we have done, remains as it is. It can no longer be altered.

If existence rules time, then what we call "the past" is the real existence. It is no longer a possible existence. It cannot be lost, and it has become immutable. Possible existence ends at death. What dies becomes immortal. The mystery of the past is that it passes away only in time, but not in existence. What passes away in time remains in real existence.

Existence in time

From a temporal perspective, however – that is to say, in our consciousness – what has happened is past. And it is obvious that what belongs to the past, that which has happened, no longer exists. It is no longer in the realm of our experience; it is only in the realm of our remembering. It is only the present existence that exists (in the emphatic sense of that term) in time. Past existence no longer exists, and future existence does not yet exist. According to Augustine's theory of time, which left a profound mark on the West, remembering allows us to reach into the realm that no longer exists and to bring the past into the present. Thanks to hope, we reach into the realm of that which does not yet exist and bring that which is future into the present. The difference is that we remember real existence, whereas all that we can do in hope is to imagine possible existence. In the powers of remembering and hoping, our soul becomes creative in our consciousness. We draw that which does not exist, and that which does not yet exist, into present-day existence. Just as God creates being out of the absolute nothing, the *ouk on,* so we, as God's image, create out of the relative nothing, the *mê on,* that which exists in the present. Time rules existence, and we draw distinctions between past, present, and future existence. In this distinction, it is only present existence that possesses pure being; past and future being belong to the category of non-being.

The times begin and end in present existence. The present is not only the point in time between past and future. If one follows Kierkegaard, the present "moment" is also seen emphatically as an "atom of eternity." In reality, however, the present is not a temporal, but a spatial concept: the subject of the experience of time is present or absent. Time comes out of the future and passes through the experience of those who live in the present into the past.

For Augustine, time is the embodiment of the transience of all that exists. Everything ends in universal death. *Chronos* is the brother of *thanatos.* If one looks in the other direction, seeing the present from the times of the future and the past, the present accompanies the subject as long as he or she lives. It is not a transient point in time along the temporal trajectory, but is the *kairos* in which future possibilities are seized and realized. *Kairos* is a brother of *zoê,* of life.

Remembering

The English word "remembering" means "joining up anew." Those who remember take their past into their present, and at the same time integrate their present into their past, becoming the contemporary of many times. They can compare their present with their past, thereby acquiring orientation for their future. When one remembers, one's past and one's present become contemporaneous. The sounds of the past are still in our ears when we hear the sounds of the present, and this is how we perceive melodies. The words of the past are still in our memory when we hear the words of the present, and this is how we understand what is said. Otherwise, we could neither recognize a melody nor understand words.

It is, however, not the case that we attempt to hold fast to something that becomes ever more remote as time goes by, and that we find this increasingly difficult as time goes by. Memories do not in the least disappear over the course of time. In old age, our long-term memory is in fact better than our short-term memory. The strength of remembering depends on repetition. It is only through memorizing that we develop the memory. It is good to transport ourselves back into past times, in order to impress on our memory what we experienced then.

When we remember, we are not neutral vis-à-vis our past. The present-day interests also determine the filter of our consciousness through which we remember past events. And the interests that direct our remembering change, in keeping with the specific present that we are experiencing. History on the large scale "needs to be rewritten again and again"; and on the personal scale, one's life history is perceived and narrated differently, again and again. But it is not only the present that leaves its mark on memories. Memories too leave their mark on the present.

We shall now look at memories that oppress us and memories that make us happy.

There are past events and past experiences that we cannot get rid of. They are not at all "past." They oppress us, and they are present experiences, although they happened long ago. The pain pierces us; the guilt humiliates us; the shame aggrieves us; the disgrace weighs us down; and grief for the person we have loved never leaves us. Such experiences do not pass away with time. Time does not heal wounds of this kind. The growing distances in time do not make such experiences a thing of the past. Such experiences must be healed, if they are to pass away. Experiences of guilt must be forgiven, if they are to become our past. If such experiences are "healed" and "forgiven," we are mercifully freed of the obligation to remember, and we can allow the events that call forth these experiences to rest in the past. We can forget them. Without the merciful forgetting of such experiences, which oppress the present, life would be simply impossible. They would suffocate us and deprive us of every hope of a different life.

The inability to forget is a torment

We can also suppress painful experiences and shut them away in the cellar of the subconscious, in order to bring them under our control. Although suppression is regarded as a violent act, it does give freedom to lead a different life. Suppression succeeds best when we throw ourselves into our work, for then we are obliged to think of something else and have no time for reflection. However, suppression and a deliberate non-remembering cost a great deal of mental energy and paralyze the strengths we need for a new life. And in that case, one lives alongside oneself. What we suppress is not past, nor does it disappear: it is merely something of which we are no longer conscious. What we suppress from consciousness exerts in the subconscious a lasting influence on our life. If we open up the suppressions, everything is present in the depth of memory just as we once experienced it: the terror, the guilt, the shame, the grief. There are no temporal distances in the depths of the experiences that we remember: everything that happened is there, and so is the way in which we experienced it. Through the suppression that we practice every day, these experiences will not be healed – or at any rate, not consciously. This is why they are just as painful and burdensome as they were on the first day. But there is also an activity of the subconscious that accepts the painful experiences that have been suppressed; it gets accustomed to them, so that they no longer cause suffering. And we can let this activity take its course. When we remember, and put a stop to the suppressions, our experiences are often altered. But when we consciously memorize the experiences, we genuinely welcome them into our life. We begin to live with them; they no longer cause us to break down and to suffer. For years, my experiences of death in the war made me wake up in the night, bathed in sweat, until I consciously pictured them and accepted them into my life. After that, these memories actually helped me to fall asleep, after so many years.

On the other hand, unredeemed promises and unfulfilled hopes likewise do not pass away with time: they accompany us as long as we live. They exist in time, and they came into being in time, but they transcend the times because they announce a future that no present has as yet attained. When we remember them or, even more strongly, when we ponder on them, we discover the future in the past. In what is past, we see an openness to the future that still awaits its realization. We discover possibilities that were not yet realized in the past. For all real existence is always surrounded by a plethora of possible existence. Only a small part of the possible was realized. This is why we can come back to the unrealized possibilities and realize them today.

We never remember only what happened, and how it happened. We always remember also what was possible and what could have happened. Let us take two examples. The "primal European catastrophe" of the First World War happened, but was it inevitable? Every historical investigation of the possibilities in 1914 concludes that war was not inevitable but could have been prevented. If one only asks the historical question "How did it actually happen?" one is paying homage to a hidden belief in fate: "It had to happen in this way." One is looking for the iron laws of necessity in real existence, not for the possibilities in real existence. The second example is the reunification of the two parts of Germany in the events of the year 1989/1990. No one thought this was possible, because most people "realistically" saw only what actually existed in East and West and wanted to continue their own present in the future. This blinded them to the surprisingly new possibilities of the future. As Heraclitus said, "One who does not hope for the unexpected will not find it." Most Germans' sense of possibilities had been overwhelmed by their sense of reality. "We did not believe it was possible," they said, and when it happened, they reacted to the "miracle" by saying: "This is crazy!"

If we integrate the unfulfilled hopes of the past into our expectations of the future and link our own hopes with those of past generations, we become their contemporaries and they become ours. We welcome that for which they lived, worked, and died, and we take our place in the great traditions of the future. The great hopes of human beings owe their existence to their humanity, with which they are indissolubly linked. This is the hope of life with which we are born. This is the hope of existence that gives us every morning the certainty that we exist. This is the hope of happiness that lets us look for the fullness of life. This is the hope in God that sustains us from day to day.

The loss of the ability to remember is a torment

Our memories are as varied as life itself. And this is why one cannot sort them neatly into categories or draw distinctions among them. They also change in the impact they make on our present-day consciousness: something painful can become full of hope, and something full of hope can suffer a bitter disappointment. I should like to discuss two functions of memory that have a special character: the disturbing and the dangerous memories.

We find the disturbing memories in the realm of the suppressed past. These are the "sore points" in our past. They do not fit our present life, but they make themselves felt and disturb our self-image. Here, I have in mind two influential cultural personalities in Germany in the post-war years, who were vocal critics of National Socialism and of the former Nazis. They were active in conservative politics, but then it emerged that one of them had been a member of the National Socialist Party and the other had done voluntary military service in the SS. Disturbing memories are important, because they bring us to truthfulness.

The "dangerous memories" of which Marcuse and Metz speak remind of what once was possible. These may be negative dangers or positive hopes. In both cases, what once was possible cannot again be made impossible. One negative example is the atomic bomb that was dropped on Hiroshima in 1945. Since then, the danger of universal nuclear death has existed. A positive example is the French Revolution of freedom, which, as Kant said, is a historical sign that can never be forgotten. Every dictatorship, whether of a social class, a race, or a party, is threatened by this dangerous memory of freedom, as we see even in the Arab world today.

"Dangerous memories" include other people's memory of their sufferings that we have caused, and of their dead who were our victims. They remind us of something that we do not want to recognize, something that we have suppressed. The Jewish and Polish memories of Auschwitz are a "dangerous memory" for us Germans. The memory of the Polish officers who were murdered at Katyn is a "dangerous memory" for Russians. The memory of the Muslim Bosnians killed at Srebrenica is a "dangerous memory" for the Serbs. "Dangerous memories" are the threatening memories that others have of us. They show that memories are not first and foremost self-referential, but are always relational. Common memories create social community, and "dangerous memories" make us aware of societal and political circumstances that have been destroyed.

To live with disturbing and dangerous memories is not a torment: it is full of hope.

Forgetting

"Seeking to forget makes exile all the longer; the secret of redemption lies in remembrance." These words are inscribed on the Jewish Holocaust Remembrance Center at Yad Vashem in Jerusalem. They were formulated by Elie Wesel on the basis of an aphorism of Baal Shem Tov.

We find the opposite proposition in Friedrich Nietzsche: "It is completely impossible to live, if we do not forget."[1] The "historical meaning" robbed the philosopher of sleep. He was so weary of reflective remembering that he wanted to live "almost without memory," "happy like an animal." He recommended direct action and the spontaneous life to the bourgeois of his days, who went in for excessive reflection.

In the experiences of our old age, however, forgetting becomes a sickness. We cannot recall the names of acquaintances, we cannot find the words we want, and we can no longer remember what we heard yesterday. The name for the involuntary, helpless forgetting is "Alzheimer's." With this forgetting, the dying of the brain cells begins. This sleep of forgetting is an ineluctable sickness that leads to death.

As every biblical dictionary shows, "forgetting" has negative overtones in the Old Testament. This is the reason for the continuous exhortation: Do not forget! Remember! "Zachor: Remember."[2] This is directed primarily against those human beings who forget God. One who forgets God abandons God and does not keep the commandments of his covenant: "Take care that you do not forget the Lord" (Deut. 6:12); "They forgot God, their Savior, who had done great things in Egypt" (Ps. 106:21). The opposite of forgetting God is remembering God: "I will remember your name from one generation to the next" (Ps. 45:18); "I will remember your wonders of old" (Ps. 77:12). Much more frequently, however, the complaint is made that Yahweh has forgotten Israel and God has forgotten humankind. Psalm 44 is a moving testimony to this: "All this has come upon us, yet we have not forgotten you, or been false to your covenant" (44:17). Accordingly, God is reminded of his fidelity to the covenant:

> *Rouse yourself! Why do you sleep, O Lord?*
> *Awake, do not cast us off forever!*
> *Why do you hide your face? Why do you forget our affliction*
> *and oppression?*
> *Rise up, come to our help.*
> *Redeem us for the sake of your steadfast love! (44:23-26)*

This cry to the God who forgets and is absent runs through the literature of exile in the Old Testament: "How long, O Lord? Will you forget me forever?" (Ps. 13:2); "The Lord has forsaken me, my Lord has forgotten me" (Is. 49:14). What is forgotten is abandoned. One who is abandoned gets lost. This cry against God's forgetting culminates in the New Testament in Jesus' cry as he dies: "My God, why have you forsaken me?" (Matt 27:46).

Only something that was promised can be forgotten. The Old Testament protest against God's forgetting presupposes God's covenant with his people and his covenantal promises. Only something that was once chosen and accepted can be abandoned. The cry of those forsaken by God presupposes a strong, positive experience of the love of God. As Jesus dies, his cry to God is so penetrating precisely because it is a reaction to Jesus' baptism, where Jesus heard the word of his God: "You are my Son, the Beloved; with you I am well pleased" (Mark 1:11).

In the New Testament, Christian forgetting is wholly at the service of the hope of God's coming and hence has a positive connotation. At Luke 9:62, Jesus proclaims: "No one who puts a hand to the plow and looks back is fit for the kingdom of God." And Paul goes so far as to affirm: "One thing I do: forgetting what lies behind and straining forward to what lies ahead" (Phil. 3:13). This is not a forgetting due to a weakness of memory or to ingratitude, but a conscious and intentional forgetting in the sense of no longer recalling. What existed in the past no longer concerns us; the old has passed away and has been replaced by the new. In Christian hope, the future is more important than the past, and awaiting is greater than remembering. Christians are beginners.

But the Christian hope too has its anchor in the memory: "Remember Jesus Christ" (2 Tim. 2:8). This refers to the coming of Jesus Christ into this world. Not every life gives grounds for hope, but the life of Jesus is a great promise. With the raising of Jesus from the dead, the future of God has been opened up once and for all to humankind, to all that lives, and to the cosmos. This is why the resurrection of Jesus Christ is the crux of hope in God in history. To use the language of Psalm 44: it is not only the resurrection of Jesus, but also the raising up of God in a world that has forgotten him, the waking up of God in the story of Jesus, and God's rebellion against the powers of evil and of death that crucified Christ. In order to be sure of this future of God in one's own experiences of the history of injustice, violence, and death, one must return again and again into this "origin" of Christ. This takes place in the Lord's supper or eucharist. Paul quotes the words "Do this in memory of me" at 1 Cor. 11:26 and adds: "until he comes" (11:26), thereby making this act of remembering the memory of a great hope.

Apologizing and Forgiving

A sincere apology belongs to an ethic of reciprocity, and free forgiveness belongs to an ethic of graciousness. Through a sincere apology, a just social relationship is re-established; through free forgiveness, one lets go and a new beginning is created. If one sees the apology only in relation to a just retribution, it becomes a legal matter, and difficult. If one sees the forgiveness only in the gracious act of freeing from guilt, it easily becomes a cheap and ineffective grace. In our culture, we do not have to choose between apology and forgiveness. As Aaron Lazare has said, they are inseparable in practical terms.[3]

The apology

The expression *Ich entschuldige mich* has crept into the German language.[4] It is the exact opposite of a sincere apology, for if I have incurred guilt, if I owe someone something, it is impossible for me to absolve myself of that guilt. I must ask for absolution from the guilt. I must first blame myself, not exculpate myself. I must accept the guilt for a wicked action or for a failure to act. Only those in relation to whom I have incurred guilt can absolve me of that guilt. The German apology in the form of a self-absolution is the false kind of apology and is often used as a way of self-assertion: "But I have apologized!" This actually prevents a sincere apology.

Sincere apologies are an essential component of societal peace. Sincere apologies have the power to heal broken promises and shattered relationships. They dissolve the resentment and the wish for retribution and revenge that have arisen because of injustice and violence, insults and affronts. For the victims, this is a path to the re-establishing of their dignity, their self-respect, and their honour; for the perpetrators, the apology is a path to liberation from their burden of guilt and shame. It is not unjust actions but failures to give help that make the greatest number of sincere apologies necessary. One was not there for one's children when they needed one; a sick friend was expecting a visit, but one put it off; one did not reply to an invitation, thereby hurting the person who had given it; or one failed to defend a person who was attacked.

Through the request for forgiveness, broken social relationships in both personal and societal life (and, not least, in political life) are healed, because this request re-establishes the self-respect of those concerned. The very request for pardon itself raises those concerned from the humiliation they have experienced and expresses the confidence that they have the strength and the authority to forgive. With the request for forgiveness, perpetrators recognize their guilt, or the debt that they owe, and lay the restoration of their own self-respect in the hands of those in relation to whom they have incurred guilt. They make up through their own self-abasement for the humiliation that they have inflicted on them; they take on themselves the affront that they have inflicted on them by confessing: "I am sorry."[5] These words have shrunk down (even in contemporary German) to the hollow exclamation "Sorry!", but in their original meaning they disclose a profound truth. By transposing myself into the suffering of others whom I have offended, I take their suffering on myself: "I am sincerely sorry. I wish that it had not happened."

This empathy of perpetrators with the victims of their actions or omissions is one essential element of a Christian apology. A second element is the insight that one has done wrong, or that one has failed to do what is right. This consciousness of injustice leads to the acknowledgement of guilt. One has become guilty, or one owes something, and one is ashamed. This path into the acknowledgement of guilt and the acceptance of shame is hard for every human being, because this is a path into self-abasement in the presence of the one in relation to whom one has incurred guilt. Seen in isolation, this asks too much of a person, because no one can live without self-respect. This is why many self-justifications arise in such a situation; other people are accused, or one excuses oneself by referring to difficult situations, or one wallows in self-pity. Without a strong confidence that the victims will desist from their accusations when they are asked for forgiveness, perpetrators cannot cast themselves into the dust before their victims without destroying themselves inwardly. This is why the victims must take a step in the direction of the perpetrators and allow them to hope that they can be set free from their guilt. A space of trust around perpetrators and victims must be created, for it is only in this space that the recognition of guilt, shame, and the request for forgiveness are possible for the perpetrators, and that the victims can emerge from their hurt and humiliation and can be willing to accept the apology. Other persons, the neighbours who are neither perpetrators nor victims, but are associated with both of them, have the responsibility for such a space of trust. Through their fellowship with both, they can form a protective space of this kind. They can motivate and act as witnesses. Such a space must not only offer protection and an atmosphere of trust; it must also offer a context where changes and new beginnings are possible, that is to say, a space full of hope for situations that are bogged down, relationships that are broken, and living environments that have congealed in bitterness. In an ethic of reciprocity, this space of trust is the shared order of morality and law. It has been damaged and must be restored, and both the perpetrators and the victims need it.

First apologizing, then forgiving

The process of apologizing that I have described above is difficult and risky. Perpetrators confess guilt, feel the suffering that they have caused, and offer to make reparation – with the risk that they may be rejected. Victims must bid farewell to their resentment and hurts, and also to the role of "victim" that is sometimes taken. They must accept the apology and encounter the perpetrator differently than as a "perpetrator." They must respect the person of the perpetrator, while they forgive what the perpetrator has done. This process is unpleasant and certainly disagreeable for both sides, but it is prescribed by ritual. It is a process in accordance with the law of retaliation: "an eye for an eye, a tooth for a tooth" (Deut. 21:24). The process of apologizing becomes a process whereby the perpetrator punishes himself. This is the law of reciprocity, taught by Moses and Confucius. The reverse is: "Do not do to anyone else what you do not want anyone to do to you," or, more simply: "What you do to me, I do to you." If the perpetrators go through the process from confession to repentance and to reparation, they must be forgiven, because they have re-established the legal order of reciprocity. One celebrated example is King Henry IV's penitential walk to Canossa in 1077, through which he compelled Pope Gregory VII to lift his excommunication of the king.

In the Christian vocabulary, this is the process of penitence, of conversion, and of a turning around. It is, however, accompanied by the act of the free forgiveness of guilt, and this makes it a process that liberates the perpetrators from the burden of their guilt and the victims from their humiliation. As the New Testament understands it in Luke 15, penitence is joy: we see this in the parables of the finding of the lost sheep and the return of the Prodigal Son. Penitence is not an act of self-punishment, but a turning around into the confidence that guilt will be forgiven.

Penitence without forgiveness is self-punishment. Forgiveness without penitence does not even touch the burden of guilt. Forgiveness and penitence belong together – but how? There are three paths:

First, the forgiveness of guilt is the beginning. Only guilt that is forgiven can be confessed without resulting in self-destruction. Self-respect is rooted in the forgiveness of sins, which makes possible the freedom from one's own self. The confession of guilt can be made without self-humiliation.

Second, the forgiveness of guilt is the goal and the end of the process of apologizing. This, of course, makes the forgiveness uncertain, because no one knows whether they have already repented correctly and carried out all the necessary works of penance.

Third, the forgiveness of guilt can accompany the process of apologizing in all its stages and can be given in part if the confession is truthful, the repentance is genuine, and the willingness to make reparation is credible. Penance and forgiveness are intimately linked here, as two sides of one and the same process. This is why the forgiveness takes as long as the penance.

I find the first way convincing, because it is ultimately also the presupposition of the third way.

Forgiving

Experiences are my starting point in this section. When one's guilt is forgiven, it no longer clings to one, and one can confess it without destroying oneself. The self is kept safe in a great affection, and one is no longer judged in accordance with one's misdeeds or omissions. This distinction between people and their actions is the great liberation that is brought about by the forgiveness of guilt.

I remember how, in 1945, I was brought to Scotland as a prisoner of war, to do forced labour. The Scottish workers with whom we constructed roads encountered us with a great kindness, although we had been their enemies only a short time before that and we had prisoners' numbers on our backs. They were hospitable, and they put us very much to shame. This made it possible for us to live with the terrible images from Bergen-Belsen that were exhibited in our camp. We could bear the burdens of our people's guilt without suppressing them, and without hardening our own hearts. This would not have been possible if we had experienced justified reproaches or contempt: we would have curled up in our own shells.

In 1947, with other prisoners, I attended the first international student conference in Swanwick/Derby. A group of Dutch students came up to us and wanted to talk with us. They told us that Christ was the bridge on which they were coming to us and that without Christ, they could not talk to us. They spoke of the Gestapo terror in their country and of Jewish friends who had been sent to the extermination camps. Our first steps were tentative, but we too were able to walk on this bridge and to confess the guilt of our people and ask for reconciliation. For me, this was the hour of liberation from a heavy burden. I could breathe freely, and I returned with new courage to my prison camp.

A well-known example of how forgiveness can lead to repentance is the moving story of Ernst Werner Techow. He was the only one of those who assassinated Weimar Republic's foreign minister Walther Rathenau in 1922 who did not flee to escape his responsibility but gave himself up to justice. He was sentenced to 15 years in prison. A few days after her son's murder, Walther Rathenau's mother wrote to Techow's mother: "Tell your son that I forgive him in the name and in the spirit of my son, just as God may forgive him, when he makes a full admission of guilt to his earthly judge and does penance before his heavenly judge . . . May these words give your soul peace." After his early release, Techow joined the French Foreign Legion. He had read Rathenau's writings while he was in prison, and he kept Mrs. Rathenau's letter. After the truce between Germany and France in 1940, he left the Foreign Legion and went to Marseilles, where he helped more than 700 Jews escape from their murderers to Spain and North Africa. It was Mrs. Rathenau's forgiveness that had brought about this conversion.

But what do forgiving (*vergeben*) and pardoning (*verzeihen*) mean?

To forgive something means renouncing one's claim to reparation or revenge, and acquitting one's debtor. The prophet Micah says of the God who "forgives" human sins: "He will tread our iniquities under foot. You will cast all our sins into the depths of the sea" (7:19). God forgives "for his name's sake" (Ps. 79:9). This is why God "will abundantly pardon" (Is. 55:7); indeed, God forgives "all your iniquity" (Ps. 103:3). When God forgives human sins, God is not reacting to human beings' apologies; God acts freely, out of immense kindness. Forgiving thus means not enforcing the right that one has vis-à-vis other persons, but remitting the guilt and no longer remembering it.

In the Bible, the forgiveness of guilt or of sins is derived from the theology and ethics of the sabbatical year. According to God's commandment, every seventh year was a sabbatical year, and every 49th year (seven times seven) was a "year of remission" (jubilee year), which began on a day of atonement. In this year, guilt is remitted and slaves are set free; the earth lies fallow in order to restore its generative strength (Lev. 25:10). When Peter asks: "How often must I forgive my brother, when he sins against me?," Jesus replies: "Seventy times seven" (Matt. 18:22), thereby locating the forgiveness of sins in the messianic jubilee year that dawns with his coming.

These sabbatical years meant the restoration of the original just relationships in God's people: "Then each one shall return to his goods and to his clan." All the unjust relationships that have come into being over the course of time are to be dissolved. The debts that have piled up are remitted, and the debt slaves are set free. These acts of forgiving are described in detail in Leviticus 25.

The prophetic theology of Isaiah promises a new servant of God who raises up the poor in the Spirit of the Lord, sets the prisoners free, and proclaims a "year of the Lord's favour" (Is. 61). Jesus enters into the sphere of this prophetic expectation and proclaims (according to Luke 4:19) this "year of the Lord's favour" here and now. His Sermon on the Mount, which speaks of the love of enemies, his acts of forgiving sin, and his demand that one forgive 70 times seven (Matt. 18:22) all go beyond the jubilee year and are to be understood as the beginning of the messianic Sabbath. But the messianic Sabbath is nothing other than the kingdom of God. This trajectory in the Old Testament tradition is important for the expectation of the kingdom of God, because it describes the relationships to God, in society, and to the earth in the kingdom of God. The forgiveness of sins and the remission of guilt are therefore a prerogative of believers and the apostolic task of Christians: "If you forgive the sins of any, they are forgiven them" (John 20:23).

Forgiveness in the name and in the Spirit of God is not linked to any conditions, because it reacts, not to the human debtor, but to the messianic Sabbath of God. The extreme love of enemies that Jesus taught in his Sermon on the Mount is a reaction, not to the enmity, but to the merciful Father, and it descends like the sun and the rain on both bad and good: "Be perfect, therefore, as your heavenly Father is perfect" (Matt. 5:43-48). The link of forgiveness to the perpetrator's penance does not correspond to the biblical context of forgiveness in the sabbatical year. The turning away of the perpetrator from injustice and violence is the expected consequence of the forgiveness of his guilt – not its precondition. The parable of the return of the Prodigal Son is to be read as a parable of the joy of the merciful father who goes to meet him.

After the war, I heard the story of a Russian woman who gave bread to some German prisoners of war who were being driven through her village. When the Russian soldiers tried to forbid this, she said: "I have given bread to Russian prisoners who were driven by the Germans through our village, and I will also give you bread when you are brought through our village by the secret police." Bonhoeffer's criticism of "cheap grace" (*Nachfolge,* 1938), and his attempt to link forgiveness to penance, are mistaken: grace is not merely cheap, it is free of cost, for otherwise it would not be grace. In the kingdom of God, "the water of life is free of cost" (Rev. 22:17), and this is anticipated as a shining light in forgiveness in human history, which is so heavy with guilt. But grace is costly: it costs God unending patience with us human beings, and it costs Christ the life that he laid down for us and for our reconciliation, as Bonhoeffer rightly said.

The biblical tradition presents a puzzle that is hard to solve: on the one hand, God forgives freely and for the sake of his name alone, while on the other hand, according to Isaiah 53, his servant redeems human beings from their sins through his vicarious sufferings: "Upon him was the punishment that made us whole, and by his bruises we are healed" (53:5). And we read that, on the one hand, Jesus freely forgives sins (Matt. 9:2, 6) as only God can forgive sins (Mark 2:7), while on the other hand, he "was handed over to death for our trespasses and was raised for our justification" (Rom. 4:25). Does forgiveness come through free grace, or because of the vicarious divine suffering? This puzzle has been resolved in favour of the vicarious suffering, declaring that God never forgives sins otherwise than in view of the vicarious suffering of Christ for the sinners and the guilty. Others, however, have rejected the idea of Christ's vicarious suffering as an archaic myth of "expiatory suffering," and have affirmed only the free, gratuitous forgiveness of sins.

I believe that both solutions are unsatisfactory. The forgiveness of sins is a precious gift and act of kindness that causes pain, in both God and human beings. In human terms, I must conquer myself and turn away from the anger that rejects the love that comes to meet me. This is why I assume that behind the free and universal forgiving on the part of God "for his name's sake" there also lies a great patience on his part with inconsistent human beings who oppose him (Rom. 2:4). This kindness, forbearance, and patience on God's part finds its human expression in the vicarious suffering and dying of the new servant of God, Jesus Christ. In the suffering of Christ, there is revealed a suffering by God that is forgiving and therefore creative. In the resurrection of the Christ who is given over to death for us, there is revealed God's passionate concern that the victims should have life and that the perpetrators should be free from guilt and sin.

The "justification that leads to life" (Rom. 5:18) must not be reduced to forgiveness, because the forgiveness of sins is only the precondition for the beginning of the new life. And justification goes far beyond a symmetry between guilt and forgiveness: "But where sin increased, grace abounded all the more" (Rom. 5:20). Paul Ricoeur calls this the "logic of the 'how much more'": how much greater is the forgiveness than the sin, the remission of guilt than the guilt itself, and the future than the past. Indeed, as Paul says at Romans 8:34, how much greater is the significance of the resurrection of Jesus than the significance of his death. Christ died for the forgiveness of our sins, but he was raised so that we might begin anew the life that is righteous.

Forgiveness for Hitler?

Last year, a man whom I did not know phoned me from Las Palmas and asked, after a lengthy conversation: "Can't we just forgive even the Nazis and be reconciled with Hitler and his comrades?" He admitted that he had several former Nazis among his neighbours and that he asked himself, when he was in church: "'As we forgive those who trespass against us' . . . even them?" I was so surprised by his question that no good answer occurred to me. I had reflected on reconciliation with Poland, with Israel, in South Africa, and in the southern states of the USA, but not of reconciliation with the people who had cost me five years of my life in war and in captivity.

This is why I posed this theological-political question in the closing discussion of the symposium in Bad Boll. Mrs. Assmann pointed out that, in terms of the history of mentality, the "1933 generation" was "de-Nazified" by the Western occupying powers after 1945, and they reassumed their positions and pensions from 1951 onwards, in keeping with Law 131. When Adenauer and Globke were in power, the Nazi past was covered over by what Hermann Lübke called a "communicative refusal to mention" it. In the Peace of Westphalia, which ended the Thirty Years' War in 1648, there was likewise an agreed *perpetua oblivio et amnesia,* an agreement that all sides would forget (as Christian Meier has shown).[6] It was only in this way that the former Nazis could play an active part in the rebuilding of West Germany, where they were needed; most of them were invited to join the conservative Christian Democratic Union/Christian Social Union. This deliberate and politically desired "communicative refusal to mention" began to break down only in 1966, with the generation conflict. More than 20 years passed in Germany after the end of the war before it was possible to look the truth in the face, and this was possible only for another generation, the "1968 generation." Now that the generation of the surviving perpetrators and victims is dying out, the direct experience is passing over into indirect memory. The following generations will no longer feel guilty, but they will have to bear the responsibility for the "sins of the fathers," that is, for the consequences of the Nazi dictatorship, whether they want to or not – just as my generation, the "1945" generation, had to bear the consequences of the "1933" generation and of the Second World War.

Reconciliation with the Nazi period cannot be prescribed. I believe that it can manifest itself only in the three steps of penance and conversion:

First, the full truth must be brought to light, without consideration for the persons involved or for the reputation of the German people in the world.

Second, the shame and grief of heart must lead to a collective change of the people's attitude: in this case, a change from the submissiveness vis-à-vis authorities to the democratic responsibility of the citizens.

And third, one must take the first step in offering "reparations." They should not be made only after accusations have been levelled. They must be generous, not stingy.

In steps such as these, the Nazi period is accepted. It is a part of one's own history that is no longer suppressed or bracketed off.

These 12 years of German history must not be reduced to an accident or a cultural break. These years belong to German history and to European history, and they will remain in our memory. There is a good sign in Berlin of how this can happen: in the centre of the German capital, there is a memorial, not to the "Unknown Soldier" of the Second World War, but to Auschwitz. We are told that we are living in the "post-war period," but that is correct only in a chronological sense. In the truest sense, we are living in the "post-Auschwitz period."

Similarly, the Protestant church struggle and the emergence of a "Confessing Church" must not be reduced to an "episode" of German ecclesiastical history. The attempt of the "German Christians" to surrender their Christian identity by means of accomodation is a temptation that always exists. The church of Christ cannot become the "religion of society" or a civic religion.

An amnesty for the perpetrators and their hangers-on does not mean amnesia with regard to what they did or allowed to be done. On the contrary, it means remembering. But there is no amnesty for the victims, and amnesia offends them doubly. The fate of the victims is an open question to which we have no answer.

The Forgiveness of Sins . . . and Who Justifies the Victims?

In 2010, the cases of sexual abuse in the Catholic Church and at the Odenwald School and other pedagogical institutions showed that, up to now, we in the churches and in the public arena know how we ought to deal with the perpetrators, but are speechless before the distress of the victims. The perpetrators are identified by name, but most of the victims remain anonymous. In the case of the perpetrators, we ask how they came to commit their abominable actions; but in the case of the victims, we do not look for ways to help them emerge from their shame and disgrace. In the public arena of our society, we are oriented to the perpetrators; we forget the victims. One sad example of this is the public concentration in Germany on the Red Army Fraction terrorists. Their names are mentioned, and their story is presented in documentaries and films. Federal presidents are asked to grant them an amnesty. But not even the names of their non-prominent victims, the drivers and police officers who were shot dead, are mentioned. No one is interested in what happened to them and in the lives of their families. They are not perpetrators, but merely victims.

The Reformation doctrine of justification has its origins in the mediaeval sacrament of penance. The power of evil is called "sin": we say that sins are forgiven exclusively through the grace of God in faith. This is correct, but it is only half the truth, because the "sinner" is the one who commits the evil. And what of the victims of their sins? In the justification of sinners, we have only our guilt in view, and we ask for the "forgiveness of guilt." And what of the victims in relation to whom we have incurred guilt? Both the Lutheran and the Catholic doctrines of justification and grace have only the perpetrators of sin in view, never their victims. Like Roman law, the Roman sacrament of penance and the Reformation doctrines of justification are one-sidedly oriented to the perpetrator.

This, however, is already the case in the apostle Paul's teaching on sin and grace. He writes honestly and self-critically in the letter to the Romans: "I do not do the good I want; but the evil I do not want is what I do. Now if I do what I do not want, it is no longer I that do it, but sin that dwells within me" (7:19–20). Why does he not see those to whom he has done evil, and those to whom he has failed to do good? Why is he concerned only with himself?

If we compare what he says about the "sin that dwells within me" with the Jesus of the gospels, it is striking that the first thing Jesus Christ sees is the sick, the poor, and the outcasts of his people, and that "he had compassion" on the wretched people (Matt. 9:36). He did not look at the sins of the perpetrators, but at the victims of injustice and violence. He brought these victims the message of the kingdom of God. He told them that it belongs to them, he healed them, and he welcomed them into his fellowship. He opened up the broad space of God to those for whom "good society" had no future. This is why the new evaluation of values dawns with the gospel of Jesus. This is the new evaluation of which his mother Mary sings in revolutionary words: "He has brought down the powerful from their thrones, and lifted up the lowly" (Luke 1:52).

When we read the Psalms of the Old Testament, we find the righteousness of God always on the side of the weak and the poor, the victims of injustice and violence: "The Lord works vindication and justice for all who are oppressed" (Ps. 103:6; 146:7). God's righteousness creates justice. God not only declares thereby what is good and evil, nor does he only repay good with good and evil with evil, like the usual redistributive justice (*justitia distributiva*): he creates justice where injustice has taken place. He sets the victims of sin back on their feet and frees them from their humiliation. Only in this way, and only with this as the goal, is his righteousness a righteousness that restores the perpetrator of the sin. Justification (*justitia justificans*) is thus first of all a righteousness that creates justice for the victims of evil; in the second place, it is then also a righteousness that restores the perpetrators of evil.

We shall investigate this more closely with regard to the perpetrators and the victims. We begin with the perpetrators, not because they are more important, but because there is an ancient and well-proved ritual for their restoration. A similar ritual for the justification of the victims has still to be found.

The sacrament of penance for the perpetrator

The perpetrators of sin are restored through the sacrament of penance and the forgiveness of their sins in three steps:

The first step is through the confession of the sin that they have committed or allowed to happen (*confessio oris,* "confession of the mouth"). The first step is always the step from the darkness of suppression and keeping silent into the light of truth. Those who confess their guilt detach themselves from the sin "that dwells within" them and expel it from themselves. This is not easy, because the public admission of guilt is always linked to a self-humbling. I identify with my evil actions and my omissions. As we saw in the South African Truth and Reconciliation Commission, this is almost impossible for the perpetrators of extreme injustice, the murderers and torturers. They need a protective space for this. This can be the confessional and the priest's seal of confession; in any case, however, it must be a space in which the forgiveness of sins by God is already present. Since God forgives, sinners are able to confess their sins without destroying themselves. It is a good

Protestant insight that we recognize our sins by means of the law and confess them candidly in the light of the gospel. Since the perpetrators of evil and those who have failed to do good have only a short memory (if, indeed, they have a memory at all), they depend on the memory of the victims if they are to hear the truth about themselves. They look at themselves with the eyes of their victims, in order to come to true self-knowledge, because the victims always have a long memory in the insults of their soul and in the wounds of their body. This became inescapably clear at the Holocaust conferences in the USA.

The second step is the change of heart, *contritio cordis,* the turning away from the paths that led to the evil action or to the failure to do the good, and the turning around to love life and to do good. In the tradition of the sacrament of penance, this was understood personally, and the personal dimension is important even today. Only persons who have been changed can change bad situations. But in the "1933 generation," the personal was thwarted by the political. And my own "1945 generation" were similarly unable to lead personal lives. We were cheated of our own life, both militarily and politically, and deprived of our freedom. Today, however, there is another factor: the break with the dictatorial systems that produce so much injustice. We can no longer live at the expense of the poor. We cannot enjoy our life at the cost of the earth and of our weaker fellow creatures. We need both personal conversion and a new political and economic orientation of our life in common.

Finally, the perpetrators enter into a new and just fellowship with their victims if they do everything possible to remove the damage that they have caused. This is called "reparation" (*satisfactio operum*), although we all know that nothing that has been done can be undone. No one can "master" evil past, and nothing that has been destroyed through injustice and violence can be made well again. But every reparation is a beginning in view of a new and just fellowship between the perpetrators and their victims, a fellowship that must be sought and also found through good deeds. One good example is the Protestant *Aktion Sühnezeichen* ("Action Reconciliation/Service for Peace"). The German Penal Code (§46a) calls this the "perpetrator-victim-agreement" or restorative justice.

A new ritual for the justification of the victims

For the perpetrators of sin, the churches have developed this helpful sacrament. For the sinners, the Reformers proclaimed the forgiveness of their sins in the faith that justifies. These two paths complement each other, but both are oriented to the perpetrators. What becomes of the victims of their sins? We need a new ritual for the justifications of the victims of sin. I offer a proposal:

In the *first step*, the victims of injustice and violence must emerge not only from the suffering that was inflicted on them, but *a fortiori* from the humiliation they have endured. In the victims of sexual violence, there is also the shame at the degradation they have suffered, and this shuts their mouths. They hide; they want to forget and to remain anonymous. This is why they need a free space where their pains are acknowledged, where they can shout aloud about what has happened to them. They need open ears that acknowledge what they have suffered and that listen to them, because the first requirement is that they rediscover their self-respect. The perpetrators' confession of guilt can help them here, but the victims do not need to wait for this, because they also need to be freed from their focus on the perpetrators. They need not be "victims" forever. In the God who "does justice for those who suffer violence," because God acknowledges them, they can rediscover their indestructible personal dignity, which no one could impair or steal. Other people must learn not only to hear the confession of the perpetrators, but also to take seriously the laments of the victims and to loosen their tongues in order to free them from their unbearable memories. This requires the protective space of a community that acknowledges them. Break the fetters of your shame! What you suffered has not touched your soul! Forget every public self-pity and every private self-hatred! Communicating to sympathetic people is the first step into the light of truth. Only the truth can set the victims free. In the case of the victims of sexual abuse in the Catholic Church, whom I mentioned above, the oppressive silence often lasted for 30 years, before they spoke the first words in public – and people listened to them.

The *second step* is to raise the victims up from their degradation, so that they lift up their heads to God. The victims of evil also need to change direction, to be raised up from the depths of shame into the broad spaces where life is affirmed. This is the experience of a life that is loved, after the crushing experience of having their life insulted.

The *third step* can then lead them not to respond to the evil that they have suffered by inflicting the same evil on the perpetrators, but rather to overcome evil with good. This is difficult, but liberating: everyone who suffers injustice dreams of revenge, and this is perfectly natural. The one who has made me suffer needs to experience the same suffering, and then we are quits; the equilibrium in justice is re-established. Whether we call it revenge or retaliation or justice, we are satisfied when the perpetrator is punished – but are we not left with a sour aftertaste?

"Do not be overcome by evil," as says Paul rightly says (Rom. 12:21). This also applies to the evil with which evil is repaid: free yourself from the evil that is in you because of the humiliation you have experienced! Do not put yourself on the same level of malice as the perpetrator! One who repays evil with evil will feel that he is no better than the perpetrator. One who murders the murderer is himself a murderer. Free yourself from the evil that has penetrated you without your will.

Paul continues: "But overcome evil with good." When we forgive our debtors, we do good not only to them, but also to ourselves. We overcome the evil that has penetrated us. Forgiveness not only makes it possible for the perpetrators to turn around from their evil paths, but also liberates the victims from hatred, from vengeance, from shame, and not least from being focused on the perpetrator. The forgiveness of guilt means liberating the one who has incurred guilt; it does not mean self-healing, as some modern psychotherapists say. Self-healing can occur as a grace, but it is not the primary goal of the forgiveness of sins; if it were the primary goal, the victims would be held captive in the circle of their own selves and would not be set free. This forgiveness must not be a sign of weakness. It must be a sign of sovereignty vis-à-vis the wretched servants of evil. One who is sovereign does not "re-act," but acts creatively and takes the first step. We can learn how this happens if we look at Martin Luther King's letter to the prisoners in Birmingham, Alabama, in which he calls on the descendants of the black slaves to have compassion on the souls of the whites, which are full of hatred because they are full of fear; or at Nelson Mandela, who returned after more than 25 years in the prison on Robben Island with a free and sovereign soul, and liberated his country from the evil fetters of apartheid.

The primary concern in the confession and the forgiveness of guilt is not the perpetrators, but the end of the evil "that must go on begetting evil" (to quote Schiller). The perpetrator is a servant of evil, and the victim suffers evil. One need not think of the evil that genuinely exists as a moral error on the part of a person who is *per se* good. Perpetrators have not merely "made a mistake": the evil that they did overpowered them and drove them to action because they had handed themselves over to the evil. This is why it is not the evil that must be separated from the human being, but the human being from the evil. In biblical language, this occurs when the perpetrator dies to the evil, so that it no longer has any power over them, and they are reborn in the fellowship to Christ to a new life in righteousness. Victims of the evil must free themselves from the effects of the evil that has penetrated their lives against their will, such as anger, rage, bitterness, and depression. When victims "forgive" the perpetrator, make no accusations of guilt, and do not demand any retribution, they liberate themselves from the evil that wants to breed in them. The victim need not be concerned about the fate of the perpetrator. The victim's primary concern must be to overcome the evil to which they have fallen victim. The important thing is not to acquit the perpetrator, but to put an end to the evil of which the perpetrator has become the servant. And this happens in the forgiveness of guilt. The perpetrator evokes the compassion and mercy that are due to one who is possessed by evil. The servants of evil, no matter why they behave thus, are miserable and wretched human beings. They are healed through forgiveness, not through punishment. Retribution would merely confirm them in their slavery. Forgiveness confronts them with the great alternative, namely, life.

At this point, I would like to tell a story from the parish of Bremen-Wasserhorst, where I was pastor from 1953 to 1958. This story was a living memory in all the houses in the village, and it was related with a mixture of horror and admiration. On 21 November 1945, ten

Polish forced labourers broke into the Kapelle farm on the banks of the Kleine Wümme river and murdered the Hamelmann family. The mother and the four daughters died at once, but the father, Wilhelm Hamelmann, who was severely injured after being shot several times, crawled to the nearest neighbour. The English military police soon identified the murderers in a nearby camp for displaced persons. Four of them were condemned to death and shot in 1946; the youngest was 21 years old. Wilhelm Hamelmann was a committed Christian: "My Christian faith was the source of strength on which I was able to draw, so that I could overcome in everything." From the hospital, he told those who had gathered to bury his family in the Wasserhorst cemetery that one must forgive rather than retaliate. It was his desire that no word should be spoken at the grave that could lead to a new hatred. "When one bears in mind that these were not only prisoners of war, but also civilian prisoners who had been deprived of their freedom, one can understand the urge to retaliate." Twenty years later, after he had worked to secure the release of the murderers of his family, who had been condemned to life imprisonment, he personally collected them from the Hamburg-Fuhlsbüttel penitentiary. Wilhelm Hamelmann was a consistent follower of Jesus. This evoked not only admiration in the parish, but also incomprehension: he seemed to them to come from another world, although he did not belong to any sect. He was the president of the Workers' Welfare Association in North Bremen and was always actively involved in society. He is unforgotten in the parish.

Letting Go and Beginning

The forgiveness of guilt means liberation for both the perpetrators and the victims of evil. The perpetrators are acquitted of the guilt that weighs them down. The victims liberate themselves from the evil that they have suffered. Perpetrators must learn to let go of their past deed, which can catch up with them at any time. Victims must let go of their evil memory. This, however, is possible only if forgiveness is the precondition of a new beginning. If forgiveness is an action that is directed only to the past, it brings about nothing more than the

restoration of the state of affairs that led to the evil that was committed and suffered. And in that case, the forgiveness of guilt would be
merely a momentary "interruption" of a bad state of affairs; after the
interruption, things would continue as before.

In the theology of the apostle Paul, the forgiveness of sins through
Christ's gift of himself for sinners is only one side of the justification
of the godless. The other side is his resurrection "for our righteousness" (Rom. 4:25). This side weighs more heavily, because "where sin
increased, grace abounded all the more" (Rom. 5:20). The traditional
Lutheran reduction of the justification of sinners to the forgiveness
of their sins destroys their hope in the event of justification, because
it fails to see the significance of Christ's resurrection and deprives the
sinners of their future.

The forgiveness of guilt is not only a presupposition of the new
beginning; it is also a consequence of the new life. Without the beginning of the new, the forgiving of guilt and the pardoning of insults will
always have something willed, something forced about it. "*Incipit vita
nova.*" Then it is easy to let go, and forgiving is a spontaneous act. "I
forget what lies behind and strain forward to what lies ahead" (Phil.
3:13). This, of course, applies first and foremost to the victims of evil.
When they have found a new life, they forgive and let go what they
have suffered. But does this also apply to the perpetrators? I believe
that it will be easier for them to ask for pardon and forgiveness when
they too have the prospect of an alternative life. How are they to do
penance if they see no end to the reproaches? How are they to change
course if they know where they are coming from but not where they
are to go?

It is only the future that makes the past past. It is only hope that
allows the memories to come to rest. It is only beginning the new that
allows one to forget the tormenting past. It lets us go, and we let it go.
When the new comes, the old passes away.

It was Hannah Arendt who taught us to understand freedom as
the initiative of something new, something unforeseeable and unique.
Freedom does not yet consist in the fact that we can do something. Freedom does not yet consist in the many possibilities that we have. Freedom means that we ourselves take the initiative and begin something

new with what we can, in the possibilities that we have. Human beings are free if they are beginners. According to Hannah Arendt, this is simply because we are "born."[7] With every birth of a new human being, a new beginning comes into the world. This sounds strange, because animals too are born, but they are not as free as human beings. But it goes back to the biblical creation narrative: "In the beginning God created heaven and earth." God created the human being as his image. Hannah Arendt quotes Augustine: "In order that a beginning might be made, the human being was created." With the creation of the human being, the "principle of the beginning" appeared in the world, and it remains in the world for as long as human beings exist. This in turn means that freedom was created along with the human being. Our likeness to God lies in our free creative power, that is to say, the ability in the human being to posit the divine beginning. "The drive to take the initiative lies in the beginning itself, which came into the world with our birth. We act in accordance with this beginning when we ourselves begin something new on our own initiative."

It is indeed true, in principle, that we can begin something new at every moment, but every moment in our life story is determined positively or negatively by the past. Although we are born for freedom, we are born into unfreedom. And we forfeit our freedom in the course of our life by incurring guilt. We get burdened down and entangled, and we cannot free ourselves from such situations. This is why every new beginning is preceded by a letting go of the past and by an *exodus* from its prisons. The freedom to begin something truly new is due to a "rebirth." A new life begins. This beginning is like a birth, a new entry into life. Every new beginning is preceded by a departure from an imprisonment that is caused by others, or from an immaturity that is one's own fault. Once we are free from the alienations of the past, the goal of the rebirth also becomes clear: namely, the fullness of free life.

Every liberation from an oppressive past begins with the pain caused by this imprisonment, the pain that arises when one becomes conscious of one's unfreedom – either because one is a slave to guilt, or because of insults that one cannot forget – but is no longer willing to submit to one's fate. When freedom draws near, the chains begin to be painful. These pains are signs of life. If one becomes consciously aware of them, the fetters of the tired soul, which are generated by fatalism and apathy, burst asunder. The love of life breaks through and seeks a new and cheerful beginning.

The Apocalypse of the Past:
The "Angel of History" and the "Angel of Hope"

At the end of this essay, we return to its beginning and reflect on its title. The mystery of the past presses on toward its revelation, for otherwise it would not be a mystery. The past cries out to be redeemed from its immutability. The charnel houses of history cry out for resurrection, the ruins wait for the construction of a new world. The past is not past: it is present, full of unfulfilled expectations, because it is "past future."

Apocalypse means not "the end of the world" but the revelation of the mysteries of history. These are, on the one hand, the discoveries of what lies hidden: "There is nothing hidden that does not come to light." These are the openings of the archives of the secret services (in Germany, the publication of the files of the secret services of Communist Eastern Germany). The apocalypse also brings light into the darkness of crimes committed by the state: "the truth will set you free," even when it is implacable and embarrassing. On the other hand, apocalypse means bringing into the light of day the hidden promises of the past. The hopes of past generations were disappointed. Hopes with regard to life went unfulfilled and therefore cry out for justice. They are a tormenting hunger for peace, and no passage of time can eliminate their presence.

With regard to the revelation of this mystery of history, two angelic figures have always fascinated me, since the apocalypse does not come unprepared. It is announced beforehand by angels – unexpected, underivable, sudden apparitions that posit the signs of the end. Whoever has ears, let them hear; whoever has eyes to see, let them see.

In 1921, under the impact of the mass murder in the First World War, Walter Benjamin made a brilliant interpretation of Paul Klee's *Angelus Novus*, which has since then been known as the *Angel of History* and has been the subject of many commentaries. My second angel is the *Angel of Hope,* painted wonderfully by Simone Martini in 1315. It can be admired in the Uffizi Gallery in Florence. Both angels are equally close to me. When I wrote my study of Christian eschatology, *Das Kommen Gottes,* in 1995, reproductions of both these angels were on my desk.

The *Angel of History* gazes at something from which it is moving further and further away:

> His eyes are wide open, his mouth is open, and his wings are outstretched . . . His face is turned to the past. Where we see a chain of events, he sees one single catastrophe that unceasingly piles ruins on ruins and hurls them before his feet. He would indeed like to linger, to waken the dead and to put together what has been shattered. But a storm is blowing from paradise. The storm has caught in his wings and is so strong that the angel can no longer fold his wings. This storm drives him inexorably into the future to which his back is turned, while the heap of ruins before him grows skywards. What we call progress is this storm."[8]

Is this a criticism or a confirmation of belief in progress? Is the "storm from paradise" paradisiacal, or the storm that expelled human beings from paradise? I assume that it is the expulsion from paradise that links the future of history with progress, and the past with the catastrophic heaps of ruins that progress leaves in its wake. The saving angel is a "luckless angel" (Gerschom Scholem) who can do nothing against the doom of history. The angel cannot awaken the dead and put together what has been shattered. It cannot even "linger." It is so rigid from horror that it can no longer fly. Benjamin had this vision of the *Angel of History* after the murders and the ruins of the First World War. His *Angel of History* is indeed powerless in face of the fields of ruins of the past, but it is also an expression of the longing for redemption that stands between the past and the future.

My second angel is the *Angel of Hope.* The prophet Malachi saw it; Mary "heard" its promise and took it to heart. This angel of hope not only looks back with anger or grief at the charnel houses of history. The angel also looks with eyes wide open into the future redemption and announces to Mary, in the midst of history, the birth of the divine child. This angel too is borne by a storm wind. The storm of the divine Spirit blows in its wings and garments. This is not a "storm from paradise," but the storm from the future of God that will awaken the dead and clear up the fields of ruins of the past. It is the storm of the resurrection of the dead and of the restoration of all things.

The *Angel of History* looks back in powerlessness; the *Angel of Hope* looks ahead in the power of the redemption. Perhaps both angels belong together. Perhaps they are one and the same angel, since Paul Klee called his angel *Angelus Novus*.

Apocalypse is the uncovering of that which is hidden, that is to say, of the truth, since the Greek noun *a-lêtheia* ("truth") means "that which does not lie hidden." Truth is the outcome of the apocalypse. In the biblical traditions, the truth of history is linked to the day of God, for then everything that has remained hidden, dark, and mysterious here will come to light. The day of God is the day of all days and brings light into all the nights of history. Then the books will be opened; then everything that is past, temporally speaking, will enter into the eternal light of the truth; then everything will be revealed in the judgment of God. How are we to think of this? In the presence of eternity, everything that has happened sequentially in time will be contemporary and present. The day of God is the day of truth. Then all things and all events will appear as they truly were. Then that which is hidden in the human being will be revealed, and we will know ourselves as we have always been known by God (1 Cor. 13:12). On the day of God, we will know what we see of God and of ourselves here only in a "mirror darkly." In the judgment of the world, the entire world will be brought to its truth. In the human consciousness, this is reflected in the conscience, which is as it were God's judgment seat in our soul. The pangs of conscience uncover our lies, and a good conscience brings us into truth with ourselves. When historians look at history, they are obligated to the truth. History is not the judgment of the world, but the memory of history stands in the light of the judgment of the world. The historian must uncover that which is hidden and liberate what is suppressed and brought to silence. Secret files and the records of the state secret services must be brought into the light of the truth and published. The Truth Commissions must bring into the light the truth about the dictatorships. This must be done without consideration for living persons and the next generations. In view of the day of God, we must break the silence and the command not to speak. Only the truth can make the past free.

Apocalypse is the raising of the dead. Death passes away on the day of God, and as the mediaeval pictures drastically show, the dead climb out of their graves in order to gather for the encounter with their truth. Originally, this was not meant in a moral sense: the victims are raised in order to confront the perpetrators with the truth of their deeds and to let them experience justice. It was only at a later date that the special righteousness of the victims was transformed into a general judgment of good and evil deeds. One who perceives the mystery of the past senses that the dead of Auschwitz are not dead: they are here, and they demand justice. The Germans of my generation know in their consciences that we will meet the dead of Auschwitz. Our history with them is not over; it will not be over until the day of God. Christianity has an image for the raising of the dead, namely, the resurrection of the crucified Christ. In this image, the general resurrection of the dead on the day of God is depicted. This is a return of the dead, a transformation of the dead, who are transformed into eternal life. The universal raising of the dead is the human part of the great transformation of the transient world into the world that cannot pass away, the transformation that is envisioned as the new creation of all things into the eternal creation. And once again, it is angels who announce this "eschatological moment" with the sound of the last trumpet, as the Revelation of John relates.

Finally, apocalypse means the restoration of all things. Nothing is lost, and nothing must be held fast. In one of Paul Gerhardt's poems, Christ says:

"Let go, dear brothers,
what torments you, what you lack:
I restore all things."

Notes

Chapter 1. A Culture of Life in the Dangers of This Time

1. Delivered as the Keynote Lecture at Beijing Forum, 2010.
2. Hölderlin, "Patmos," lines 3–4.
3. Ibid., lines 1–2.
4. For the full text of Obama's speech, see http://www.huffingtonpost. com/2009/04/05/Obama-prague-speech-on-nu_n_183219.html.
5. See his *The First Three Minutes: A Modern View of the Origin of the Universe* (New York: Basic Books, 1993).

Chapter 2. The Hope of the Earth

1. Max Scheler, *Die Stellung des Menschen im Kosmos* [1927] (Munich: 1947).
2. G. Pico della Mirandola, *Uber die Wurde des Menschen* (Oration on the Dignity of Man) (Munich: 1990).
3. For the development, cf. A. Koyre, *Von der geschlossenen Welt zum unendlichen Universum* (Frankfurt: 1969). For the theoretical discussion, J. Moltmann, *Wissenschaft und Weisheit. Zum Gespräch zwischen Naturwissenschaften und Theologie* (Gütersloh: 2002).
4. R. Descartes, *Discours de la Méthode* [1692] (Mainz: 1948), 145.
5. A. Zakai, *Jonathan Edwards' Philosophy of Nature: The Re-enchantment of the World in an Age of Scientific Reasoning* (London: 2010).
6. The Earth Charter (2000), Preamble. www.earthcharter.org.
7. J. Moltmann, *Gott in der Schöpfung: Ökologische Schöpfungslehre* (Munich: 1985), 194.

8. D. Staniloae, *Orthodoxe Dogmatik* (Gütersloh: 1985), 294.

9. I adopt this apt expression from R. Bauckham, *Bible and Ecology: Rediscovering the Community of Creation* (London: 2010), 37.

10. A Gehlen, *Urmensch und Spätkultur* (Bonn: 1956), 265.

11. Moltmann, *Gott in der Schöpfung*, 106; K. Barth, *Kirchlliche Dogmatik* Ill, 1-4 (Zurich: 1947–1951).

12. Basil of Caesarea, *Über den Heiligen Geist* (Freiburg: 1967), 75.

13. Hildegard of Bingen, *Lieder* (Salzburg: 1969), 229.

14. Earth Charter.

15. M. White, *Isaac Newton, The Last Sorcerer* (London: 1998).

16. R. Sheldrake, *Das Gedäachtnis der Natur. Das Geheimnis der Entstehung der Foren in der Natur,* 9th ed. (Munich: 2001), 9–15.

17. J. Lovelock, *Gaia: A New Look at Life on Earth* (Oxford: 1979); J. Lovelock, *The Ages of Gaia: A Biography of Our Living Earth* (Oxford: 1988); J. Lovelock, *The Revenge of Gaia Why the Earth Is Fighting Back – and How We Can Still Save Humanity* (London: 2008). For the discussion, cf. Celia Deane-Drummond, "God and Gaia: Myth or Reality?" *Theology* 95 (1992), 277–85.

18. L. Boff, "Die Erde als Gaja Eine ethische und spirituelle Herausforderung," *Concilium* 45 (2010), 276–84.

19. Denzinger, *Enchiridion Symbolorum* (Freiburg: 1947), nr. 1785 and 1806.

20. K. Barth, *Nein! Theol. Ex. Heute* 14 (Munich: 1934).

21. K. Barth, *Kirchliche Dogmatik* IV/3, 125ff.

22. H.-J. Iwand, *Nachgelassene Werke* I (Munich: 1952), 290f.

23. For more detail cf. J. Moltmann, *Erfahrungen theologischen Denkens: Wege und Formen christlicher Theologie* (Gütersloh: 1999), 68–84.

24. J. Moltmann, *Die Quelle des Lebens: Der Heilige Geist und die Theologie des Lebens* (Gütersloh: 1997).

Chapter 3. A Common Earth Religion

1. Donella H. Meadows, Jorgen Randers, Dennis L. Meadows, and William H. Behrens, *The Limits to Growth: A Report for the Club of Rome's Project on the Predicament of Mankind* (New York: Universe, 1972).

2. Carl Friedrich von Weizsäcker, *Die Bedingungen des Friedens* [The conditions for peace] (Frankfurt: Vandenhoeck + Ruprecht, 1963), 9, 11.

3. Ernst Ulrich von Weizsäcker, *Erdpolitik: Ökologische Realpolitik an der Schwelle zum Jahrhundert der Umwelt* [Earth policy: Ecological *Realpolitik* at the dawn of the century of the environment] (Darmstadt: Wissenschaftliche

Buchgesellschaft, 1991); Ernst Ulrich von Weizsäcker, *Factor Four: Doubling Wealth, Halving Resource Use* (London: Earthscan Ltd.), 1998.

4. Not only crude oil, but all the earth's raw materials are limited. When the supply of uranium, iron, copper, and so on becomes too expensive due to growing demand and dwindling resources, the "refuse industry" of today will become a recycling industry, so that the consumption of raw materials can be replaced by a loop of recyclable materials.

5. This has been aptly shown by Theodor Sundermeier in *Religion – Was ist das?* [Religion – what is it?] (Frankfurt: Lembeck, 2007).

6. Jürgen Moltmann, "Theologische Kritik der politischen Religion" [A theological critique of political religion], in *Kirche im Prozess der Aufklärung* [Church in the process of enlightenment], ed. Johann Baptist Metz, Jürgen Moltmann, Willi Oelmüller (Munich/Mainz: 1970), 11–52.

7. See Jan Assmann, *Herrschaft und Heil: Politische theologie in Altägypten, Israel und Europa* [Lordship and salvation: Political theology in ancient Egypt, Israel and Europe] (Munich: Carl Hanser, 2000).

8. Jörg Rieger, *Christ and Empire: From Paul to Postcolonial Times* (Philadelphia: Fortress Press, 2007).

9. Pico della Mirandola, *On the Dignity of Man* (1486).

10. Jürgen Moltmann, *Ethik der Hoffnung* [Ethics of hope] (Gütersloh: Gütersloher Verlagshaus, 2010), 128ff.

11. James Lovelock, *Gaia: A New Look at Life on Earth* (Oxford: 1979); James Lovelock, *The Ages of Gaia: A Biography of Our Living Earth* (Oxford: Oxford University Press, 1988); James Lovelock, *The Revenge of Gaia: Why the Earth Is Fighting Back – And How We Can Still Save Humanity* (London: Penguin, 2008). There is some discussion as to whether the earth can be described as "living." If we apply the term "living" only to things that can reproduce, then no, the earth is not "alive." However, if we see the earth as the source and habitat of other life, then we can indeed call it "living" to a greater extent. Only in a comparative sense does it mean anything to call the earth an "organism": much more than just a lump of matter and energy, the earth can, in the interplay of its ecosystems, be compared to an "organism," but it is something greater than any of the organisms that inhabit it. For it is also meaningful to talk of the earth as a "nature subject," as Ernst Bloch proposed: in its reactions to what happens on it and beyond it, earth shows itself as more of an active subject than a passive object. Fundamentally, though, planet earth and the life that it brings forth are (as far as we know) a one-off, a unique creation *sui generis*; therefore, comparisons are impossible. From a theological point of view, the earth is a creative creation, and in that it is like nothing else but humanity itself. For a discussion, see Celia

Deane-Drummond, "God and Gaia: Myth or Reality?" *Theology* 95 (1992), 277–85; and Richard Bauckham, *Bible and Ecology: Rediscovering the Community of Creation* (London: Darton, Longman and Todd, 2010), 179–80.

12. Leonardo Boff, "Earth as Gaia: An Ethical and Spiritual Challenge," in *Eco-Theology*, ed. Elaine Wainwright, Luiz Carlos Susin, and Felix Wilfred, *Concilium* vol. 3 (London: SCM Press, 2009), 24–32.

13. *Tao Te Ching*, trans. Gia Fu Feng and Jane English (New York: Vintage, 1997), chap. 25.

14. Jürgen Moltmann, "TAO – The Chinese Mystery of the World: Lao Tsu's *Tao Te Ching* Read with Western Eyes," in Moltmann, *Science and Wisdom* (London: SCM Press, 2003), 172–93.

15. *Tao Te Ching*, chap. 52.

16. Jürgen Moltmann, *Ethik der Hoffnung: der Gottesbund der Erde* [Ethics of hope: God's covenant with the earth] (Gütersloh: Gütersloher Verlagshaus, 2010), 172.

17. As expressed in the Introduction to the 1990 Chicago Declaration of the Parliament of the World's Religions.

18. Such is the purpose of Rainer Maria Rilke's *Duino Elegies* (1922).

19. Dietrich Bonhoeffer's desire was to use the Old Testament message of God's justice on earth to free Christianity from the chains of being a Gnostic salvation religion and make it "this-worldly." See Dietrich Bonhoeffer, *Letters and Papers from Prison* (London: SCM Press, 2001).

20. For a discussion of the ecological significance of the Old Testament Sabbath laws, see Jürgen Moltmann, *Creating a Just Future: The Politics of Peace and the Ethics of Creation in a Threatened World* (London: SCM Press, 1983), 61–66.

Chapter 4. Mercy and Solidarity

1. Translator's note: The author quotes the older German translation here: "es jammerte ihn" (see above, in section 1). The "Good Samaritan" is known in German as the "Merciful Samaritan."

Chapter 5. The Unfinished World

1. Published in German that year as *Licht und Materie. Ergebnisse der neuen Physik: Mit einem Vorwort von Werner Heisenberg* (Hamburg: 1943).

2. The 2011 Boyle lecture was given at St Lawrence, Jewry, in the City of London on 8 February 2011. The Boyle lectures are designed to address topics which explore the relationship between Christianity and our contemporary

understanding of the natural world. Professor Moltmann's lecture was translated from the German by Margaret Kohl.

3. Jürgen Moltmann, *Science and Wisdom*, trans. Margaret Kohl (London: SCM Press, 2003), 14–57.

4. A good example can be found in John Polkinghorne (ed.), *The Trinity and an Entangled World: Relationality in Physical Science and Theology* (Grand Rapids: Eerdmans, 2010).

5. See Jürgen Moltmann, "Natural Science and the Hermeneutics of Nature," in *Sun of Righteousness, Arise! God's Future for Humanity and the Earth* (Minneapolis and London: SCM Press, 2010), 189–208.

6. Hans Blumenberg, *Die Lesbarkeit der Welt* (Frankfurt: 1983).

7. Johannes Reiter, "Bild und Sprache der Gentechnik. Zur Hermeneutik naturwis senschaftlicher Rede und Argumentation," in *Kriterien biomedizinischer Ethik: Theologische Beiträge zum gesellschaftlichen Diskurs,* qd 217, ed. K. Hilpert and D. Mieth (Freiburg: 2006), 337–53.

8. Guiseppe Tanzella-Nitti, "The Two Books Prior to the Scientific Revolution," *Annales Theologici* 18 (2004), 51–83.

9. For evidence see Moltmann, *Science and Wisdom,* 10–15

10. Max Scheler, *The Human Place in the Cosmos* [1927], trans. M. Frings (Evanston: Northwestern University Press, 2009), with reference to Spinoza and Hegel.

11. "Nature," *HistW Ph* lv, 421–78.

12. Günter Howe, *Mensch und Physik* (Witten and Berlin: 1953).

13. Jürgen Moltmann, *God in Creation: An Ecological Doctrine of Creation* (the Gifford Lectures, 1984–85), trans. Margaret Kohl (London and San Francisco: SCM Press, 1985).

14. John Polkinghorne (ed.), *The Work of Love: Creation as Kenosis* (Grand Rapids: Eerdmans; London: SCM Press, 2001).

15. Thomas F. Torrance, *Divine and Contingent Order* (Oxford: Oxford University Press, 1981).

16. Rupert Sheldrake, *The Presence of the Past* (London: Collins, 1988).

17. Cf. W. Thomsen and H. Hollander (ed.), *Augenblick und Zeitpunkt* (Darmstadt: 1984).

18. I. Prigogine and I. Stenger, *The End of Certainty: Time, Chaos and the New Laws of Nature,* trans. from French (London and New York: Free Press, 1997).

19. Carl-Friedrich von Weizsacker, *Die Geschichte der Natur* (Gottingen: 1953).

20. Georg Picht, "Die Zeit und die Modalitäten," *Hier und Jetzt. Philosophieren nach Auschwitz,* vol. 1 (Stuttgart: 1980), chap. 5, 362f.

21. Martin Heidegger, *Being and Time,* trans. J. Macquarrie and E. Robinson (London: SCM Press, 1962), 63.

22. Søren Kierkegaard, "The Possible Corresponds Precisely to the Future . . . and for Time the Future Is the Possible," *The Concept of Dread,* trans. W. Lowrie (Princeton: Princeton University Press; London: Oxford University Press, 1944), 108.

23. See Reinhard Koselleck, *Vergangene Zukunft: Zur Semantik geschichtlicher Zeiten* (Frankfurt: 1979), and Fritz Cramer, *Der Zeitbaum: Grundlegung einer allgemeinen Zeittheorie* (Frankfurt: 1993). Both follow M. Heidegger: "The primary phenomenon of primordial and authentic temporality is the future," *Being and Time,* 378.

24. See, e.g., Rudolf Bultmann, *Glauben und Verstehen* III (Tubingen: 1960): "So what is the meaning of the righteousness of God, the forgiveness of sins? . . . It is that the original relationship of creation is restored."

25. Jürgen Moltmann, "Creation as an Open System," *The Future of Creation,* trans. Margaret Kohl (London: SCM Press, 1979), 115–30, esp. 116.

26. Fritz Cramer, *Symphonie des Lebendigen. Versuch einer allgemeinen Resonanztheorie* (Frankfurt: 1998), 24.

27. I agree with John Polkinghorne's view that what best fits scientific and theological thinking at the end of the 20th century is a thinking in "temporality, top-down causality, divine vulnerability, an inclination towards openness, and recognition of creaturely selfmaking." See John Polkinghorne, *Belief in God in an Age of Science* (New Haven: Yale University Press, 1998), 74.

28. Jürgen Moltmann, "Der Kategorie Novum in der christlichen Theologie" [1965] *Perspektiven der Theologie* (Munich: 1968), 174–88.

29. Avihu Zakai, *Jonathan Edwards's Philosophy of Nature: The Reenchantment of the World in the Age of Scientific Reasoning* (London: T & T Clark, 2010), 255. How do we understand nature if we take its facts as signs? That does not exclude the *reductio ad scientiae ad mathematicam;* it presupposes the exact observation and the measuring and calculation of the facts. But it looks for their interpretation in the context of wider hermeneutical horizons. These interpretative horizons can be anthropocentric, as they are in the modern world, but they can also be theocentric, in correspondence with the reason of faith. We can make the sign language of nature clear to ourselves from our own bodies. If someone feels ill, they go to the doctor. The doctor takes their temperature, feels their pulse, takes x-rays, and so forth. The doctor first establishes the facts and then makes the diagnosis. For this, the doctor takes the facts as symptoms, as signs of an illness. If the diagnosis is

correct, the doctor can identify the illness and begin the therapy. The result is a circle between diagnosis and therapy. Can the medical interpretation of facts as signs be applied to the sciences and a hermeneutics of nature?

Chapter 6. Terrorism and Political Theology

1. C. Schmitt, *Politische Theologie: Vier Kapitel von der Souveränität,* 2nd ed. (Berlin: 1934). Translated into English by B. McNeil.

2. M. Bakunin, *God and the State* [written 1871, published posthumously 1882], Eng. trans. (New York: 1916), available online.

3. H. Meier, *Die Lehre Carl Schmitts. Vier Kapitel zur Unterscheidung Politischer Theologie und Politischer Philosophie* (Stuttgart and Weimar: 1994). Translated into English by B. McNeil.

4. Schmitt, *Politische Theologie,* 83.

5. Mary Kaldor, *Neue und alte Wege. Organisierte Gewalt im Zeitalter der Globalisierung* (Frankfurt: 2000). Translated into English by B. McNeil.

6. E. Eppler, *Vom Gewaltmonopol zum Gewaltmarkt?* (Frankfurt: 2002). Translated into English by B. McNeil.

Chapter 8. God and the Soul, God and the Senses

1. In this section, I follow M. Grabmann, *Die Grundgedanken des heiligen Augustinus über Seele und Gott in ihrer Gegenwartsbedeutung* (Libelli 90), 3rd ed. (Darmstadt: 1967). Texts from Book 10 of the *Confessions* are translated by R.S. Pine-Coffin, *Saint Augustine: Confessions* (London: Penguin Books, 1961); all other texts from Latin and German are translated by Brian McNeil.

2. Grabmann, *Grundgedanken,* 11.

3. Ibid., 12.

4. Ibid.

5. Accordingly, Scheler described the human being as *bestia cupdissima rerum novarum.* See M. Scheler, *Die Stellung des Menschen im Kosmos* (Munich: 1949), 56.

6. See W. Pannenberg, *Was ist der Mensch? Die Anthropologie der Gegenwart im Lichte der* Theologie (Göttingen: 1962), 5ff.

7. See Scheler, *Stellung des Menschen,* 46.

8. See J. Moltmann, "Theologie mystischer Erfahrung," in *Gotteserfahrungen: Hoffnung, Angst, Mystik,* 46–71 (Munich: 1979), 46ff.

9. Grabmann, *Grundgedanken,* 74.

10. Mechthild von Magdeburg, *Das fließende Licht: " Eine Auswahl mittelhochdeutsch/neuhochdeutsch,* ed. G. Vollmann-Profe (Stuttgart: 2008), 25.

11. Ibid., 47.

12. H. Kunisch, *Eckhart – Tauler – Seuse: Ein Textbuch aus der altdeutschen Mystik* (Hamburg: 1958), 67.

13. D. Mieth, *Meister Eckhart: Einheit mit Gott* (Düsseldorf: 2008), 154.

14. Kunisch, *Eckhart – Tauler – Seuse*, 65.

15. See ibid., 17.

16. See H.H. Borchert and G. Merz (eds), *Ausgewählte Werke von Martin Luther*, vol. 2 (Munich: 1938), 319ff.

17. See ibid., 235.

18. By means of this formulation, Elisabeth Moltmann-Wendel has strengthened the self-consciousness of women in feminist theology. She goes back to Martin Luther: "The sinners are beautiful, because they are loved; they are not loved because they are beautiful" [*Peccatores sunt pulchri, quia diliguntur, non ideo diliguntur, quia sunt pulchri*]. See E. Vogelsang (ed.), *Luthers Werke in Auswahl*, vol. 5 (Berlin: 1933), 392. Whatever other definitions may say, being loved makes a human being beautiful.

19. WA 40, II, 328, 17: The true subject of theology is "the human being as guilty of sin and lost, and God who justifies and is the savior of the sinful human being. Any subject in theology apart from this that is investigated or made an object of disputation is an error and a poison."

20. E. Wolf, "Die Rechtfertigungslehre als Mitte und Grenze reformatorischer Theologie," in *Peregrinatio: Studien zur reformatorischen Theologie, zum Kirchenrecht und zur Sozialethik,* vol. 2, 11–21 (Munich: 1965), 12. For a deepened and broadened doctrine of justification, see J. Moltmann, "Gerechtigkeit für Opfer und Täter," in *In der Geschichte des dreieinigen Gottes: Beiträge zur trinitarischen Theologie,* 74–90 (Munich, 1991), 74ff.

21. J. Calvin, *Unterricht in der christlichen Religio: Institutio Christianae Religionis,* rev. and trans. O. Weber (Neukirchen: 1955), 1f.

22. B. Pascal, *Über die Religion und einige andere Gegenstände,* ed. E. Wasmuth (Heidelberg: 1946), 238.

23. See R. Descartes, *Meditationen über die Grundlagen der Philosophie: Worin das Dasein Gottes und die Unterschiedenheit der menschlichen Seele von ihrem Körper bewiesen wird* (PhB 21) (Leipzig: 1948).

24. Ibid., 17.

25. K. Jaspers, *Philosophie: Philosophische Wertorientierung,* Vols. I–II (Berlin 1932), I, 15; II, 1.

26. S. Kierkegaard, *Die Krankheit zum Tode,* ed. C. Schrempf (Geneva: 1946) [Danish original: *Sygdommen til Døden*] (Copenhagen, 2018).

27. Ibid., 74.

28. See F.D.E. Schleiermacher, *Der christliche Glaube: Nach den Grundsätzen der evangelischen Kirche im Zusammenhang dargestellt,* 2nd ed. [1830/31] (Berlin: 2008), §3.

29. Ibid., §4.

30. See R. Bultmann, *Glauben und Verstehen. Gesammelte Aufsätze,* Vol. 1 (Tübingen: 1933); on this, see now M. Bauspiess, C. Landmesser, and F. Portenhausen (eds), *Theologie und Wirklichkeit: Diskussionen der Bultmann-Schule* (Neukirchen-Vluyn: 2011).

31. Bultmann, *Glauben und Verstehen,* 26ff.

32. Ibid., 33, 37.

33. Ibid., 119, 124.

34. J. Moltmann, *Die Quelle des Lebens: Der Heilige Geist und die Theologie des Lebens* (Munich: 1977), 89.

35. I recall my first prison camp in February 1945 in Belgium: 200 men in a barrack, three-story plank beds, two buckets for the night, my senses dead. I no longer wanted to feel, taste, smell, hear, or see anything. I drew my wounded soul back into a shell. All that I had left was the "inner world" and the world of dreams, until one day in May 1945, when I was on a transport and I suddenly stood in front of a cherry tree in blossom. I almost fainted. The fullness of life looked me in the eyes, and my senses awakened to life once more.

36. G. Tersteegen, *Geistliches Blumengärtlein inniger Seelen, oder: Kurze Schlussreime, Betrachtungen und Lieder über allerhand Wahrheiten des inwendigen Christenthums, zur Erweckung, Stärkung und Erquickung in dem verborgenen Leben mit Christo in Gott; nebst der Frommen Lotterie* (1751), 11th ed. (Elberfeld: 1826), I 454, I 173, III CX; on this, see J. Moltmann, "Grundzüge mystischer Theologie bei Gerhard Tersteegen," *EvTh* 16 (1956): 205–24, at 205ff. The "inner Christianity" was regarded from Johann Arnd until Tersteegen as the "true Christianity": "The inner life of the Christians shines, / although the sun burns it from without." This well-known 17th-century hymn by Christian Friedrich Richter was not given a place in the new Protestant hymnal in Germany.

37. See E. Wolf, "Die Rechtfertigungslehre als Mitte und Grenze reformatorischer Theologie," in *Peregrinatio: Studien zur reformatorischen Theologie, zum Kirchenrecht und zur Sozialethik,* vol. 2 (Munich: 1965), 11–21.

38. See K.A. Bauer, *Leiblichkeit – das Ende aller Werke Gottes: Die Bedeutung der Leiblichkeit des Menschen bei Paulus* (Gütersloh: 1971).

39. See H. Plessner, *Conditio Humana: Einleitung zur Prophyläen-Weltgeschichte* (Pfullingen: 1964).

40. See E. Bloch, *Spuren*, 2nd ed. (Berlin: 1959), 7.

41. Hildegard of Bingen, *Lieder: Gesamtausgabe* (Salzburg: 1969), 229.

42. Calvin, *Unterricht in der christlichen Religion*, I, 13f.

43. See B. Janowski, *Gottes Gegenwart in Israel: Beiträge zur Theologie des Alten Testaments* 1 (Neukirchen/Vluyn: 1993), 117ff.

44. The Earth Charter, preamble (2000), www.earthcharter.org.

45. Francis of Assisi, *Il Cantico di Frate Sole*: "Be praised, O Lord, through all your creatures, especially through my Lord Brother Sun . . . Praised be you, my Lord, through Sister Moon and the stars . . . Praised be you, my Lord, through Brother Wind. . . through Sister Water . . . through Brother Fire. . . through Sister Mother Earth."

46. See J. Moltmann, "'Du erweckst mir alle Sinne . . .': Eine Spiritualität der Sinne," in *So komm, dass wir das Offene schauen: Perspektiven der Hoffnung*, 67–81 (Stuttgart: 2011), 67ff.; see also I. Riedel, *Geschmack am Leben finden: Eine Entdeckungsreise mit allen Sinnen* (Freiburg: 2004).

47. See A. Heschel, *Der Sabbat. Seine Bedeutung für den heutigen Menschen* (Neukirchen/Vluyn: 1990); J. Moltmann, "Der Sabbat. Das Fest der Schöpfung," in *Gott in der Schöpfung: Ökologische Schöpfungslehre*), 279–98 (Systematische Beiträge 2) (Munich: 1987), 279ff.

Chapter 9. The Unfinished Reformation

1. See also H.-G. Link, *Die un-vollendete Reformation: Zur konziliaren Gemeinschaft von Kirchen und Gemeinden* (Evangelische Verlagsanstalt Leipzig and Bonifatius, 2016).

2. For this section, I refer to the lecture by J. Brosseder, "Ökumene baut Brücken: Ökumene auf dem Weg zum Reformationsjubiläum" (Munich: 2014).

3. H. Fast (ed.), *Der linke Flügel der Reformation* (Bremen: 1962).

4. J. Moltmann, "Gerechtigkeit für Opfer und Täter," in *In der Geschichte des dreieinigen Gottes: Beiträge zur trinitarischen Theologie* (Munich: 1991), 74–89; "Erlöse uns von dem Bösen," in *Im Ende – der Anfang: Kleine Hoffnungslehre* (Gütersloh: 2003), 64–90.

5. K.-A. Bauer, *Gemeinschaft der Heiligen. Leben aus dem Abendmahl bei Luther* (Freimund Verlag, 2016).

6. W. Goez, *Translatio Imperii: Ein Beitrag zur Geschichte des Geschichtsdenkens und der politischen Theorie im Mittelalter und in der frühen Neuzeit* (Tübingen: 1958); on Luther and the historiography of the Reformation, 257–304. On the theory of the ages of the world and the Quintomonarchians, see J. Moltmann, *Das Kommen Gottes: Christliche Eschatologie* (Gütersloh: 1995),

161–67; see J. Moltmann, "Die Geburt der Neuzeit aus dem Geist chiliast-ischer Theologie" (The Birth of the Modern Age from the Spirit of Chiliastic Theology), in idem, *Hoffen und Denken* (Neukirchen, 2016), 111-133.

Chapter 10. Persevering in Faith

1. This essay, originally titled "The Election and Perseverance of the Faithful," is based on a lecture delivered on 10 July 1959 at the Church Academy in Wuppertal.

2. R. Bultmann, *Glauben und Verstehen*, Vol. 1 (1933), 311.

3. On the problem as a whole, see G.C. Berkouwer, *Geloof en Volharding* (1958); O. Weber, "Die Treue Gottes und die Kontinuität der menschlichen Existenz," *Sonderheft der Evang. Theologie für E. Wolf* (1952), 131ff.; D. Bonhoeffer, *Akt und Sein*, 2nd ed. (1956). We should also mention here Bonhoeffer's beautiful letter "about patience," *Gesammelte Schriften*, Vol. 2 (1959), 541ff.

4. O.S.I., 69. On this, see P. Brunner, *Vom Glauben bei Calvin* (Tübin-gen: 1925). – Inst. III, 2.21.

5. See C. O. 47, 73, and Inst. III, 2.6, as well as C. 0.-45, 36.

6. C. O. 51, 17.

7. Inst. III, 2, 40.

8. This possibility was conceded by Duns Scotus, and was maintained by the Scotist theologians at the Council of Trent. See H. Rückert, *Die Rechtfer-tigungslehre auf dem tridentinischen Konzil* (1925).

9. See the Enchiridion of the Council of Trent, session VI, chs. 12 and 13 (Denzinger, *Enchiridion Symbolorum*, nr. 805ff.) and the corresponding anathemas 15–17 and 22 (Ibid., nr. 825–827 and 832).

10. This refers to the Thomist doctrine of certainty: *Summ. Theol.* I, 2, 122, 5ff.

11. Inst. III, 2, 40.

12. See Calvin's exposition of Rom. 8:29: C. O. 49, 159.

13. Inst. III, 2, 33.

14. O. S. I, 87.

15. Inst. III, 24, 6.

16. E.F.K. Müller, *Bekenntnisschriften der reformierten Kirche* (1903), 763.

17. *Dogmengeschichte des Protestantismus*, III (1926), 367.

18. H. Otten, *Calvins theologische Anschauung von der Prädestination* (1938), 63ff.

19. O. S. I, 89.

20. O. S. I, 90.

21. O. S. I, 88.

22. *Kirchliche Dogmatik,* II, 2 (1940), 367.

23. Inst. III, 23, 13.

24. Inst. III, 2, 12.

25. Inst. III, 2, 11.

26. Luther, *Tischreden,* V, nr. 5897; Melanchthon, *Studienausgabe,* II, 2 (1953), 596, n. 3.

27. For passages from the Reformed tradition on this subject, see J. Moltmann, *Christoph Pezel und der Calvinismus in Bremen* (1958), 94ff.

28. C. O. 39, 44.

29. Inst. III, 2, 37.

30. Inst. III, 2, 17.

31. Inst. III, 2, 21.

32. Inst. III, 2, 24.

33. Inst. I, 14, 18.

34. H. Zanchius, *Epistolarum libri 2* (Hanover: 1609), II, 440.

35. *Aufsätze zur Kirchengeschichte,* I (1921), 92.

36. W. A. Br. II, 549.

37. W. A. X, I, 1, 332.

38. W. A. V, 474.

39. E. Sormunen, quoted in O. Wolff, *Die Haupttypen der neuen Luther-deutun* (1938), 293.

40. *Loci Theologici,* ed. Preuß, IV (1865), 117.

41. For texts, see J.W. van den Bosch, *De Ontwikkeling van Bucers Praedestinatiegedachen vóór hat optreden van Calvin* (1922), 52ff. and 80ff., §9, "De elective en de volharding."

42. Inst. III, 24, 10.

43. *Enodatio* (Amsterdam: 1649), 332.

Chapter 11. The Passibility or Impassibility of God

1. Dietrich Bonhoeffer, *Widerstand und Ergebung* (Munich: Christian Kaiser Verlag, 1951), 242, 247, trans. Isabel Best, Lisa E. Dahill, Reinhard Krauss, and Nancy Lukens, *Letters and Papers from Prison,* Dietrich Bonhoeffer Works, Vol. 8 (Minneapolis: Fortress Press, 2010).

2. J. K. Mozley, *The Impassibility of God: A Survey of Christian Thought* (Cambridge: Cambridge University Press, 1926).

3. Bertrand R. Brasnett, *The Suffering of the Impassible God* (London: SPCK, 1928).

4. I have continued this discussion in *Trinität und Reich Gottes* (Munich: Christian Kaiser Verlag, 1980), trans. Margaret Kohl, *The Trinity and the Kingdom of God* (London: SCM, 1981), ch. 2; Jurgen Moltmann, *In der Geschichte des dreieinigen Gottes* (Munich: Christian Kaiser Verlag, 1991), trans. John Bowden, *History and the Triune God* (London: SCM, 1991) II.2 (in response to Karl Rahner's critique).

5. Paul S. Fiddes, *The Creative Suffering of God* (Oxford: Oxford University Press, 1988).

6. Mozley, *The Impassibility of God,* 177–83.

7. Ibid., 178.

8. It is the problem of negative theology that its negations do not in themselves point to God, but to nothingness.

9. *Large Catechism* (1529), First Commandment.

10. Personalism in modern German theology has its origins in Martin Buber and Ferdinand Ebner's work in the early 1920s. See Christoph Schwobel, *Gott in Beziehung: Studien zur Dogmatik* (Tübingen: Mohr Siebeck, 2000).

11. American process theology has its origins primarily in the mathematician and philosopher Alfred North Whitehead's work *Process and Reality* (New York: Free Press, 1929). One of its ancestors was William James. See Catherine Keller, *On the Mystery: Discerning God in Process* (Minneapolis: Fortress Press, 2008).

12. Hegel encouraged the German theology of history later pursued by Wolfhart Pannenberg and others in *Offenbarung als Geschichte* (Gottingen: Vandenhoeck & Ruprecht, 1961), trans. David Granskou, *Revelation as History* (London: Sheed and Ward, 1979).

13. For an eschatologically orientated theology, see Jürgen Moltmann, *Theologie der Hoffnung* (Munich: Christian Kaiser Verlag, 1964), trans. James W. Leitch, *Theology of Hope* (London: SCM, 1967); Jürgen Moltmann, *Das Kommen Gottes* (Gutersloh: Christian Kaiser Verlag, 1995), trans. Margaret Kohl, *The Coming of God* (London: SCM, 1996).

14. We owe this approach to Karl Barth's theology of revelation; see his *Kirchliche Dogmatik* (Munich: Christian Kaiser Verlag, 1935–67), trans. and ed. G. W. Bromiley et al., *Church Dogmatics* (Edinburgh: T&T Clark, 1936–77).

15. Mozley, *The Impassibility of God*, 178.

16. Ibid.

17. Jürgen Moltmann, "God's *Kenosis* in the Creation and Consummation of the World," in John Polkinghorne (ed.), *The Work of Love: Creation as Kenosis* (Grand Rapids, Mich.: Eerdmans/ London: SPCK, 2001), 137–52.

18. Emil Brunner, *Dogmatik* Bd. 2 (Zi.irich: Zwingli-Verlag, 1950), 31.

19. W. H. Vanstone, *Loves, Endeavour, Loves, Expense: The Response of Being to the Love of God* (London: DLT, 1977), 120.

20. Karl Rahner, *Schriften zur Theologie*, Bd. 5 (Zurich: Benziger Verlag, 1962), 183–221, trans. Karl H. Kriiger, *Theological Investigations 5* (Baltimore/London: Helicon Press/DLT, 1966).

21. Mozley, *The Impassibility of God*, 179.

22. Ibid., 180.

23. Bernard of Clairvaux, *Sermones in Canticum Canticorum*, Sermon 26, in: P. Migne (ed.), *Patrologia Latina* 183 (Turnhout: Brepols, 1844–55), 906.

24. Benedict XVI, encyclical *Spes Salvi* (Rome: Libreria Editrice Vaticana, 2007), 75. The Pope here cites Bernard's thesis as a sound solution to the problem.

25. Anselm of Canterbury, *Proslogion* 8.

26. Thomas Aquinas, *Summa Theologiae;* quoted in J. B. Cobb and D. R. Griffin, *Process Theology: An Introductory Exposition* (Louisville: Westminster John Knox Press, 1976), 45. Cf. Catherine Keller, *On the Mystery,* 125–27.

27. Friedrich Schleiermacher, *Glaubenslehre,* H. R. Mackintosh and J. S. Stewart, trans. and eds (Edinburgh: T.&T. Clark, 1928), §85.

28. Karl Barth, *Kirchliche Dogmatik II/l,* 416.

29. Karl Barth, *Kirchliche Dogmatik III,* §8.

30. Aristotle, *Metaphysics* XII, 1073a10.

31. Abraham Heschel, *The Prophets* (New York: Harper and Row, 1962), chs 14 and 18.

32. Mozley, *The Impassibility of God,* 180.

33. Ibid.

34. Ibid., 181.

35. Bernd Janowski, *Gottes Gegenwart in Israel: Beitriige zur Theologie des Alten Testaments* (Neukirchen: Neukirchener Verlag, 1993), II.5.

36. See Jürgen Moltmann, *Der gekreuzigte Gott* (Munich: Christian Kaiser Verlag, 1973), trans. R. A. Wilson and John Bowden, *The Crucified God:*

The Cross of Christ as the Foundation and Criticism of Christian Theology (London: SCM, 1974).

37. Mozley, *The Impassibility of God,* 181.

38. Ibid., 182.

39. Ibid.

40. Ibid., 183.

41. Moltmann, *The Trinity and the Kingdom of God.*

42. H. J. Eckstein and M. Welker (eds), *Die Wirklichkeit der Auferstehung* (Neukirchen: Neukirchener Verlag, 2002); N. T. Wright, *The Resurrection of the Son of God* (London: SPCK, 2003).

Chapter 12. The Mystery of the Past

1. Friedrich Nietzsche, *Vom Nutzen und Nachteil der Historie für das Leben,* in *Werke,* ed. K. Schlechta, Vol. 1 (Munich: 1954), 213.

2. Yosef Hayim Yerushalmi, *Zachor: Erinnere Dich. Jüdische Geschichte und jüdisches Gedächtnis* (Berlin: 1968).

3. Aaron Lazare, *On Apology* (Oxford: 2004).

4. Translator's note: This expression functions in the same way as the English expression "Excuse me," but it literally means "I excuse myself, I absolve myself of blame." This section contains an extensive play on words that are not translatable into English.

5. Translator's note: In German, *Es tut mir leid*: literally, "It causes me to suffer." See the noun "suffering" in the following sentences.

6. Christian Meier, *Das Gebot zu vergessen und die Unabweisbarkeit des Erinnern:. Vom öffentlichen Umgang mit schlimmer Vergangenheit* (Munich: 2010).

7. Hannah Arendt, *Vita activa oder Vom tätigen Leben* (Munich: 1960).

8. Walter Benjamin, *Illuminationen* (Frankfurt: 1961), 272.